The Pembro...
PREMIER GUI...

DESIGNED AND PUBLISHED BY
Eden Publications Ltd
01646 682296
WRITTEN BY David Merchant,
Matt Drabble with contributions by
local sources
EDITED BY Mary Thomas
PHOTOGRAPHY BY Eden
Publications Ltd

Everyone needs a place to think and my place is Pembrokeshire. I grew up here – my bedroom looked out across Milford Haven and for as long as I can remember I've sat and watched the boats sailing past Pembroke Dock – the ferries to Ireland, trawlers from the Bristol Channel, laden tankers from the Middle East – adventures from another world outside my window.

As little boys we learnt to row up and down the River Cleddau from the slip way at Front Street to Lawrenny and back. Our weekends were spent on the beaches of Freshwater and Barafundle. Saturdays and Sundays were always for walks along the coast path – chewing over the past week and thinking about the days to come.

On this ancient coast and its weather beaten shores the cares of the world wash away when you walk over sunken forests that covered Wales millions of years ago.

Pembrokeshire is still the place I return to – the Preseli Mountains where we had picnics, Tenby and the boat to Caldey Island, Broad Haven Beach where we swam in freezing waters – they are the places which anchor my travels everywhere else in the world – the compass to steer by.

Everyone always says you are bound to feel a tie to the place where you were born and brought up but Pembrokeshire exerts a kind of magnetism that makes you yearn for it when you've been away too long. The light is magical – the coastline is mesmeric – the sea hypnotises with its menacing beauty and danger and the people are entrancing.

CONTENTS

Welcome

It is always our great pleasure to welcome all visitors to Pembrokeshire, and we hope that you can use our guide to maximise your stay. Pembrokeshire is a county steeped in history, myths and legends through the centuries. The evidence of the sweeping changes throughout Pembrokeshire are evident everywhere you look, from drowned prehistoric forests, to Iron Age Forts and Bronze Age burial chambers. This guide book has been painstakingly researched and written, covering the whole of the county. We update our photographs for every new edition, as we feel that it is important to constantly strive to improve our guide for the benefit of all our readers. Included in the book are Beach Guides, Maps, Town Guides, Arts and Crafts, Castles and Monuments, Where to eat Guides, Pembrokeshire Events lists, Cycling and Walking Routes, Premier Attraction Guides, Car Tours, as well as fantastic historical facts and stories on Pembrokeshire's towns and villages. We hope that this guide will serve a very practical purpose during your stay with its maps and guides, to eating out, attractions and places of interest to visit and after your stay you will be able to take the time, sit back and read through all the background information about the places that you visited. We genuinely hope that you enjoy your visit to our beautiful county and that you can use our guide to get the most out of your holiday. Please enjoy your stay.

Bienvenue

Chers visiteurs, c'est toujours avec grand plaisir que nous vous accueillons, tous et toutes, dans le Pembrokeshire. Nous espérons que notre guide vous aidera à profiter de votre séjour au maximum. Le Pembrokeshire est un comté imprégné d'histoire, peuplé de mythes et de légendes qui s'étalent sur plusieurs siècles. Où que porte votre regard, vous verrez la preuve des changements profonds qui ont bouleversé le paysage, des forêts préhistoriques inondées aux forts de l'âge du fer, sans oublier les chambres funéraires de l'âge du bronze. Ce guide a fait l'objet de recherches minutieuses et a été rédigé avec soin. Il couvre la totalité du comté. Nous mettons nos photographies à jour à chaque nouvelle édition car nous pensons qu'il est important de toujours chercher à améliorer notre guide, pour qu'il profite à tous nos lecteurs. Ce livret contient entre autres un guide des plages, des cartes et des plans, un guide sur les villes, une section sur l'artisanat, un guide des châteaux et des monuments, une section « où manger », le calendrier des manifestations dans le Pembrokeshire, les promenades à faire à pied et en vélo, un guide sur les attractions de premier choix, les excursions à faire en voiture, ainsi que de nombreux faits historiques et anecdotes passionnants sur les villes et les villages du comté. Nous espérons que ce guide répondra à un but très pratique pendant votre séjour, grâce à ses cartes et ses plans, sa section « où manger », ses attractions et sites intéressants ; et aussi, qu'après votre séjour, vous pourrez prendre le temps de lire toutes les informations de fond sur les lieux que vous aurez visités. Nous espérons vraiment que vous passerez un séjour merveilleux dans notre beau comté et que notre guide vous aidera à profiter au mieux de vos vacances. Nous vous souhaitons un excellent séjour.

Croeso

Pleser pob amser yw croesawu ymwelwyr i Sir Benfro a hyderwn y defnyddiwch yr arweinlyfr i wneud y gorau o'ch arhosiad. Ar hyd y canrifoedd bu Sir Benfro'n sir wedi'i thrwytho mewn hanes a chwedlau. Gwelir tystiolaeth o'r newidiadau sydd yn Sir Benfro ymhob man o goedwigoedd cynhanesyddol boddedig i siambrau claddu'r Oes Efydd ac Amddiffynfeydd o'r Oes Haearn. Ceir ôl ymchwil a chofnodi trylwyr yn yr arweinlyfr hwn gan ymdrin â'r sir gyfan. Rydym yn diweddaru lluniau ar gyfer pob rhifyn gan ein bod yn ei theimlo'n bwysig i ymdrechu'n gyson i wella'n cyfeirlyfr er budd ein darllenwyr. Gyda'r arweinlyfr hwn gwelwch Arweinlyfr Traethau, Mapiau, Arweinlyfr i Drefi, Celf a Chrefft, Cestyll a Chofadeiliau, Canllawiau ar le i fwyta, Rhestr Digwyddiadau Sir Benfro, Teithiau Cerdded a Beicio, Arweinlyfr i'r Prif Atyniadau, teithiau Ceir, ynghyd â ffeithiau a straeon hanesyddol gwych am drefi a phentrefi Sir Benfro. Gobeithiwn fydd yr Arweinlyfr yn werthfawr fel rhan o'ch ymweliad a bydd cyfle gennych i eistedd nôl a darllen gwybodaeth gefndirol y llefydd yr ymwelwch â hwy. Rydym yn wirioneddol yn gobeithio byddwch yn mwynhau eich ymweliad i'n sir brydferth ac y bydd yr arweinlyfr yn eich cynorthwyo i gael y mwyaf allan o'ch arhosiad. Mwynhewch eich ymweliad!

Willkommen

Es ist uns immer ein großes Vergnügen, alle Besucher in Pembrokeshire willkommen zu heißen, und wir hoffen, dass Sie unseren Leitfaden bestens für Ihren Besuch verwenden können. Pembrokeshire hat eine Jahrhunderte alte Geschichte, Mythen und Legenden. Überall in Pembrokeshire finden Sie Zeugnisse umgreifender Entwicklungen, von überfluteten vorgeschichtlichen Wäldern bis zu Festungen aus der Eisenzeit und Gräbern aus der Bronzezeit. Dieser Leitfaden beruht auf sehr gründlicher Forschung, wurde sehr sorgfältig verfasst und befasst sich mit der ganzen Grafschaft. Für jede neue Ausgabe aktualisieren wir unsere Fotos, denn wir meinen, dass es wichtig ist, unseren Leitfaden zum Nutzen aller unserer Leser fortlaufend zu verbessern. Das Buch enthält Strandleitfäden, Karten, Stadtführer, Kunst und Kunsthandwerk, Burgen, Schlösser und Denkmäler, Restaurantführer, Veranstaltungen Pembrokeshire, Rad- und Wanderwege, Führer zu leitenden Attraktionen, Autotouren sowie fantastische historische Fakten und Geschichten über die Städte und Dörfer von Pembrokeshire. Wir hoffen, dass Ihnen dieser Leitfaden mit seinen Karten und Führern, Restaurantempfehlungen, Attraktionen und Sehenswürdigkeiten auf Ihrem Besuch sehr nützlich sein wird. Nach Ihrem Besuch können Sie sich dann die Zeit nehmen und die Hintergrundinformationen für die Orte nachlesen, die Sie besucht haben. Wir hoffen wirklich, dass Sie Ihren Besuch in unserer schönen Grafschaft genießen und dass dieser Leitfaden Ihren Besuch noch verbessert. Genießen Sie Ihren Besuch!

PEMBROKESHIRE

Ferry to Rossl...

Strumble Head

Pen Brush

Pwll Deri

Trefasser

St Nicholas

Aber Mawr

Tre

Abercastle

Granston

Porthgain

Trevine

Mathry

A487

Square & Compass

Castle Mor

Abereiddy

Llanrhian

B4330

Croesgoch Treglemais

Tretio

Llanhowel

Llandeloy

St Davids Head

Treleddyd-fawr

Rhodiad-y-Brenin

North Bishop

Whitesands

B4583

Whitchurch

Middle Mill

Brawdy

Hayscastle

Point St John

St Justinian

St Davids

A487

PE

Bishops and Clerks

Ramsey Sound

Solva

Pen-y-cwm

Roch

South Bishop

Ramsey Island

St Non's Bay

Caerfai Bay

Green Scar

Dinas Fawr

Newgale

Simpson Cross

Pelcomb

Lambsto

Nolton Haven

Nolton

Druidston

Haroldston West

ST BRIDES BAY

Stack Rocks

Broad Haven

Little Haven

Broadw

B4327

Walwyn Castle

Talbenny

St Brides

PEMBROKESHIRE COAST NATIONAL PARK

Tie

Skomer Island

Wooltack Point

Martins Haven

Marloes

Hasguard

Herbrandston

Sandy Haven

ne Smalls

Midland Isle

Pembrokeshire Coast Path

St Ishmaels

Milford Haven

Grassholm Island

Broad Sound

Gateholm Island

West Dale Bay

Dale

Dale Point

Milford Haven

Angle Bay

Skokholm Island

St Ann's Head

Angle

Rhoscrow

Ferry to Rosslare

Sheep Island

Freshwater West

Castle

Blucks Pool

Linney Head

7

CARDIGANSHIRE

Pen-yr-Afr
Pwllgranant
Tre-Rhys
Ceibwr Bay
St Dogmaels
Moylgrove
Monington
Glanrhyd
CARDIGAN
Penparc
Blaenporth
Beulah
Llangoedmor
B4570
Llechryd
B4323
Pont Hirwaun
Brongest
Cenarth
Cwm-cou
Cilgerran
Abercych
Newcastle Emlyn
Aber Ara
Rhoshill
Boncath
Newchapel
Penrherber
B4332
Capel Iwan
Cwm Morgan
Nevern
Berry Hill
Tredrissi
Felindre Farchog
Eglwyswrw
Blaenffos
Bwlch-y-groes
Cilrhedyn
335m
Llanfair-Nant-Gwyn
Star
362m
Trwyn-y-bwa
Newport Bay
Cwm-yr-Eglwys
Parrog
Newport
Brynhenllan
Dinas Head
Dinas (island)
Pwllgwaelod
Fishguard Bay
Bryn-henllan
Dinas
A487
Carningli Common
Crosswell
Whitechurch
Hermon
Tegryn
Cwm Morgan
Lower Town
Fishguard
Llanychaer
Cilgwyn
311m
Mynydd Melyn
Mynydd Caregog
Brynberian
PEMBROKESHIRE COAST NATIONAL PARK
Crymych
Pentregalar
Llanfyrnach
Dinas
Trelech
Trewn
Pontfaen
Tafarn-y-bwlch
MYNYDD PRESELI
536m
Foel Eryr
Mynachlogddu
265m
Blaenwaun
Cwmbach
Trelech-ar-Betws
B4313
Mynydd Cilciffeth
Morvil
Foel Cwm-cerwym
368m
Foel Drych
Glandwr
B4299
Little Newcastle
Puncheston
Castlebythe
Mynydd Castlebythe
Rosebush
Llandre Isaf
Hebron
Maesgwynne
Cwmfelin Mynach
Gellywen
St Dogwells
Tufton
Woodstock
Henry's Moat
Maenclochog
Llanglydwen
Login
Wolfs Castle
Ambleston
New Moat
Llangolman
Efailwen
CARMARTHENSHIRE
Spittal
Llys-y-frân Reservoir
Llys-y-frân
Llanycefn
Llanboidy
Scolton
B4329
Clarbeston
Pen-ffordd
Llandissilio
Henllan Amgoed
Llangynin
Meidrim
B4298
Great Rudbaxton
Clarbeston Road
Bletherston
Rhydywrach
Cwmfelin Boeth
Whitland Abbey
Picton Ferry
Bancyfe
Poyston Cross
Wiston
Gelli
Llawhaden
Clunderwen
Llanfallteg
A40
Crundale
HAVERFORDWEST
Robeston Wathen
Canaston Bridge
Llanddewi Velfrey
Whitland
Trevaughan
Llwyn-y-brain
Pwll-trap
St Clears
Merlin's Bridge
The Rhos
Slebech Park
Picton Park
A40
Narberth
Crinow
Princes Gate
Lampeter Velfrey
River Taf
AA77
Llanddowror
Lower Freystrop
Landshipping
Minwear
A4115
Cold Blaw
B4315
B4314
Templeton
Tavernspite
Llandawke
Freystrop
Hook
Llangwm
Martletwy
Yerbeston
Ludchurch
Crunwear
Red Roses
B4314
Llansadurnen
Brook
Laugharne
Sardis
PEMBROKESHIRE COAST NATIONAL PARK
Cresswell
Reynalton
Llanteg
Marros
A4066
Pendine
Houghton
Lawrenny
Jeffreston
Begelly
Kilgetty
Stepaside
Amroth
Wiseman's Bridge
Burton
West Williamston
Cresselly
Redberth
East Williamston
Saundersfoot
Saundersfoot Bay
Cleddau Bridge
Co?heston
Milton
Carew
Sageston
Monkstone Point
Pembroke
A477
Carew Cheriton
B4318
New Hedges
Tenby Roads
A4075
Lamphey
St Florence
Gumfreston
Tenby
St Catherine's Island
CARMARTHEN BAY
Kingsfold
Hodgeston
Penally
B4584
Jameston
A4139
Lydstep
Caldey Sound
Petrox
Freshwater East
Manorbier
St Margaret's Island
Monastery
Stackpole
Cheriton or Stackpole Elidor
Old Castle Head
Caldey Island
Stackpole Head
Broad Haven
St Govan's Head

8

PEMBROKESHIRE'S ULTIMATE BEACH GUIDE

Barafundle

It is no surprise that many visitors to Pembrokeshire come here first and foremost for the county's magnificent sandy beaches. No fewer than 30 of Pembrokeshire's beaches qualified for The Keep Wales Tidy Award. There are 12 beaches which have European Blue Flag Awards and 30 beaches have Green Coast (rural) awards. So whether you are a sun worshipper, watersports fanatic, boat owner or you simply love the seaside, Pembrokeshire is an idyllic place to enjoy the great beach holiday.

SOUTH COAST

Amroth

AMROTH (1)

Amroth is a charming coastal village where time seems to have stood still. The beach is punctuated by a series of groynes that help

protect the village from winter storms and rough seas. The Western end marks the start of the renowned 186 mile Pembrokeshire Coastal Path. Parking is good along the seafront and in the village.

WISEMANS BRIDGE (2)

The beach's claim to fame is that it was used in 1944 for rehearsals of the D Day landings under the watchful eye of Sir Winston Churchill himself. The beach is sandy and it's possible to walk to neighbouring Saundersfoot at low tide. Parking is limited.

COPPET HALL (3)

Coppet Hall is a popular beach which has extensive parking facilities. It also affords access to Saundersfoot village.

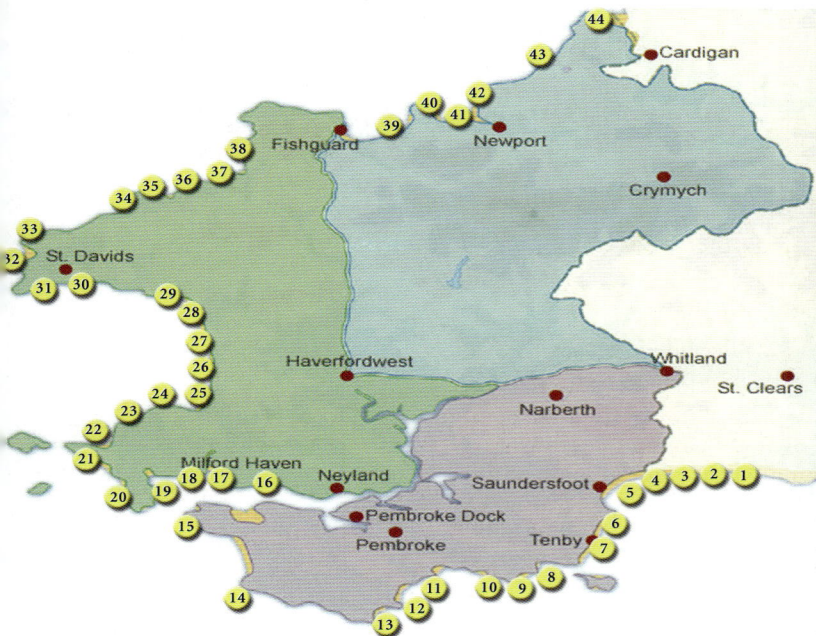

Saundersfoot

SAUNDERSFOOT (4)

Saundersfoot is one of the area's most popular resorts and it's easy to see why. There is everything for the family including a superb beach and a range of shops, cafes and restaurants. There is also a picturesque harbour plus extensive parking facilities.

MONKSTONE (5)

Monkstone (Saundersfoot) is unsuitable for families as access is down very steep steps. Those hardy enough to make the journey will find a beautiful stretch of sand but no facilities. Entry to the beach is through Trevayne Farm off the B4316 near New Hedges. There is a small charge for parking.

TENBY NORTH (6)

Tenby is one of the most popular seaside resorts in Wales. A medieval walled town with narrow streets, it stands on a rocky headland which divides its two main beaches. The award winning North Beach has first class facilities together with a picture postcard harbour and sandy beach. Because of the town's narrow streets, visitors are advised to park in one of the large car parks outside the town walls, all of which are within walking distance of the beaches.

TENBY SOUTH (7)

Tenby's South Beach offers a large expanse of fine sand. A firm favourite with people

Tenby

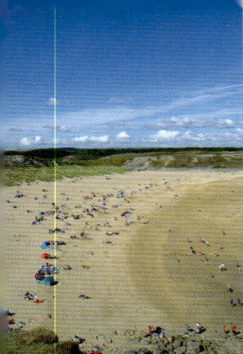

Broad Haven South

holidaying at the nearby Kiln Park Holiday Village. The beach, which is backed by cliffs on which the town stands, offers unlimited views of Caldey Island which is inhabited by monks. Facilities are excellent.

LYDSTEP HAVEN (8)

Lydstep Haven is a privately owned beautiful sheltered bay for which there is an admission charge. Characterised at either end by wooded cliffs, Lydstep boasts a slipway to cater for the many boats and pleasure crafts using the bay. One of the area's main features is the Smugglers Cave, which can be explored even at high tide.

SHRINKLE HAVEN (9)

Skrinkle Haven is an absolute gem of a beach sheltered by tall cliffs. However, access is down very steep steps and a winding path. There is a car park above the beach but no other facilities.

MANORBIER (10)

Manorbier is very popular with surfers. Overlooked by a medieval castle and the 12th Century church of St James, the beach is the home to a stone cromlech known as the King's Quoit. The sandy beach is served by a large car park, (charges during summer) together with parking areas on the road above the beach.

Manorbier

FRESHWATER EAST (11)

Freshwater East is a wide, sweeping crescent of sand and shingle backed by dunes and grassy headlands. Popular with boat owners, divers, fishermen and surfers alike, it has a holiday village and caravan site close by. Parking and toilets are available near the beach.

BARAFUNDLE (12)

Barafundle is surely one of Pembrokeshire's most beautiful beaches, it is however only accessible from the coastal path. Owned by the National Trust, the nearest parking is at Stackpole Quay about half a mile away. Due to its remote location the beach itself has no amenities, but there is a tearoom at Stackpole Quay.

BROAD HAVEN SOUTH (11)

Broad Haven South is a superb sheltered beach popular with sun worshipers. Another of the National Trust owned beaches, it offers excellent parking for both those visiting the beach or those using it as a gateway to the area's many fine walks.

FRESHWATER WEST (11)

Freshwater West is a haven for surfers. They are drawn to the area by the big Atlantic rollers so it seems only natural that the beach has been used for the Welsh National Surfing Championships. However, it can be dangerous to swimmers because of strong rip currents and hazardous quicksands so families with small children should be on their guard.

Freshwater East

Barafundle

WEST COAST

Dale

West Angle Bay

WEST ANGLE BAY (15)

West Angle Bay is another beautiful location, very popular with visitors and local inhabitants alike. Low tides reveal rock pools, which youngsters can explore. The beach houses the remains of an old lime kiln now partly overgrown. There are excellent walks along the cliffs offering spectacular views. Parking and other facilities are good.

GELLISWICK (16)

Gelliswick is the headquarters of the Pembrokeshire Yacht Club and offers an excellent slipway for boats. A large sand and shingle beach, facilities include toilets, free parking and the nearby shops of Milford Haven.

SANDY HAVEN (17)

Sandy Haven beach is sandwiched between the village of Sandy Haven and Herbrandston. Just below Herbrandston lies a sandy beach, which at low tide offers superb views of the estuary. Unsuitable for swimming however, because of unpredictable estuary currents. Parking on both sides of the western and eastern sides of the estuary are limited.

LINDSWAY BAY (18)

Lindsway Bay is not suitable for bathing, but because of its position to the Milford Haven Waterway, it makes an ideal place for walking, bird watching and collecting shellfish. Enveloped by cliffs and large rocks, it also offers good views of St. Ann's Head from both the beach and the cliff top. South of the bay is Great Castle Head, the site of an Iron Age Fort. The beach is devoid of amenities and parking is a quarter of a mile away.

DALE (19)

If it's watersports you're interested in then this is the place to be. Dale is home to yachting, windsurfing and a watersports centre. It is also attractive to the sub-aqua fraternity because of its wreck sites. Facilities in the attractive village overlooking the sea are good and there is a large carpark opposite the shingle beach.

WEST DALE (20)

West Dale is a stunning secluded cove, but its sand and shingle beach can be dangerous to swimmers because of undertows and unpredictable currents and hidden rocks. Access is via road or footpath through Dale, but parking is limited and there are no amenities.

MARLOES (21)

Marloes sands is a magnificent beach, characterised by outcrops of rocks and a large crescent of golden sand at low tide, which was inhabited from prehistoric to medieval times and which still bears the remains of 5th century huts. Another feature are the Three Chimneys - horizontal beds of rock, more than 400 million years old. The National Trust has a car park half a mile from the beach, but the nearest facilities are about a mile away in the village of Marloes.

MARTINS HAVEN (22)

Martins Haven is a small north facing cove with a pebble beach. Boat trips operate from here to the Skomer Nature Reserve. Facilities include toilets and parking.

MUSSELWICK (23)

Musselwick Sands is a fine sandy beach that is only exposed at low tide. Access is difficult and visitors need to be aware that the tide could cut them off. There are no amenities and parking at the start of the long footpath to the beach is limited.

ST. BRIDES HAVEN (24)

St. Bride's Haven is a sheltered cove with a beach of shingle, pebbles and rock pools, enhanced at low tide by sand. Interesting features near the beach include an early Christian Cemetery with stone lined graves and the remains of an old limekiln. There is limited parking near the church.

LITTLE HAVEN (25)

Little Haven is a small sandy cove with a slipway for small boats, including the local inshore rescue boat. There is a pay and display car park close to the beach and numerous facilities including pubs offering food and drink and other useful shops.

BROAD HAVEN WEST (26)

Broad Haven (west) is a large magnificent expanse of sand, which runs the entire length of Broad Haven village. It is a favourite with bathers and watersport enthusiasts, and also has a great deal to interest geologists with an abundance of different rock formations. The village offers good facilities and a choice of car parks.

Little Haven

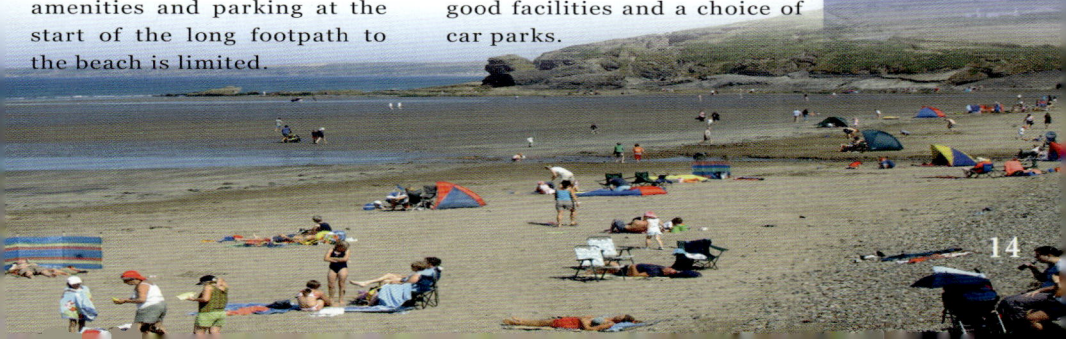

Broad Haven

14

DRUIDSTON HAVEN (27)

Druidston Haven, whilst being a long sandy beach, is not suitable for bathers because of strong currents. Enclosed on three sides by steep cliffs, access to the beach is by two footpaths. However, there is only limited parking on the roadside and there are no amenities.

NOLTON HAVEN (28)

Nolton Haven is a beach of sand and shingle with cliffs on either side. A red flag flying warns of danger to swimmers. There is a National Trust car park above the beach.

NEWGALE SANDS (29)

Newgale Sands is another broad expanse of sand exposed to the Atlantic gales, which acts as a magnet to surfers and other watersports enthusiasts. During summer lifeguards designate areas for swimmers and patrol this excellent beach. There is a shop, two cafes and a pub. Parking areas are good.

WEST COAST

CAERBWDI BAY (30)

Caerbwdi Bay is a small sheltered beach of rock and pebble with sand visible at low tide. Close to St. Davids, it is reached along a half mile footpath leading from the A487 Solva to St. Davids road where there is limited parking. Although popular with walkers, the beach has no facilities.

CAERFAI BAY (31)

Caerfai Bay is the nearest beach to St. Davids and is popular with bathers, although at high tide the beach is covered leaving only rocks and boulders. A feature of the bay is the unusual purple sandstone along the cliffs, which was used to build St. Davids Cathedral. Parking is available above the beach, but there are no facilities.

WHITESANDS (32)

Whitesands, or to give is its Welsh name Traeth Mawr, is consistently rated one of Wales' very best seaside resorts. A large sandy beach in a magnificent setting,

Whitesands is well known for its views, glorious sunsets and crystal clear water. It is understandably popular with safe swimming and surfing areas designated by the lifeguards who patrol here during the summer months. If you can drag yourself away from the beach, there are some stunning walks with memorable views over the St. Davids Peninsula and Ramsey Island. Facilities at the beach are good and include a large car park. As an added bonus St. Davids, Britains smallest city is close by with its many attractions and ancient cathedral.

PORTHMELGAN (33)

Porthmelgan is a sandy and secluded beach close to Whitesands. Access is along the coastal path from St. Davids or the car park at Whitesands.

ABERIEDDY BAY (34)

A few miles along the coast towards Fishguard will bring you to Aberieddy Bay which is vastly different to other beaches in the county in that it is covered in black sand. This is the result of waves constantly pounding the slate cliffs on either side.

Tiny fossil graptolites can be found in pieces of shale, which have geological importance and should not be removed. Nearby is the Blue Lagoon, a deep flooded slate quarry, which serves as a reminder that the area was quarried until 1904 when the slate was shipped all around Britain. A large car park overlooks the beach but bathers should take car when going into the waters because of undercurrents.

TRAETH LLYFN (35)

Half a mile away from Aberieddy is Traeth Llyfn, a beautiful sandy beach whose only access is down steep steps. The beach is enclosed by cliffs and can be dangerous for swimming, especially in rough seas because of strong undertows. There is also the possibility of getting cut off by the incoming tide. There are no amenities although there is a small clifftop car park within walking distance.

TREFIN (36)

Trefin is not suitable for bathing because of rocks and an unstable cliff, but there are excellent walks and views along the coast in both directions. Above the beach where parking is very limited, there are the remains of an old mill.

Abereiddy Bay

Trefin

Whitesands

16

Newport Sands

Pwllgwaelod

ABERCASTLE (37)

Abercastle is an attractive sheltered harbour much favoured by fishermen, boat enthusiasts and walkers. Picturesque cottages overlook the shingle beach, which has a small car park. Above the beach to the right lies Carreg Samson, a 4,500 year old burial chamber.

ABERMAWR (38)

Abermawr is a large sheltered beach covered in pebbles, which is rarely visited by lots of people. Access is along a short path from the road where parking is limited and although there are no other amenities, the beach is well worth visiting. Like other Pembrokeshire beaches the low tide reveals the remains of a drowned forest.

PWLLGWAELOD (39)

Pwllgwaelod near Dinas Head is a small attractive sandy beach with views of Fishguard Bay and its harbour. It offers good cliff walking, a nature trail and the beach at Cwm-Yr-Eglwys.

CWM-YR-EGLWYS (40)

Cwm-Yr-Eglwys is a petite eye-catching cove popular with families. Overlooking the picturesque shingle and pebble beach are the remains

of the 12th Century church of St. Brynach, which was destroyed during a fierce storm in 1859. The storm also wrecked over 100 ships. Access is along a narrow country lane off the main road between Fishguard and Cardigan, but is very much worth a visit. There is limited parking in a private car park.

NEWPORT PARROG (41)

The historic town of Newport stands near the mouth of the River Nevern where there are two beaches, one on either side of the estuary. The Parrog is on the southern side and although this is the more sheltered beach, unpredictable currents may make bathing dangerous. However the area is rich in prehistoric sites, including the Pentre Ifan burial chamber.

NEWPORT SANDS (42)

By far the more popular of Newport's two beaches, this vast expanse of sand on the northern side of the Nevern Estuary is backed by dunes and a golf course. A favourite spot for beach games and all manner of watersports, visitors should be careful of the dangerous currents around the mouth of the river. There is a large car park above the beach and limited parking on the sand.

CEIBWR BAY (43)

Ceibwr Bay is an ideal base for coastal walks as the area boasts the highest cliffs in Pembrokeshire. The spectacular coastal scenery includes the Witches Cauldron (a cave, blowhole and natural arch) together with incredible folding of the cliff rock strata. Another attraction is the sight of Atlantic grey seals swimming offshore or basking on the rocks. Access to Ceibwr Bay is along a narrow road from the village of Moylegrove with limited parking above the bay

POPPIT SANDS (44)

Situated at the mouth of the Teifi Estuary, Poppit Sands is a large expanse of sand which marks the northern border of Pembrokeshire and the northern end of the Pembrokeshire Coastal Path. The proximity of the beach to the town of Cardigan has made it very popular with visitors. Bathers should be aware of dangerous currents and heed the warning signs and lifeguard flags. The beach is backed by sand dunes and mudflats, both of which are sensitive, fragile environments important to wildlife, so should be avoided. Facilities close to the beach are good and include a large car park.

Ceibwr Bay

Cwm-Yr-Eglwys

18

TENBY & THE SOUTH COAST

"Little England beyond Wales", is the affectionate term by which South Pembrokeshire is known. The description owes its origin to the Normans who effectively created a linguistic and cultural divide between the north and south of the county when they arrived in Pembrokeshire in 1093. Today this divide still exists. South Pembrokeshire is much more English than it is Welsh, while in North Pembrokeshire the reverse is true. However to visitors the difference is purely academic, and, if anything adds to the variety of this unspoiled corner of West Wales. There are four main holiday centres in South Pembrokeshire, Tenby, Saundersfoot, Pembroke and Narberth. Tenby and its near neighbour Saundersfoot are among Britain's favourite seaside resorts, while the ancient town of Pembroke, which celebrated 900 years of history in 1993, boasts one of Britain's best preserved medieval castles. Narberth too is an historic town with a Norman castle. All four centres are close to the countless visitor attractions and places of interest, and each provides an ideal base for exploring the glorious South Pembrokeshire coastline and countryside.

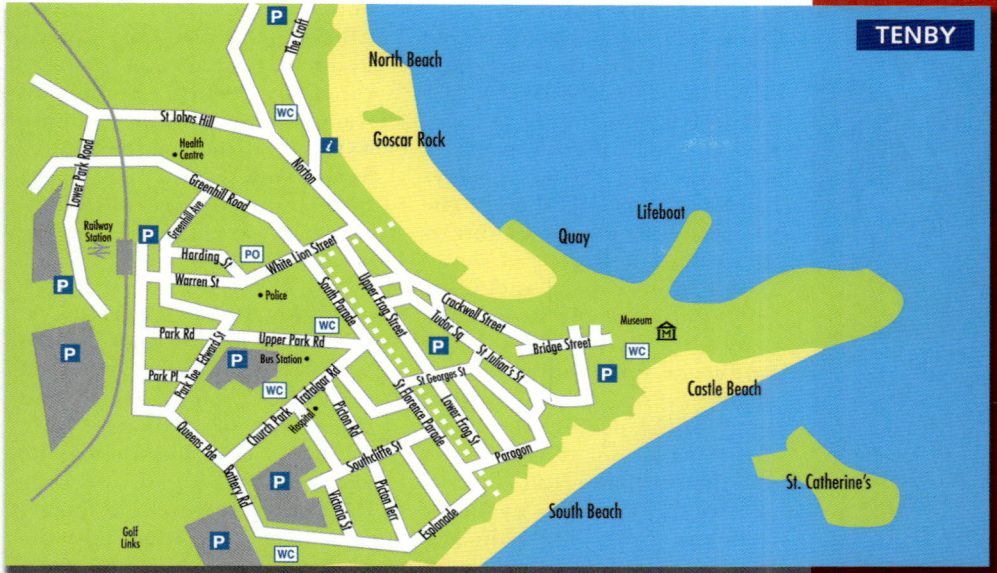

Map labels:

North Beach
Goscar Rock
Lifeboat
Quay
Castle Beach
St. Catherine's
South Beach
The Croft
St Johns Hill
Health Centre
Norton
Greenhill Road
Railway Station
Greenhill Ave
Harding St
White Lion Street
PO
Warren St
Police
South Parade
Upper Frog Street
Crackwell Street
Tudor Sq
St Julian's St
Bridge Street
Museum
Park Rd
Upper Park Rd
Bus Station
Park Ave
Edward St
St Georges St
Park Pl
Trafalgar Rd
Picton Rd
St Florence Parade
Lower Frog St
Queens Pde
Church Park
Hospital
Southcliffe St
Paragon
Battery Rd
Picton Terr
Victoria St
Esplanade
Golf Links

Tenby

Distances: Fishguard 36m; Haverfordwest 19m; Milford Haven; 19m; Narberth 10m; Pembroke 10m; St. Davids 35m; Saundersfoot 3m; Carmarthen 27m; London 247m

Little has changed in Tenby since wealthy Victorians provided the finance to develop the town into one of Britain's most attractive holiday resorts. The Victorians came here for the good of their health, but it was the birth of the coming railway in 1866 which saw a ground swell of visitors. Were those early visitors to return today, they would no doubt be surprised to discover that Tenby is almost as they had left it and has seemingly escaped what many would regard as the "plague" of modern development. Much of the 13th century wall which surrounds Tenby is still intact and the narrow streets, freshly recobbled to imitate a bygone age are still packed tight with shops and places to eat. Although the bathing machines have long gone, the beaches have still retained their appeal. Both the North Beach and South Beach are a mecca for holidaymakers. The picturesque harbour too is unchanged except for the boats. In Victorian time Tenby's link with the sea was dominated by the boats of a once thriving fishing industry as opposed to the leisure craft, which now shuttle visitors to Caldy Island, home to a Reformed Order of Cistercian Monks. Tenby also offers a great deal away from the beach and here are some of the resort's most popular attractions.

Tenby

20

Tudor Square, Tenby

Tenby Harbour

TENBY MURAL

Described as a panorama of Tenby's history, this magnificent mural by local artist Eric Bradforth is a highly decorative and informative work of art gracing Tenby's refurbished Market Hall. The mural, which measures 32ft by 8ft reveals a wealth of detail about Tenby's past, including the building of the town walls together with the arrival of the Pembroke and Tenby railway in July 1863. It also depicts many of the people who made their mark on the town. A detailed explanation of the painting's content is available from the Tenby Museum and Art Gallery.

CASTLE HILL

Overlooking Tenby harbour, and with panoramic views across Carmarthen Bay to Worms Head and the Gower Peninsula, Castle Hill is where you will find the Welsh national memorial to Prince Albert, Consort to Queen Victoria, which was inaugurated by Prince Arthur in August 1865. Another tribute to the Victorians is the replica bandstand, built in 1991 where regular musical performances are given every summer.

TENBY HARBOUR

Small, picturesque and brightly coloured by the neat painted cottages and spectrum of summer sail, Tenby harbour has a magnetic attraction. To sit on the harbour wall watching fisher men cast their lines and the boats sailing to and from Caldy Island is a pleasurable way of whiling away the time. Alternatively you can explore the lifeboat station passing Laston House on the way, where in the 19th century, Sir William Paxton played his part in helping to put Tenby on the map as a fashionable resort.

Tenby, from the sea

TUDOR MERCHANT'S HOUSE

Tenby's 15th century Tudor Merchant's House is the oldest furnished residence in the town. Standing on Quay Hill, between the harbour and Tudor square, its authentic furniture and fittings recreate the atmosphere of the period and illustrate the manner in which a successful Tudor merchant and his family would have lived. Three of the interior walls bear the remains of early Frescoes. Owned and managed by the National Trust, the house is open between March and October.

for further information call 01834 842279 or 01558 822800

TENBY LIFEBOAT STATION

Tenby is fortunate to have two lifeboats, the Hayden Miller and the smaller inshore rescue boat, the Georgina Stanley Taylor. The old lifeboat station, which is still standing, was established in 1852. The new lifeboat station is open to the public from the end of March to the end of October, between 10am and 4.30pm 7 days a week and most summer evenings until around 9pm. The new lifeboat, the Hayden Miller has been in operation since March 2006.

for further information go to www.tenby rnli.co.uk

Tenby's new Lifeboat Station

22

Caldey Lighthouse

CALDEY ISLAND

A visit to Caldey Island is like stepping onto a different world. The monastery and ancient churches combine with the sea air and quiet, beautiful surroundings to create Caldey's unique atmosphere of timelessness and peace. Caldey is more than just an island with a monastery. You can enjoy a snack at the Tea Gardens, try the unique perfumes made on the island, visit the Chocolate Factory and Weaver's Shop, choose an unusual gift or send a postcard franked with the island's special stamp. You can watch a video about the life of the monks and explore the Old Priory and the island's simple and inspiring churches. A walk up to the Lighthouse offers spectacular views of the Pembrokeshire coast and beyond. You can also follow the waymarked cliff and woodland paths, or simply relax on the sandy beach at Priory Bay. Caldey is a 20 minute boat trip from Tenby. Boats run every 20-30 minutes between 10am and 5pm from Easter to the end of October. Sailings are Monday to Saturday from May to September and Monday to Friday in April and October with selected saturdays. A full range of products can be found at the Caldey Island shop, Quay Street, Tenby.

Visit www.caldey-island.co.uk

DE VALANCE PAVILION

This impressive 500 seater hall in Upper Frog Street in the heart of Tenby hosts a great variety of entertainment throughout the year.

for details of 2008 entertainment and events ring 01834 842730

TENBY ARTS FESTIVAL
Saturday 20th - 27th September 2008

Many visitors and local residents have discovered over the years that one of the best times to be in Tenby is at the time of the Arts Festival in late September. Traditionally it opens with a weekend of family fun, launched by a grand parade of entertainers through the streets of the town, followed by a free concert at the harbour. The main eight-day Festival provides a feast of music, dance, cinema, poetry, art, drama and talks in a diverse programme featuring international names as well as local artists. The 2008 programme includes the famous cellist Julian Lloyd Webber; the world renowned pianist Noriko Owaga, who makes a welcome return; the Edinburgh Camerata, who will present a delightful Sunday afternoon concert; and the captivating gypsy-style music of the Amigos. Additionally a must for visitors to Wales is the music of a Welsh Male Voice Choir, as well as other musical ensembles. There will be Arts and Crafts displays and workshops. Notable in the programme of talks will be one by Roy Haggar, whose family have been making and showing films in and of Pembrokeshire for generations. A national daily rated last years Festival in the top five in the U.K.

Programmes will be available in the Summer from Information Centres, libraries and other outlets throughout Pembrokeshire. Tel:01834 845341 or visit www.tenbyartsfest.co.uk

FRIENDS OF PEMBROKESHIRE NATIONAL PARK

Do you love Pembrokeshire National Park?. Most visitors do because of the stunning coastal scenery, unspoiled sandy beaches, hidden coves and wide estuaries, spectacular cliffs, abundant flora and fauna and above all, the magnificent 186 mile long coastal path. The only coastal national park in the UK is worth protecting and the Friends aim is to protect, conserve and enhance the Park and safeguard its future. The organisation does this in a variety of ways: not least by encouraging the National Park Authority in its statutory role and also campaigning against any proposals which might threaten the peace and beauty of the landscape. Among other things, the body organises work parties which enhance the Park, undertakes guided visits to places of interest not always accessible to the general public, arranges education programmes and generally contributes to the life of the Park. Members also enjoy a regular newsletter and a discount on National Park goods.

More friends are needed to protect and enhance this lovely area, so why not join now. Full details can be found on the websitewww.fpnp.org.uk, Tel: 01646 680392 pick up a leaflet from any Pembrokeshire Tourist Information Centre

SILENT WORLD AQUARIUM

Silent World Aquarium and Reptile Collection is one of the most fascinating, intriguing and memorable visits the Tenby area has to offer, and one of the few that are indoors - a refuge in bad weather, but best seen on a sunny day, it's quieter! Housed in an attractive 19th century chapel of rest close to the North Beach, The Aquarium displays a collection of over 200 species of British Marine Life, some exotic fish such as Seahorses and Amphibians like the Axolotl. TheReptile,Amphibian and Creepy Crawlies from around the world are in over 30 displays upstairs. You will also find a themed gift and book shop, fresh ground coffee and a fine pot of tea.

NORMANDIE

BAR · ACCOMMODATION · RESTAURANT

The Normandie is a vibrant, colourful bar and restaurant with rooms, nestled between the Historic Town Walls and Upper Frog Street in the picturesque harbour town of Tenby, on the beautiful coast of West Wales. Emphasis here is on great beers, good wines, delicious freshly made food and comfortable spacious ensuite bedrooms.

The Normandie Upper Frog Street Tenby
Tenby Pembrokeshire West Wales
Tel. 01834 842227
Web: Normandietenby.co.uk
info@Normandietenby.co.uk

Tenby Museum

7

TENBY & THE SOUTH COAST

TENBY LEISURE CENTRE
Facilities include swimming pool and children's learner pool, multi-purpose sports hall and fitness room.

For more information ring 01834 843575. See activity section

TENBY MUSEUM AND GALLERY
Founded in 1878, Tenby Museum and Art Gallery is one of Tenby's main indoor attractions with the reputation of being one of the best local museums in the country. Situated on a spectacular site in part of the medieval castle, overlooking castle beach and Caldey Island, the Museum is a pleasant place for visitors of all ages to explore. The galleries show the geology and archaeology of Pembrokeshire, its natural history, its bygones and the changing aspects of Tenby's developments up to the present day, including an exhibition on the history of Tenby harbour and the lifeboat. The Local History Gallery features an exhibition on the story of Tenby, featuring the history of the town from the 10th century. Minor exhibits include the last invasion of the British mainland by the French in 1797 and the story of piracy around the area. The art gallery concentrates on artists with close local associations and works by others which portray Tenby and its locality. Augustus John was born in Tenby and his sister Gwen, now highly regarded, was brought up

here. There is a permanent exhibition of their works, and a Gwilym Prichard exhibition is planned for June 28th to August 3rd 2008. Other artists represented in the permanent collection include John Piper, David Jones, John Knapp-Fisher and Tenby born artist Nina Hamnett. The second art gallery features regularly changing exhibitions and has included shows by Graham Sutherland, Philip Sutton and David Bellamy to name but a few. Tenby Museum and Art Gallery is open throughout the year. Full access for disabled visitors. Research facilities. Admission charges and concessions apply.

For information and opening times ring 01834 842809

Penally

Nestling just west of Tenby is the pretty hillside village of Penally, which overlooks Tenby's golf course and South Beach. Penally is a well kept village complete with Post Office, shop and pubs together with a good choice of accommodation including a first class hotel, the Penally Abbey, camping and caravan sites. A feature of the village is the 13th century church of St. Nicholas, which houses a memorial to the victims of the Tenby lifeboat who drowned when it capsized in 1834. Penally's proximity to Tenby, Lydstep, Manorbier, Freshwater East and Pembroke makes it an ideal holiday spot.

RITEC VALLEY QUAD BIKES, PENALLY

Ritec Valley Quad Bikes offers the ultimate in Quad bike entertainment whatever the weather, all year round.

Trail Riding is our serious activity (Minimum age 16) and needs to be booked in advance. We use 250cc semi-automatic sports quads (You need to be able to use gears).

We have over 12km of groomed routes to test every ability.

Arrive and Drive is for all ages and is carried out on Automatic quads (Minimum age 6). Arrive and Drive is for everyone under 16, families wishing to ride together or for seasoned quad bike addicts looking for a quick fix. No need to book, just Arrive and Drive.

We are open ALL YEAR but have a limited opening profile during the winter months.

For full info, please phone 01834 843390, check our website out. www.ritec-valley.co.uk Or email us on: info@ritec-valley.co.uk

Ritec Valley Quad Bikes

HEATHERTON COUNTRY SPORTS PARK, ST. FLORENCE, TENBY

Situated in acres of picturesque parkland near the village of St. Florence, Heatherton offers a great day out for families of all ages, with a bonus - there is no entry fee. You only pay for the activities that you participate in. Economies can also be made through family packages and group deals. Attractions include: The Maize Maze, Pirates of the Caribbean Adventure Golf, Coarse Fishing, Paintball Games, Clay Pigeon Shooting, Pistol Shooting, Karting Track, Bumper Boats, Baseball, 18 Hole Pitch and Putt Course and Horse Riding Centre.

For further information ring 01646 651025

Horseriding at Heatherton Country Sports Park

Penally from Tenby Golf Course

St. Florence

Once a medieval harbour standing on an inlet to the sea, St. Florence is a picturesque village of great charm and pretty cottages and boasts a past winner of the national "Wales in Bloom" competition. Here you will discover one of the areas's last surviving areas's last surviving curious round chimneys, which are often described as Flemish in style. Also of interest is the 13th century parish church, featuring a Norman tower.

St. Florence

Saundersfoot

This bustling village is about three miles from Tenby, lying at the foot of a picturesque wooded valley. With its attractive harbour and extensive sandy beaches, it has established itself as a popular centre for sailing, fishing, watersports and traditional seaside holidays. Originally a small fishing village and home to two shipyards by the 1800's, Saundersfoot was suddenly caught up in the excitement of the black gold rush when high quality anthracite was discovered locally. Such was the demand for this coal that in 1829 the harbour was built, connected by rail to six mines. The railway ran along what is now The Strand and the coal was exported worldwide. It was not until the Second World War that coal shipments ceased, but by this time another flourishing industry was putting the village on the map - tourism. The rest they say is history.

Saundersfoot

30

Pembrokeshire
Tourist Information Centres
www.visitpembrokeshire.com

SAUNDERSFOOT TIC
The Barbecue
Harbour Car Park
Saundersfoot
SA69 9HE
01834 813672
saundersfoot.tic@pembrokeshire.gov.uk

TENBY TIC
Unit 2
Gateway Complex
Upper Park Road
Tenby
SA70 7LT
01834 842402/04
tenby.tic@pembrokeshire.gov.uk

PEMBROKE TIC
The Commons Road
Pembroke
SA71 4EA
01646 622388
pembroke.tic@pembrokeshire.gov.uk

FERRY TERMINAL TIC
Irish Ferries
Pembroke Dock
SA72 6JZ
pembrokedock.tic@pembrokeshire.gov.uk

MILFORD HAVEN TIC
94 Charles Street
Milford Haven
SA73 2HL
01646 690866
milford.tic@pembrokeshire.gov.uk

NEWPORT TIC
2 Bank Cottages
Long Street
Newport
01239 820912

HAVERFORDWEST TIC
19 Old Bridge
Haverfordwest
SA61 2EZ
01437 763110
haverfordwest.tic@pembrokeshire.gov.uk

OCEAN LAB
The Parrog
Goodwick
SA64 0DE
01348 874737
fishguardharbour.tic@pembrokeshire.gov.uk

FISHGUARD TIC
The Town Hall
The Square
Fishguard
SA65 9HE
01437 776636
fishguard.tic@pembrokeshire.gov.uk

KILGETTY TIC
Kingsmoor Common
Kilgetty
01834 814161

**PEMBROKESHIRE COAST NATIONAL
PARK VISITOR CENTRES**
www.pembrokeshirecoast.org.uk

ST. DAVIDS VISITOR CENTRE
The Grove
St. Davids
SA62 6NW
01437 720392
enquires@stdavids.pembrokeshire.org.uk

Amroth

The small coastal village of Amroth sits on the Pembrokeshire and Carmarthenshire border, just seven miles from Tenby and four miles from Saundersfoot. It is a wild and beautifully unspoilt location. In summer the wonderful expanse of gently shelving sand, exposed at low tide, makes it a favourite beach for families and anglers alike. The village, spread along the narrow seafront, lacks the frills of bigger resorts but has an undeniable charm together with plenty of good facilities, including restaurants, pubs, gift shops, caravan parks and holiday homes. Attractions close by include Colby Woodland Garden, which is owned by the National Trust, and Pendine Sands, a resort made famous in the 1920's by speed king Sir Malcolm Campbell. In April 1926, Parry Thomas set a new World Land Speed record of 171.02mph driving his car "Babs". The following year he died at the wheel of "Babs" while attempting to regain the record. The car was buried in the sand by local villagers with the consent of his family and was recovered for restoration in March 1969.

Amroth

Pendine Sands

Wiseman's Bridge

A tiny hamlet, best known for its inn and rocky beaches, nestles on the coast between Saundersfoot and Amroth and at low tide it is possible to walk across the sands to either. You can also walk to Saundersfoot through the tunnels that once formed part of the all important railway link between local mines and Saundersfoot harbour.

Wiseman's Bridge

Kilgetty

Before the bypass was built, the main road into South Pembrokeshire from the east went through Kilgetty village. However, the place remains an important centre for visitors, with its Tourist Information Centre, railway station, supermarket and shops, and it's close to several major attractions. The neighbouring village of Begelly is well known for Folly Farm and Begelly Countryside Gardens and is a short distance west of Kilgetty as are the villages of Broadmoor and East Williamston, where there are first class caravan parks, a pub and a village shop.

Stepaside

It is hard to believe now but in the 19th century this quiet little hamlet was a hive of industrial activity after the Pembrokeshire Iron and Coal Company built the Kilgetty Ironworks here in 1848. Iron ore, in plentiful supply from seams along the cliffs between Amroth and Saundersfoot, was smelted in the blast furnace using locally produced limestone and coal and the iron transported to Saundersfoot harbour by railway. However, from the outset, the ironworks were beset by major problems and ceased operations less than forty years after going into production.

COLBY WOODLAND GARDEN

Described by the National Trust as one of their most beautiful properties in Pembrokeshire, the garden is part of the Colby Estate, which was established by John Colby, the 19th century mining entrepreneur. The garden is a spectacular blaze of colour from early spring to the end of June. On site is a National Trust shop where refreshments are available, along with a gallery, plant sales, toilets and a car park.

for more information
01834 811885

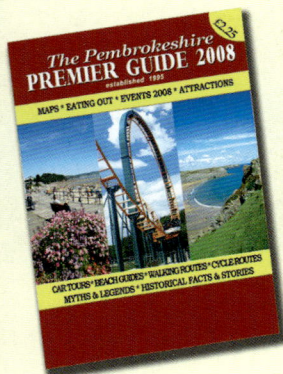

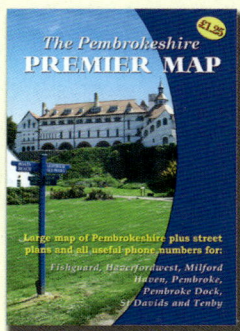

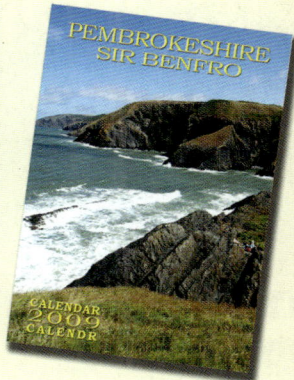

34

THE BIER HOUSE

The Bier House in the centre of the village was built in 1900 to house the parish bier, a funeral hand cart that was used to carry the dead to the burial ground. Now the building has been restored and provides an information point relating to the history of the parish.

Manorbier

Manorbier is a small seaside village midway between Tenby and Pembroke, and is best known for two striking features, the beach and a well preserved medieval castle. The castle, which enjoys a spectacular location overlooking the bay, was the birthplace of Gerald of Wales, a much respected medieval writer and a man of many talents whose two major works are still in print today. But Gerald wasn't the only one to find inspiration in Manorbier, George Bernard Shaw spent several months there, and prior to her marriage in 1912 Virginia Woolf was a regular summer visitor.

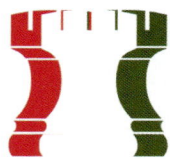

Lamphey

The village of Lamphey is the site of what is left of the Bishop's Palace, built in the 13th century by the Bishops of St. Davids and now in the care of Cadw who are responsible for Welsh Historic Monuments. The centuries old ruins are an evocative reminder of the great power enjoyed by the medieval Bishops of St. Davids. The comfortable palace buildings were set among well stocked fish-ponds, plump orchards and an extensive vegetable garden. In its heyday Lamphey boasted an impressive 144 acre park, a deer herd, windmill, two watermills and a dovecote. The palace's finest architectural features include the great hall built by Bishop Henry de Gower in the 14th century and the 16th century chapel.

for opening times and admission prices ring the Pembrokeshire Tourist Information and Visitor Centre on 01646 622388 or CADW (Welsh Historic Monuments) on 01443 336000

Lamphey Palace

37

Pembroke

Distance: Fishguard 26m, Haverfordwest 10m, Milford Haven 5m, Narberth 15m, St. Davids 26m, Tenby 12, Carmarthen 32m, London 252m.

Pembroke is a small but charming walled town with a genteel atmosphere and 900 year old history and much to recommend it to visitors. Like many other Welsh towns, Pembroke grew up around its medieval castle. This magnificent structure, the birthplace of Henry VII enjoys a spectacular location offering breathtaking views from the top of its famous keep. The castle is in a very good state of repair having undergone an extensive restoration programme that started as far back as 1928. Throughout the year the castle is the venue for many important events, several of which are traditions rooted firmly in the towns medieval past. The castle also plays host to such attractions including Shaskespearean productions, medieval banquets, military tattoos and displays by the Sealed Knot Society.The Norman Conquest saw Pembroke develop into the main base from which the invaders increased their stranglehold on West Wales. The town became a major market centre with regular fairs. Now every October this tradition is still remembered when the town celebrates the Pembroke Fair which attracts visitors from far and wide.

Pembroke Castle

PEMBROKE

CORNSTORE

To the casual observer there is little physical evidence to indicate Pembroke's important role in the maritime trade of Wales. However on the North Quay we have one remaining warehouse, "The Cornstore", an impressive three storey stone building which provides a little insight into the style of structure that was constructed to meet the needs of the maritime and Pembrokeshire trade in general. It would have been an expensive structure to erect and provides a clue to the potential wealth that had gathered in Pembroke by the mid-eighteenth century. Today the building is back in use after being subject to an award winning restoration. The building is currently occupied by Vintage Interiors who offer the most inspirational selection of furniture, accessories, textiles and accent pieces for the home in Pembrokeshire. In addition a wide range of personal accessories, handbags, jewellery and local arts are available. The Quayside Cafe offers freshly prepared light lunches and real Pembrokeshire Cream Teas.

for further information ring 01646 684290

39

The vast majority of Pembroke's shops, banks, restaurants and many of its most impressive Georgian houses are to be found along Main Street, a pleasant thoroughfare with facades ranging from Tudor to modern. Here visitors will discover an interesting mix of retail outlets, including those run by the Pembrokeshire Coast National Trust and Pembroke Visitor Centre. Another of the town's attractions is Mill Pond, formed by one of two tidal creeks. It's a popular beauty spot with visitors and locals alike because of the wildlife it attracts. Swans, herons, cormorants and if you are lucky enough even otters can be seen along this peaceful stretch of water. As visitors can explore Pembroke, they will see evidence of the town's ancient and extensive walls, which are a throwback to the 13th century, when the townsfolk demanded that stone walls be built to protect their cottages from raiders. It took thirty years to complete the task. Since the Norman Conquest 900 years ago, Pembroke's fortunes have been mixed. Under Norman rule, it established itself as an important trading port and hit a peak between the 17th and 19th centuries, exporting goods around Europe only to fall into decline with the coming of the railway. The situation was compounded by the gradual silting up of the shallow river entrance and in 1977, Pembroke was designated an outstanding Conservation Area.

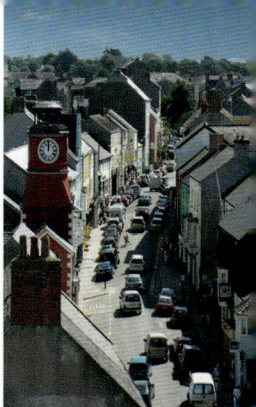

PEMBROKE FESTIVAL 2008

Now in its sixth successful year Pembroke Festival continues to showcase the best local musicians and artists encouraging new talent.

In addition to the established favourites; Battle of the Bands, World Music Night and the Celtic Fiddle Competition the Festival now has a host of other attractions on offer including a Farmers Market, hands-on wildlife activities, walks and talks and an art exhibition and competition. This years Festival will conclude with a pageant that involves the whole community and reflects the heritage of the historic walled town.

Pembroke Festival 2008 takes place 4th to 7th September 2008

For more information Tel: 01646 680090 www.pembrokefestival.org

PEMBROKE VISITOR CENTRE

Built in 1993 to coincide with the town's 900th birthday celebrations, this is an integral part of Pembroke's superb new Tourist Information Centre. Displays and exhibits tell the story of Pembroke and there is a choice of books, maps and souvenirs on sale.

tel:01646 622388

PEMBROKE CASTLE

Pembroke Castle is one of the best preserved medieval castles in Wales. Open to visitors all year round, it is an intriguing place to explore. The wide walls are honey-combed with a seemingly endless system of rooms, passageways and spiralling flights of narrow stone steps; interpretive displays and informative panels give a fascinating insight into the castles origins and long history. One of the most impressive features is the distinctive round keep, which was built soon after 1200. It is 75ft high and the views from the top in all directions are nothing short of magnificent. From this lofty position it is easy to understand why the Normans were well aware that the site was ideal for fortification, a low rocky peninsula between two tidal creeks offering superb natural defences. They quickly established a wooden fortress and in 1200 work began on the castle itself. Harri Tudor(Henry VII) was born in Pembroke Castle on 28th January 1457 of an Anglesey family. In 1485 he returned from exile in France, landing at Millbay on the Milford Haven waterway. From there he marched a growing army of largely untrained volunteers across country to Bosworth Field in Leicestershire to confront Richard III. Against the odds, Henry's forces defeated Richard and Henry became King of England. So ended the War of the Roses and began the Tudor dynasty.

For opening times and charges call
01646 681510 or 684585

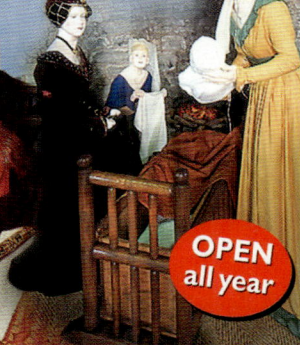

Pembroke Dock

Pembroke and Pembroke Dock are alike in only one respect: both have experienced fluctuating fortunes. There the similarity ends, because as a place of any significance Pembroke Dock has a very short history. In the early 19th century it was nothing more than a small coastal village known as Paterchurch. But when in 1814 the lease expired on the Royal Naval Dockyard in Milford Haven, the Admiralty decided to move its shipbuilding operation across the water and further from the mouth of the estuary and Paterchurch was designated the ideal site. Hence began an amazing transformation, which saw naval architects lay out the distinctive grid pattern of wide streets so characteristic of today's Pembroke Dock. The prosperous new town grew uparound the thriving dockyard and many fine ships were built here. These included HMS Tartar the first steam man of war, HMS Conflict, the first propeller driven war ship and several royal yachts. When the dockyard closed in 1926 it had produced more than 260 ships and the town's population exceeded 3000. But it was not long before ships were replaced by a totally different kind of boat. In 1930 a major part of the dockyard site was transferred from the Admiralty to the Air Ministry, and in the following year the Royal Air Force established a seaplane base, operated by Southampton flying boats of 210 Squadron. 1938 saw the arrival of the squadron's first

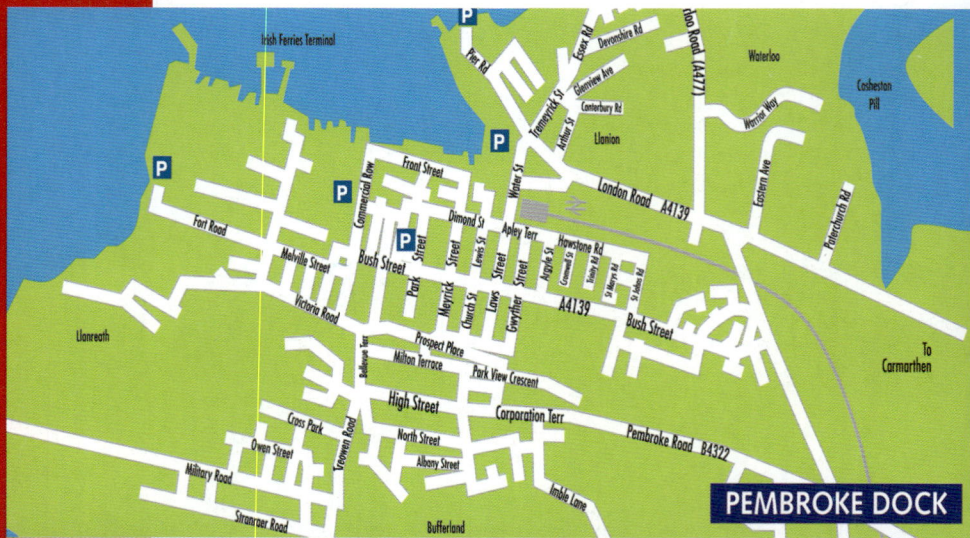

PEMBROKE DOCK

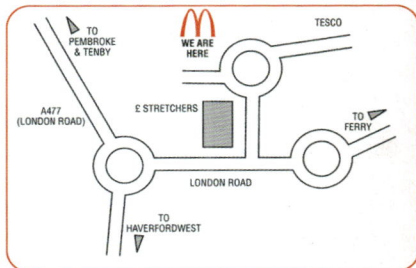

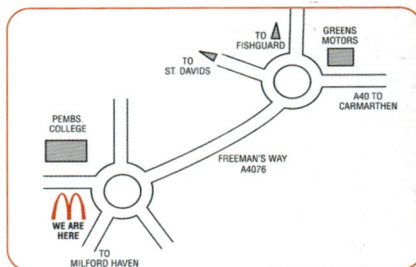

TENBY & THE SOUTH COAST

The Gun Tower Museum

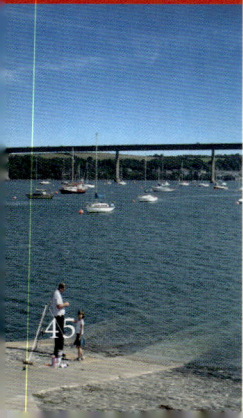

Pembroke Dock

Sunderland flying boat, the aircraft with which Pembroke Dock is most associated. During the Second World War the Sunderlands gave sterling service and eventually stayed on here until 1957. Even today the aeroplanes are far from forgotten, and on several occasions their spirits are revived in startling fashion. In March 1993, for example, during one of the lowest tides of the century, three men discovered the remains of a rear gun turret and fairing, part of a Sunderland flying boat of 201 Squadron that crashed in the Haven Waterway during a training exercise in March 1954. Today Pembroke Dock is better known as a ferry port with excellent boating and watersport facilities. The Cleddau toll bridge, at 150 feet high, gives spectacular views over the waterway in all directions. The Cleddau Bridge is, in fact, a very significant landmark because once you have crossed it to the waterway's northern shore you have left South Pembrokeshire behind.

THE GUN TOWER MUSEUM

The Gun Tower formed part of the fortifications of the Milford Haven waterway. The tower's specific role was to help defend and protect the Royal Naval Dockyard, though in the event the only threat came from the air raids in the Second World War, long after the dockyard had closed. Built in 1851 to repel "unwelcome guests", the imposing dressed stone tower now welcomes visitors with open arms. Visitors are offered an intriguing experience of the life lived by Queen Victoria's soldiers and marines, who waited, in these cramped quarters, for the French invasion that never came. Three floors of colourful models, pictures and full scale displays include life sized soldiers and many authentic relics. These build up an exciting picture of Pembrokeshire's military history. A splendid panoramic model shows us the town's Royal Dockyard. Here 250 warships were built, along with five elegant Royal yachts. A whole room is devoted to the RAF. During World War Two, Pembroke Dock was the world's largest operational flying boat base. Important features include an original working roof cannon and the basement magazine, where 20,000 lbs of gunpowder were stored, plus an educational video. Among new exhibits are a 12 ft wingspan model Sunderland flying boat and a display of authentic World War II aircrew uniforms and equipment.

for all information call
01646 622246

45

The Castlemartin Peninsula

The Castlemartin Peninsula, which is also known as the Angle Peninsula, typifies the unique appeal of South Pembrokeshire in that it has many special features of interest to many different groups. The magnificent scenery which unfolds along the coast path and the profusion of wild flowers and butterflies to be found here captivates photographers, walkers, artists and naturalists. Birdwatchers flock here for the colonies of guillemots, razorbills, kittiwakes, choughs and other species that nest along the cliffs and rock formations. To geologists, the peninsula presents some outstanding examples of fissures, sea caves, blowholes, natural arches and stacks, the result of continual sea erosion of the carboniferous limestone cliffs. Anthropologists have been excited by the discovery of bones and implements in caves which 20,000 years ago gave shelter to the regions earliest known human inhabitants. Historians are enchanted by such mysteries as tiny St. Govan's Chapel and by the remains of Iron Age Forts and other ancient sites. For visitors who are here to simply enjoy a holiday, there are attractions such as the Bosherston Lily Ponds and the superb beaches of Barafundle, Broad Haven, Freshwater West and West Angle Bay to savour. The peninsula is also well known for it's 6000 acre Ministry of Defence tank range. This means that a large section of the coastline is inaccessible, one of the very few places in Pembrokeshire that the coast path is diverted inland, but there is some compensation to visitors in that on certain days a spectator area enables you to watch the tanks in action as they fire live ammunition at a variety of still and moving targets. Much of the southern half of the peninsula, including the tank range, was once part of the Stackpole Estate. This embraced more than 13,000 acres and was on of the most substantial land holdings in Wales. Until 1688 the estate was owned by the Lort family of Stackpole, but in that year it changed hands when Elizabeth Lort married Alexander Campbell of the Cawdor Estate in Scotland. It was the enterprising Campbells who created the Bosherston Lakes and Lily Ponds. They also planted a great variety of trees and introduced many unusual and innovative ideas to the estate, including the building of a

Freshwater East

Stackpole Quay

stone icehouse, an 18th century refrigerator in which dairy produce was stored. In 1976 the National Trust acquired 2000 acres of the estate and is now responsible for its management. Sadly though, the mansion that stood on the estate, Stackpole Court, was demolished in the 1960's.

Freshwater East

From the small coastal village of Freshwater East, visitors are ideally placed to explore the stunning coastline of the Castlemartin Peninsula. Stackpole Quay, Barafundle Bay, the Bosherston Lily Ponds and Broad Haven Beach are all within very easy reach along the coast path, while only Barafundle is inaccessible by road. Freshwater East is also a popular resort in its own right. The Trewent Park holiday complex provides self-catering accommodation close to the beach and there are shops, a touring caravan park and other facilities.

Stackpole

Stackpole has its name in Norse origins, and the village as it stands today is in a different place from its original medieval site, having been moved by the Campbells in 1735 to accommodate growth of the Stackpole Estate. The centre

of the old village is about half a mile to the southwest, marked by the remains of a preaching cross.

Close to the present village are interesting areas of woodland, Castle Dock, Cheriton Bottom, Caroline Grove and Lodge Park, which were planted as part of the estate 200 years ago. There are species here from all over the world, many of them brought in from London's Kew Gardens. The woods are managed by the National Trust, who have created several miles of pathways for horses and walkers.

Stackpole Quay

The National Trust owns and manages Stackpole Quay, which it acquired in 1976 as part of the 2000 acres of Stackpole Estate. This acquisition also included the stretch of coastline between here and Broad Haven, under the Enterprise Neptune initiative, a scheme launched in 1965 to save and protect Britain's precious and threatened coastline.

Stackpole Quay was originally a private quay built for the estate, so that coal could be imported and limestone shipped out from the quarry. It is claimed that this is Britain's smallest harbour, however pleasure boats are now the only craft that use the stone jetty.

There are good parking facilities here, as well as toilets and a new National Trust Information Centre and cafe. This car park is as close as you can get by road to nearby Barafundle beach, which is accessible via the coast path.

Stackpole Quay is also notable for its geological features. Fossils of old shells and corals can be seen in the rocks, and just to the east of the quay is a change in the cliff landscape where the grey carboniferous limestone gives way to deposits of old red sandstone.

facilities, but groups or event organisers should first contact the warden. Close to the quarry is the main car park for Stackpole Quay, along with the National Trust holiday cottages, carefully converted from old buildings.

for more information about holiday letting call 0870 458411 or visit www.nationaltrust.org.uk for details of the quarry facilities call 01646 661359

Stackpole Quarry

As part of its management of the Stackpole Estate, the National Trust has utilised the natural geological features of the old quarry near Stackpole Quay to create an area in which visitors, including those with special needs, can enjoy countryside recreation. Around the top of the quarry is a circular path giving spectacular vistas of the surrounding landscape and coastline. Down below, on the quarry floor, are sheltered picnic and barbeque areas and an archery bay. In addition, the cleared rock faces a present a challenge to experienced climbers and abseilers. Everyone can use the quarry's

Bosherston

For such a small village, Bosherston certainly enjoys its fair share of fame due to its proximity to several major tourist attractions in South Pembrokeshire. These include the delightful Bosherston Lily Ponds, part of the Stackpole Lakes, and Broad Haven beach. On days when the M.O.D tank range is not in use and the access roads are open, Bosherston is also the gateway to the remarkable St. Govan's Chapel and some of the best limestone cliff scenery in Europe, with coastal features such as St. Govan's Head, Huntsman's Leap, Stack Rocks and the Green Bridge of Wales.

Bosherston Lily Ponds

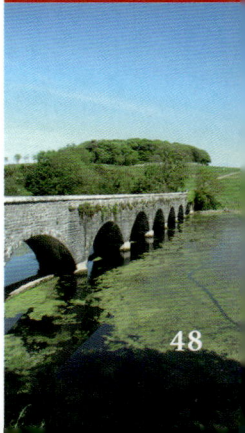

Eight Arch Bridge, Bosherston

Lilies in bloom

Broad Haven Beach

49

The village is also home to the 14th century St.Michael's Church which has an unusual cross of the same period standing in the churchyard. Much older still is a huge boulder, originating from Scotland, which was deposited at Bosherston by a moving glacier during the last Ice Age. Bosherston also has ample parking, with alternative parking above Broad Haven, and a pub, tearooms and toilets. When the tank range access road is open there is also plenty of free parking at St. Govan's.

to find out range road access times ask at any Tourist Information Centres or ring Merrion Camp on 01646 662287 or Bosherston Tearooms on 01646 661216.

Bosherston Lily Ponds & Broad Haven Beach

When the Campbells of Stackpole created the lakes and lily ponds to enhance their estate in the late 18th and early 19th centuries, they were unwittingly setting the scene for an attraction that brings thousands of annual visitors to the small village of Bosherston. Covering more

than 80 acres, the lakes and lily ponds are the largest area of fresh water in the Pembrokeshire Coast National Park and are part of the Stackpole National Nature Reserve. They are usually at their very best around June, when the lilies are in full bloom, but even in winter they provide easy and fascinating walks. They also offer good coarse fishing and are well stocked with roach, pike, tench and eels. Fishing permits are available from the tearooms in the village. There are in fact three lakes, artificially created by the deliberate flooding of narrow limestone valleys. The lily ponds occupy only the western lake, which is fed by underwater springs. Grey herons are regular visitors, and the total lakes area attracts a great variety of birds and wildlife, including coots, moorhens, mallard, teal, swans, cormorants, kingfishers, buzzards and many smaller winged visitors such as blue damseflies and emperor dragonflies. Over 20 species of duck alone have been recorded here.

St. Govan's Chapel

Remarkable St. Govan's Chapel is one of the wonders of Pembrokeshire. A tiny building hidden in a fissure in the cliff near St. Govan's car park, the restored chapel nestles at the bottom of a flight of narrow steps. It is said that if you count the steps on the way down and then count them on the way back up, the numbers won't tally. This is only one of the mysteries and legends attached to the chapel. Though it occupies the site of a 5th century hermit's cell, the age of the chapel itself is not known for sure; expert estimates put it at no older than 11th century. St. Govan is reputedly buried beneath the altar. It is also said that Sir Gawaine, one of King Arthur's Knights, lived here in isolation. Yet another legend tells of the holy well's miraculous healing powers. St. Govan's Chapel is close to St. Govan's Head, the most southerly point in Pembrokeshire and is well worth seeing for its dramatic cliff scenery. Both are accessible via the road that runs through Bosherston village.

Huntsman's Leap

According to legend, a horseman fleeing from pursuers miraculously leaped across this gaping chasm in the cliffs west of St. Govan's Chapel. On looking back he was so horrified by the prospect of what might have happened that the shock killed him anyway.

Castlemartin

In the small village of Castlemartin is a circular stone cattle pound, built in the 18th century, which now serves as a traffic roundabout. There is another connection here with cattle in that the land, rich and well drained because of the carboniferous limestone, is some of the most fertile in Wales and was at one time renowned for its high cereal yield and breed of Welsh Black cattle. Close to the village is the tank range spectator area, which when open gives free admission to cars and coaches. Just east of Castlemartin is Merrion Camp itself, where two tanks stand on display at the main gates. When the range is not in use there is access to Stack Rocks car park. From here it is only a short walk to the spectacular Green Bridge of Wales, a natural limestone arch, and the two vertical rock stacks that give rise to the name Stack Rocks. In early summer these rocks are a cacophony of calling seabirds as thousands of breeding guillemots and razorbills cling to every ledge.

Flimston Chapel

This medieval chapel, used as a barn until it was restored, is now open to visitors and stands beside a deserted farm on the Castlemartin tank range. It is accessible along the road to Stack Rocks car park, (which is open only when the range is not in use) It is dedicated to St. Martin, and in the churchyard, where boulders deposited by glaciers have been used as gravestones, stands the stone Ermigate Cross.

Angle

The village of Angle, sandwiched between the popular sandy beach of West Angle Bay and the pleasure craft which moor in East Angle Bay, is at the entrance to the Milford Haven waterway, and has a long seafaring tradition. It also has a lifeboat, housed in an impressive modern station. Among its historic buildings are a medieval fortified residence, Tower House, the scant remains of a castle, a dovecote and 15th century Angle Hall. Angle and the surrounding area is superb walking country. In addition to the delights to be discovered on the coast path, there is much to see along the Haven waterway, where supertankers and sailboats share one of the world's best natural deep-water harbours.

Green Bridge of Wales

Standing just 150 yards or so from Stack Rocks car park, the Green Bridge of Wales is an excellent example of a natural limestone arch. It was formed by the joining of two caves, each created by erosion of the rock by constant bombardment by the sea, and eventually the roof of the arch will collapse and leave a pinacle of rock, a stack standing in the sea. This is the same process that created Stack Rocks. The Green Bridge of Wales is easy to see and photograph in full profile with complete safety thanks to the wooden viewing platform constructed especially for the purpose by the National Park Authority.

WHERE TO EAT GUIDE

TENBY & THE SOUTH COAST

Tenby

D.FECCI & SONS

Award winning licensed gourmet fish and chip restaurant and take away with an extensive menu

FIVE ARCHES TAVERN & RESTAURANT

A highly recommended venue with a variety of homemade dishes on the menu see page 24

THE NORMANDIE

A vibrant, colourful bar and restaurant with rooms, nestled between the Historic Town Walls and Upper Frog Street in the picturesque harbour town of Tenby, emphasis is on great food, wines and beers and excellent accommodation. see page 26

Penally

PENALLY ABBEY COUNTRY HOUSE HOTEL

Delicious unpretencious food in beautiful surroundings.
see inside front cover

Stackpole

THE STACKPOLE INN

High quality home cooked food, including roasts on Sunday, Lunch, Dinner and daily specials.

Carew

THE CAREW INN

Excellent pub and restaurant, high quality fare with an extensive menu including many Pembrokeshire recipes.

Pembroke Dock

THE CLEDDAU BRIDGE HOTEL

Excellent a la carte restaurant serving high quality fare, combining an excellent menu with fantastic waterway views.
see inside rear cover

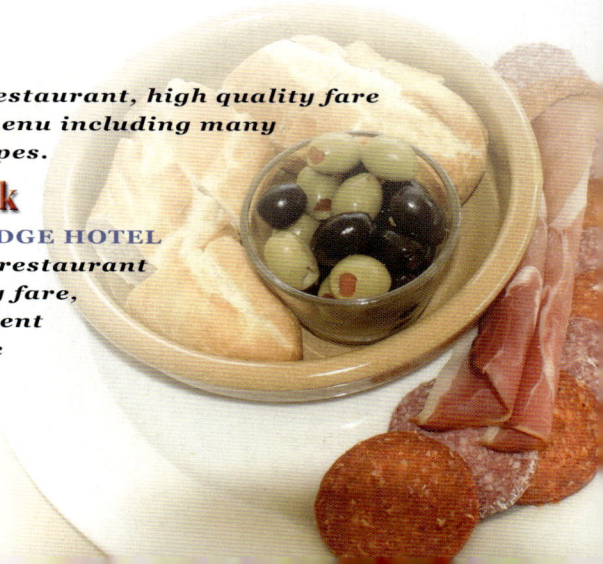

MCDONALD'S RESTAURANT
Good quality fast food for the family in a hurry.
see page 44

Lydstep
THE LYDSTEP TAVERN
Good food and fine ale in a traditional country inn.
see page 35

Lamphey
THE DIAL INN
Excellent bar food and wine, plus an imaginative evening menu.
see page 37

Pembroke
THE CORN STORE
Take refreshments in our waterside cafe with fresh locally sourced produce.
see page 39

Martletwy
CWM DERI VINEYARD AND ESTATE
Whether it is a simple cup of coffee and cake, a cream tea or a full meal, the restaurant and cafe at Cwm Deri can satisfy your needs. Using only the finest quality local ingredients from Pembrokeshire and West Wales wherever possible, our chef Daniel can cater for the food requirements of individuals or for parties of up to forty or more.
see page 175

Lawrenny
QUAYSIDE TEAROOM
Beautiful homemade cakes, Pembrokeshire clotted cream teas, freshly baked baguettes, local crab and daily specials in a magnificent waterside setting.
see page 173

WHERE TO EAT GUIDE

HAVERFORDWEST & THE WEST COAST

Haverfordwest

VINCENT DAVIES
A mouthwatering selection of home cooked food and an excellent menu in friendly surroundings. see page 74

McDONALDS
Good fast food for the family in a hurry see page 44

Broad Haven

NAUTILUS
A popular bar and restaurant with function rooms. Outstanding food in a stylish contemporary setting with stunning seafront and sunset views.

ST DAVIDS & THE NORTH COAST

Porthgain

THE SLOOP INN
A varied menu catering for all tastes and only 100 yards from the harbour. see page 124

Mathry

THE FARMERS ARMS
Charming old inn serving good homemade food in the bar or conservatory garden room.
see page 125

Trefin

ORIEL-Y-FELIN GALLERY & TEAROOM
Mouthwatering lunches, clotted cream teas, etc., using the best of Pembrokeshire produce. Les Routiers recommended
see page 126

Newport

THE CANTEEN
Teas, coffees, light lunches and full evening meals. see page 135

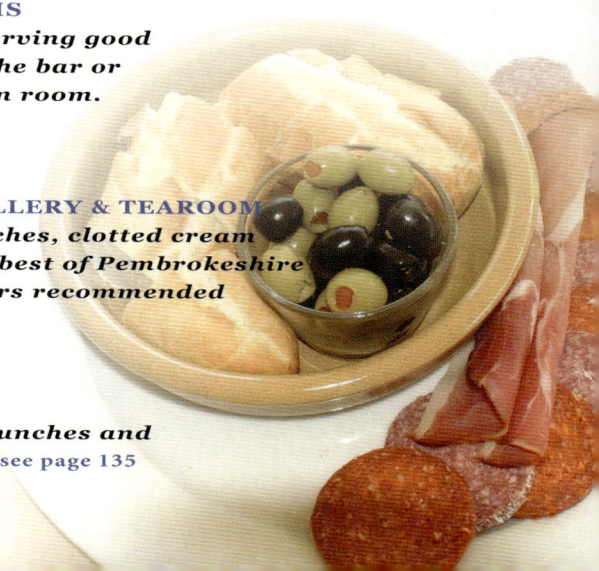

Moylegrove

PAVILION CAFE, PENRALLT NURSERY & GARDEN CENTRE

Enjoy homemade lunches, freshly made coffee and wonderful cream teas, set in a beautiful location overlooking the sea at Ceibwr Bay.

INLAND PEMBROKESHIRE

Clarbeston Road

LLYS-Y-FRAN RESERVOIR RESTAURANT/TEA ROOMS

Restaurant menu and beverages available whilst you visit see page 150 the reservoir.

Rosebush

THE OLD POST OFFICE TEA ROOMS & RESTAURANT

Good Welsh cooking from local produce.

Boncath

THE NAGS HEAD

Historic riverside pub well known for its superb pub food, interesting restaurant menu and generous portions.

Clynderwen

TREFACH COUNTRY PUB

Restaurant and fully licensed bar open all year round.

Narberth

THE CREATIVE CAFE

Paint your own pottery whilst enjoying special coffees, baguettes and homemade cakes. Now licensed.
see page 159

56

OAKWOOD
THEME PARK
Canaston Bridge

Oakwood Theme Park is a top ten UK theme park and with over 30 rides and attractions there's something for everyone. Thrill seekers can brave Speed, our newest white knuckle ride and the UK's first rollercoaster with a beyond vertical drop. Or why not try Megafobia, the award winning wooden coaster with character, you'll get off laughing and be desperate for more. Not afraid of heights? Well, what about The Bounce, a 160ft Shot 'n Drop Tower coaster which shoots riders into the air at speeds of 70 kph in less than two seconds. Or maybe you fancy cooling off on Hydro, the steepest and wettest ride in Europe!

For those who prefer a slightly slower pace we have fantastic family rides for everyone to enjoy. You can whiz around the slides of Snake River Falls, pilot your own plane on Plane Crazy or take a relaxing paddle around the Boating Lake on one of our pedaloes. Joining these great rides are The Waterfall, Bobsleigh, Spooky 3D, the Pirate Ship and many, many more the only problem is making sure you have time to squeeze them all in!

For smaller kids there's plenty of fun to be had in KidzWorld – a special world created just for children. In KidzWorld your child can lead an expedition into the under-cover adventure play-world The Lost Kingdom. WhizzKidz can experiment with more than 30 hands-on science exhibits in the indoor discovery world Techniquest. In The Wacky Factory, they'll have a ball! Equipped with thousands of soft balls, banana blasters, air fountains and levitation tables all propelled by compressed air, The Wacky Factory is an interactive play zone where kids can go wild! And for the little ones there's Playtown, where kids can ride the Clown Coaster, pilot their own jet plane or cause chaos on the roads in their own Trucks.

AND the fun doesn't stop there ... join us throughout August for After Dark when the park is open until 10pm every night when you can experience the thrill of riding our rides by night! The party atmosphere really kicks off in the Premier Theatre with our fantastic live shows every night.

Theme Park OAKWOOD
PEMBROKESHIRE

MEGAFOBIA
THRILLS BEYOND FEAR

The BEST for family FUN and thrills

Please ring: 01834 891376 or check website for 2008 opening times

Bookings and brochure requests: 01834 861889

Signposted from the end of the M4 and off the A40 at Canaston Bridge, 8 miles east of Haverfordwest

online booking at www.oakwoodthemepark.co.uk

Make sure you keep an eye out for something rather special happening during Easter 2008 when things are not quite what they seem when we reopen on 20th March with our brand new Easter show.

We've got a great variety of food for you to choose from to make sure you've got the energy to carry on all day! There's Woody's Burger Bar for family meal deals and flame grilled burgers; Dixie's Chicken Diner for finger licking southern fried chicken; the Restaurant for fish and chips and jacket potatoes; Acorn Arms for cream teas and cakes; and a variety of hot dog stalls, ice cream kiosks and sweet shops. Don't forget to visit

Oakwood's retail shops for gifts, mementoes and exclusive ride merchandise – they'll make the memories of a great day at Oakwood go on and on forever!

To make your day easier there's plenty of free parking, left luggage facilities, picnic areas, baby changing areas and we've even got kennels for your dog!

So go on ... take a ride on the wild side at Oakwood this year!

For a great family day out call for more information on 01834 861889 or visit our new website at www.oakwoodthemepark.co.uk

THE DINOSAUR PARK
Gumfreston, Tenby

At the Dinosaur Park, Tenby on the mile long Dinosaur Trail deep in the woodlands, on the board-walks over swamps where over 20 life size dinosaurs are waiting to meet you. A few tips...Mother Triceratops roars out if you get too close to baby Tiny Tops and close examination of the Pteranodon eggs brings a screech from Terry. Look out for the hissing raptors devouring a carcass (they might mistake you for lunch!). Roger the T-Rex is always hungry so steer clear of his snapping jaws and tiptoe past Eric the spitting Dilosophaur otherwise you may get wet! This is just a taste of what you'll encounter. If you survive all this, complete the free quiz and earn your 'Expert' sticker.

Visit Dino's Den Adventure Playland with a custom built indoor Adventure Playground for tougher and bigger kids alongside a brilliant Soft Play Den with 3 separate areas, and Little Tykes Toys where even the tinys can join in. Heaps of fun for everyone! It's perfect for birthday parties too.

In the Adventure Playground big kids can whoosh down the Giant Astra Slide, whilst toddlers can go on the Dippy Dinoslide. Blast away as you wiz round the Orbiter Car Circuit, drive your own motorised tractor as a Dino Keeper on Safari and dance on the water in the battery run Disco Boats .The Jungle Climb and Jurassic Challenge will also test your skills. Have fun with remote controlled Dino Buggies and Safari Rovers on a Jurassic Journey. Get your licence on the brilliant Off-Roaders Circuit or reach for the sky on the Superjumper trampolines. Super Dig with a grown-up digger for kids or try your hand at the Giant Jigsaws and Dinos and Ladders . Little ones will be busy working the Diggers in Excavator Alley or making sandcastles in the sandpit. All the family can compete on the free 18-hole Volcanic themed Adventure Golf Course, and lose each other in the Labyrinth

A changing programme of Daily Activities in our Theatre
Fossil Hunt – *every child guaranteed a fossil*
Puppet Show – *lots of participation*

Dinosaur crafts – *make something to take home*
Family Frolics – *Monster style "It's a Knockout"*
Pat-a-Pet – *at Guinea Pig Village*
Treasure Hunt – *search for dino clues*
Children's Street Entertainer – *lots of clowning around and fooling about!*

All activities are supervised so every child can take part.

In the Activity Centre Computersaurus Alley offers screens for all ages and skills- educational games and CD ROMs; examine a dinosaur egg nest and fossils and see live 'hatchlings' in an incubator. Youngsters can even climb into a nesting box and hatch a dino egg.

When you're ready to eat choose from the Rib Cage with daily "specials" and toddler size meals or sit on the Sun Terrace by the self-service kiosk, or join Dino in his Den at the Snack Bar – there's something for all tastes.

Come early for a Monster Day out for the whole family.

Dinosaur Park, Tenby located on the B4318 Sageston to Tenby road.

FOLLY FARM
Begelly, Kilgetty

Award winning attraction, Folly Farm Adventure Park & Zoo is the BIG Family Day Out, with enjoyment for all ages whether it's sunny or raining. A day at Folly Farm means so much fun, with a spectacular zoo, friendly farmyard, adventure play and an enormous indoor funfair!

Enjoy some farming fun in the Jolly Barn where you can meet friendly animals, and experience traditional farming methods first-hand, by hand-milking or bottle-feeding a goat. There are even little critters for you to handle – from the cute and cuddly to the scaly and slimy, during supervised pet-handling sessions.

See and learn about many exotic animals in Folly Farm's zoo, including rare and endangered species from around the world! Educational feeding talks take place at various enclosures around the zoo, where you can see the animals being fed, meet the zookeepers and have your animal questions answered!

Relive the fun of yesteryear in Folly Farm's amazing vintage funfair, the biggest undercover fairground in Europe! Rekindle the spirit and nostalgic atmosphere of bygone days in this incredible collection of working rides and stalls, with fantastic rides for both young and old.

Relax outside and watch the kid enjoy a high-seas adventure o the pirate ships and othe adventure play equipmen Indoors, enjoy the incredibl 'Carousel-Woods' – Wale biggest indoor adventure pla ground! An innovative ventur for the whole family, Carouse Woods contains heaps of imagi native play equipment suitabl for the adults and the childre with a magical, enchanted fores theme!

Also enjoy two new attractions the CAT "Big Dig" Digger Par and the Go-Kart track, with 1 Le Mans vehicles.

Outside, take a tranquil stro through the beautifu FollyWood Country Park and enjoy learning about our rar breed animals, follow the natur trail, and then ride back on th land train.

Folly Farm has plenty of food drink and ice cream outlets o offer, including a restaurant coffee shops, a burger bar, a gif shop and much more!

To find us all you have to do i head north from Tenby on th A478 towards Narberth, Foll Farm is less than a mile from th Kilgetty roundabout.

Look out for our brochure, call for more information on 01834 812731 or visit us at www.folly-farm.co.uk

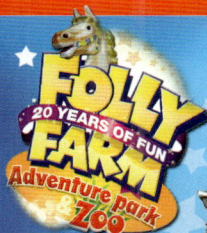

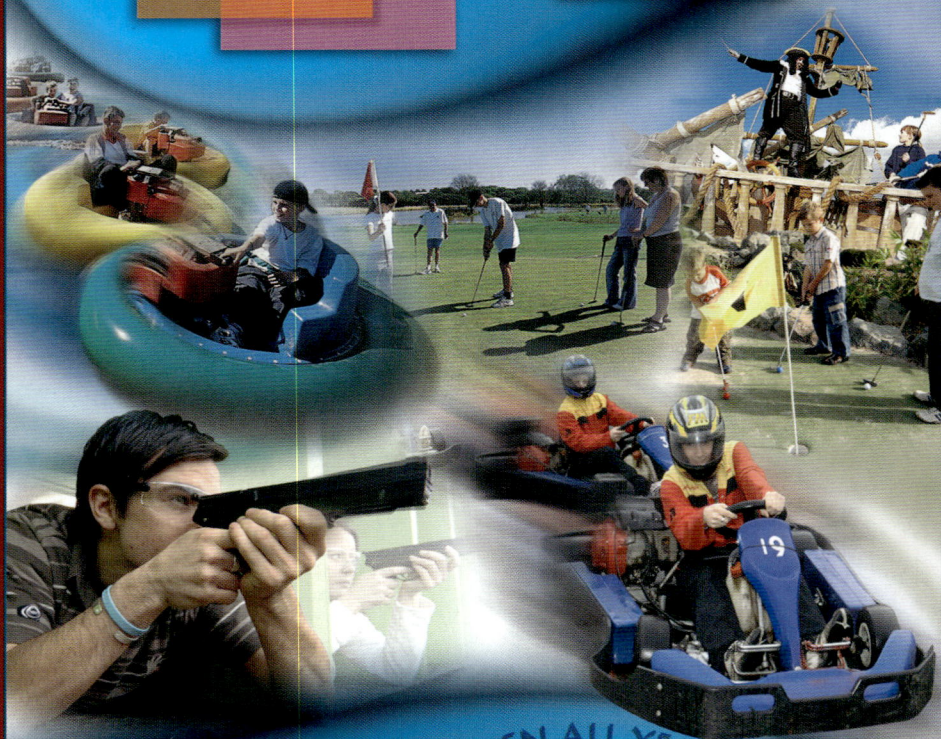
65

ATTRACTIONS LISTINGS

OAKWOOD THEME PARK
Canaston Bridge, Nr Narberth
Tel: 01834 861889
Visit: www.oakwoodthemepark.co.uk

**CC2000 FAMILY
ENTERTAINMENT CENTRE**
Canaston Bridge, Nr Narberth
Tel: 01834 891622

**FOLLY FARM
ADVENTURE PARK & ZOO**
Begelly, Kilgetty
Tel: 01834 812731
www.folly-farm.co.uk

THE DINOSAUR PARK
Gumfreston, Tenby
Tel: 01834 845272
www.thedinosaurpark.co.uk

TORCH THEATRE
St. Peters Road, Milford Haven
Tel: 01646 695267
www.torchtheatre.co.uk

**BLACKPOOL MILL,
CAVES AND CAFE**
Canaston Bridge, nr Narberth
Tel: 01437 541233

LLYS Y FRAN COUNTRY PARK
Llys y Fran, SA63 4RS
Tel: 01437 532694

PEMBROKESHIRE SHEEPDOGS
Tremynydd Fach, Berea, St. Davids
Tel: 01437 721677

SCOLTON MANOR
Spittal, Haverfordwest, SA62 5QL
Tel: 01437 731328

WELSH WILDLIFE CENTRE
Cilgerran, nr Cardigan
Tel: 01239 621600
E-mail: centre@wtww.co.uk

NANT-Y-COY MILL
*Treffgarne Gorge, nr
Haverfordwest*
Tel: 01437 741671

GUN TOWER FRONT STREET
Pembroke Dock
Tel: 01646 622246

PALACE CINEMA
*Upper Market Street,
Haverfordwest,*
Tel: 01437 767675

OCEAN LAB
Goodwick, Fishguard,
Tel: 01348 874737

CWM DERI VINEYARD
Cwm Deri Vineyard, Martletwy
Tel: 01834 891274

HEATHERTON SPORTS PARK
St Florence ,Tenby
Tel: 651025

RITEC VALLEY QUAD BIKES
*Roberts Wall
Trefloyne Lane, Penally, Tenby*
Phone: 01834 843390
Web:www.ritec-valley.co.uk

**SILENT WORLD AQUARIUM &
REPTILE COLLECTION**
*Slippery Back, Narberth Road,
Tenby*
Tel: 01834 844498

HAVERFORDWEST & THE WEST COAST

Pembrokeshire's Atlantic West Coast is a wild and dramatic landscape of spectacular cliff scenery, golden beaches and secluded coves. Offshore are the nearby islands of Skomer and Skokholm and much further out to sea, Grassholm, names which are a reminder of the days when ransacking Viking war lords and Norse settlers made their mark in the area. This coastline has nothing to compare with Tenby for size and general amenities, a fact which makes it all the more appealing to those visitors in search of peaceful isolation. Even here there are popular village resorts such as Broad Haven and Dale, which though small and very relaxing, are only a few miles from the old country town of Haverfordwest and its first class shopping and other facilities. Not surprisingly, Haverfordwest has increasingly become a major holiday base for visitors to the Dale Peninsula, Marloes Peninsula, St. Bride's Bay and even the Preseli Hills. Indeed, it is ideally placed for exploring the whole of Pembrokeshire, close to the major towns and not forgetting the small city of St. Davids. Even closer to Haverfordwest is the neighbouring town of Milford Haven with its marina and dockside attractions. From here you can catch any of the several pleasure boats which ply the Haven waterway to and from Skomer, Skokholm and Grassholm. These islands are vitally important habitats for a variety of birds and wildlife. Skomer and Skokholm are best known for their puffins, but they also support the world's largest population of Manx Shearwaters. Grassholm has a similar claim to fame, its population of 32,000 pairs of gannets makes it the second largest gannetry in the Northern Hemisphere. The waters along the coast here are of great importance too. Around Skomer and the Marloes Peninsula is one of only two Marine Nature Reserves in Britain, and the warming influence of the Gulf Stream helps support a rare species of coral. Other marine inhabitants include dolphins, porpoise and Atlantic grey seals. Another major natural attraction of the remote west is the Pembrokeshire Coastal Path, where walkers can discover the true meaning of solitude.

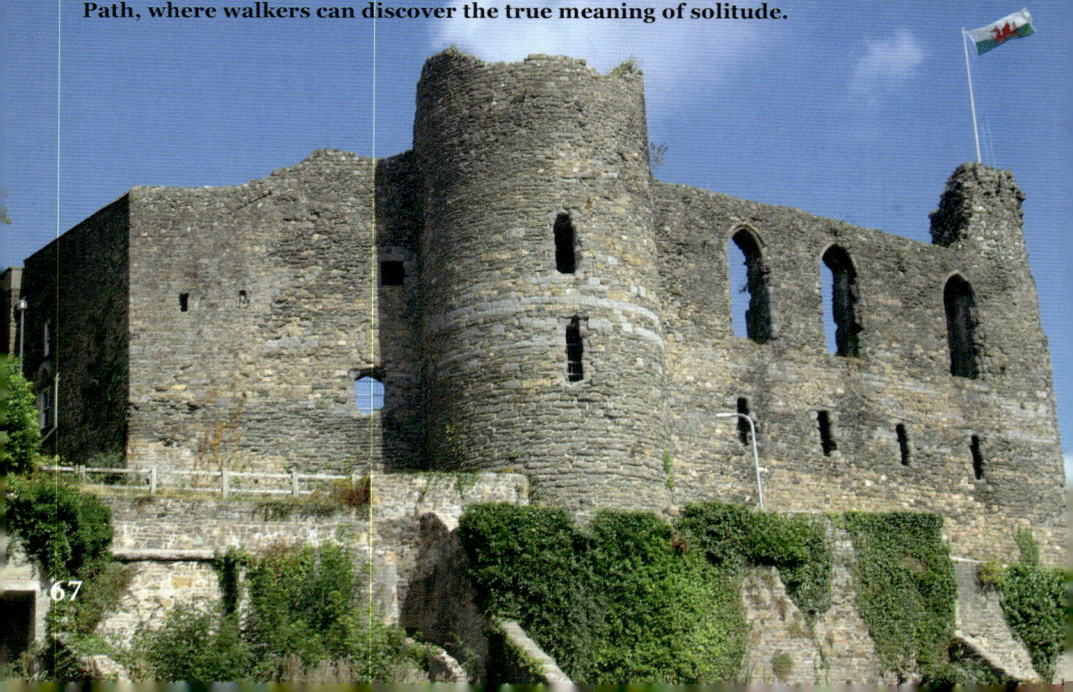

Haverfordwest

Distances: Fishguard 16m, Milford Haven 7m, Narberth 8m, Pembroke 11m, St. Davids 16m, Tenby 19m, Carmarthen 30m, and London 245m

Haverfordwest, always more English than Welsh and the county town of Pembrokeshire, is still the region's most important town, and the biggest centre for shopping and employment. Overlooking the town centre are the ruins of the medieval castle. The centre itself has a medieval street plan, but the first appearances suggest that the only buildings older than 18th century are the castle and three Norman churches of St. Mary's, St. Martin's and St. Thomas's. However, behind the new facades of many buildings are much older structures. The castle was founded prior to 1120 and rebuilt in the 13th century and only Pembroke was bigger. In 1220 the town was burnt at the hands of Llywelyn the Great, but the castle was undamaged. In 1405 Owian Glyndwr and more than 2,500 men put the town under siege, but again the castle proved impregnable. In the Civil War, Haverfordwest, like Tenby and Pembroke, was held in turn for both King and Parliament, before Cromwell ordered the castle to be slighted in 1648. He also decreed that Haverfordwest should become the county town in place of Pembroke.

The keep and substantial sections of wall are all that remain of the castle today, though it had continued to serve the town well over the centuries. In the 18th and 19th centuries it was used as a gaol, until the new county gaol was built in 1820. It has also been a police station.

St. Mary's Church is one of South Wales' finest. Built in the 13th century but substantially altered in the 15th century, it has many outstanding features, including curved oak roofs, a brass dating back to 1651 and an early English lancet window. St. Martin's with its high steeple, is the town's oldest church and has undergone much restoration. From Tudor times to the early part of this century Haverfordwest was a flourishing port. Exports included wool, skins, corn, lime and coal, and among the imports were salt, iron, leather, finished goods and French and Spanish wine. There was a regular if infrequent passenger service to London, which sailed once a month.

Haverforwest shopping

Haverforwest by the water

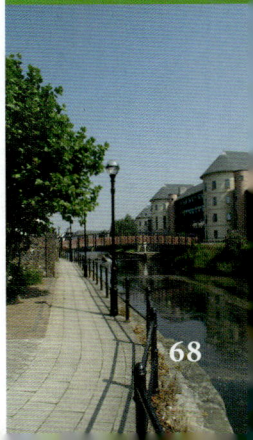

HAVERFORDWEST & THE WEST COAST

From the 18th century, many small industries such as limekilns, boatyards, collieries and quarries sprang up alongside the Western Cleddau and further downstream. Large warehouses lined the quay in Haverfordwest and the waterway was bustling with fleets of barges, coasting vessels and small steamships. The decline of the port is a familiar story in 19th century Wales. In 1853 the arrival of the first train in Haverfordwest was greeted with great celebration. Though this exciting event represented a milestone in the history of the South Wales Railway, it was also the kiss of death for the town's maritime trade. A new era in travel had dawned and shipping could not compete. Today, the once hectic quay has become the Riverside Quay Shopping Centre. A modern and attractive development, it includes a large indoor market, a reminder that Haverfordwest has for centuries been an important market town. There is a wide range of fresh local produce on sale here, along with locally made crafts and a popular open air Farmer's Market. There is also a large open air market held on Sundays on Withybush airfield.

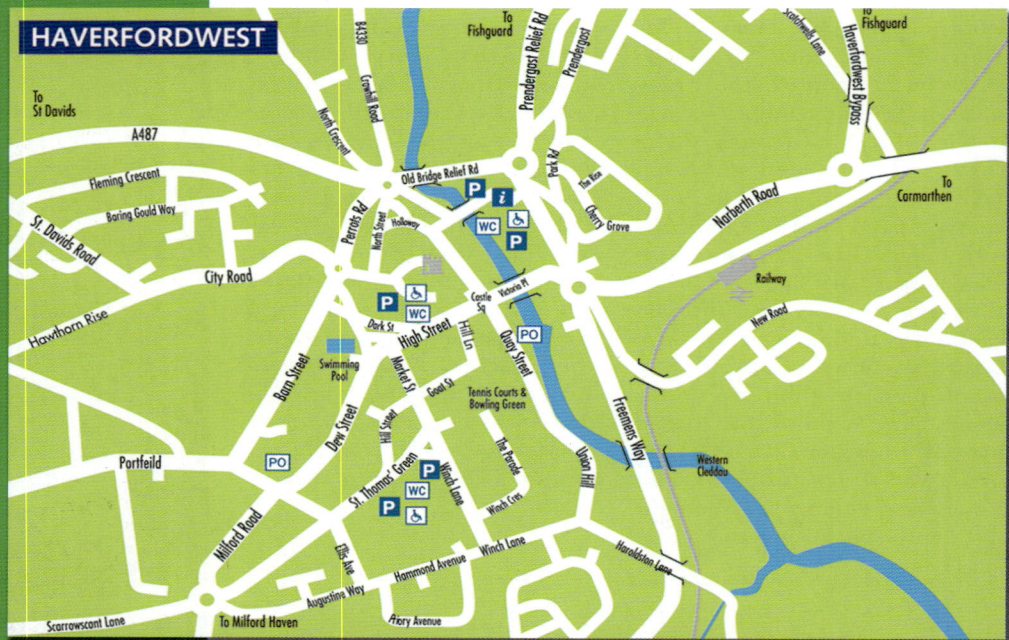

Riverside Quay, Haverfordwest

HAVERFORDWEST

PEMBROKESHIRE FISH WEEK

Pembrokeshire Fish Week 2008 is bigger and better than ever!

The celebration of everything fishy will be packed with over 150 events for families, foodies, beach-lovers, outdoor enthusiasts, anglers, and cultural devotees alike.

Choose from many seaside and outdoor activities – from boat wildlife expeditions to coastal explorer sessions, island walks, beach bushcraft lessons, and more.

Tempt your tastebuds with a choice of more than 50 foodie events – from fresh crab lunches to fish and chip suppers, seafood extravaganzas and fish cookery demos with celebrity chefs.

Children and families can enjoy fun days all over the county, snorkel safaris, rockpool rambles, crab catching, and seaside-inspired art and craft work-shops.

Would-be anglers can pick from a range of learn-to-fish days while more experienced anglers of all ages can take part in coarse or sea fishing competi-tions.

Don't miss sea shanty nights in local pubs, historical fishing exhibitions, art workshops, photography competitions and more.

Pembrokeshire Fish Week 2008 will be held between 21st and 29th June.

The annual festival, which attracted more than 15,000 visitors in 2007, is organised by Pembrokeshire County Council.

One of the annual highlights is the Celebrity Chef Fish and Shellfish Masterclass. This year, it will be hosted by Mitch Tonks, leading fishmonger, restaurateur and food writer.

"Mitch is one of the most passionate advocates of cooking and eating seafood in Britain today, and we're really looking forward to welcoming him to Pembrokeshire," said Kate Morgan, Food Officer for Pembrokeshire County Council and organiser of Fish Week.

The Masterclass will be held at the Torch Theatre in Milford Haven on June 26th.

Pembrokeshire Fish Week was shortlisted in the 'Best Event Major in Wales' category in the prestigious Welsh National Tourism Awards 2007.

"The festival is unique in that it encompasses the whole of Pembrokeshire, not just one town or area," said Kate.

"It's about using the area's assets – its coast, rivers, food, and culture – to help people experience true Pembrokeshire life."

• Sea Fair Milford Haven - a maritime festival for traditional craft and seafarers - is also taking place between 18th and 25th June 2008.

For more on Pembrokeshire Fish Week 2008, view www.pembrokeshirefishweek.co.uk

DATES FOR HAVERFORDWEST FARMERS MARKET 2008

JANUARY 4th 18th FEBRUARY 1st 15th 29th
MARCH 14th 21st 28th APRIL 11th 25th
MAY 9th 23rd JUNE 6th 20th
JULY 4th 18th AUGUST 1st 15th 29th
SEPTEMBER 12th 26th OCTOBER 10th 24th
NOVEMBER 7th 21st DECEMBER 5th 12th 19th

EASTER MARKET 21 MARCH 2008
PLANTING FOR SPRING 23 MAY 2008
HARVEST FAYRE 26 SEPTEMBER 2008
XMAS MARKETS 5, 12 and 19 DECEMBER 2008

Also at Fishguard on alternate Saturdays from 12th January 2008

Awards:
FARMA Farmers Market 2005/06
True Taste Retail Gold Winner 2005/06
FARMA Regional Winner 2005/07

The Sheep Shop

Bridge Street, Haverfordwest

In the centre of the County Town is one very special shop. Don't miss the Sheep Shop with its huge range of Welsh and Celtic Crafts, its artist's gallery area and its new delicatessen serving only Welsh foods and drinks

The Sheep Shop
32 Bridge Street
Haverfordwest
We are open:
Monday to Saturday
9.30am-5.00pm.
Tel: 01437 766844

The gallery area exhibits pictures and prints from many of Pembrokeshire's finest photographers and artists including Graham Brace, Annabel Greenhalgh, Peter James, Simon Swinfield, Adrian James and Gary Llewellyn.

The main craft shop is a treasure trove of lovely gifts: lovespoons, jewellery, cuddly toys and many presents with a 'sheepy' theme.

Complimenting the craft shop and gallery is our new delicatessen area serving a wide range of Welsh foods and drinks including locally-made chocolates, Welsh wines, beers and spirits , local cheeses, jams, honeys and pickles and, of course, real dairy ice-cream from Pembrokeshire.

We look forward to welcoming you!

Haverfordwest

HAVERFORWEST TOWN MUSEUM

See Pembrokeshire's Castles and Museums section.

HAVERFORWEST SPORTS CENTRE

tel:01437 765901

HAVERFORWEST PRIORY

Robert Fitz-Tancred, castellan of Haverforwest, who died in 1213, founded the Augustinian Priory of St. Mary & St. Thomas the Martyr. In 1536, during Henry VIII's Dissolution of the Monasteries, it was stripped of its lead roof and the stonework was plundered. Not surprisingly it became a rich source of building stone, but at various times in later years also fulfilled other roles, such as a boatyard, smithy and stables. The ruins, within easy walking distance of the towns centre are now being excavated by a team of archaeologists working with CADW (Welsh Historic Monuments), and many interesting finds have been made to date.

PICTON CASTLE

A visit to Picton is a grand day out for kids and grans, gardeners and foodies, those who like to walk and those who like to look.

The impressive 13th century castle and elegant Regency wing are surrounded by 40 acres of woodland and walled garden. Inside, guided tours provide an entertaining snapshot of 750 years of

Philipps' family history, illustrated with fine antiques and paintings set in beautifully proportioned rooms.

Outside, there's the special grandeur of avenues dominated by massive redwoods and oaks, some more than 300 years old. There's a new jungle garden planted with bananas, gingers and other exotics, and magnificent Rhododendrons bred by Picton's own gardeners.

More than 100 conifers from declining habitats have been planted to prevent extinction, including a fine Dawn Redwood (a conifer thought extinct until rediscovered in China in 1941). There's a glade of tree ferns, an avenue of Myrtles, stately Embothrium and Eucryphia ... all helping make up one of West Wales' largest rare plant collections.

All of which goes unnoticed by kids as they follow woodland trails in search of clues, exercise limbs and imagination in the adventure playground and explore the traditional maze.

Chance upon Picton on a Family Fun Day (most Wednesdays during school holidays) and you'll find a children's entertainer in the medieval courtyard, usually a face painter, perhaps a bouncy castle. What could be better than to sit outside Maria's Mediterranean Restaurant and enjoy a fair trade coffee or glass of wine, with perhaps a tortilla and salad, to the sound of youthful laughter?

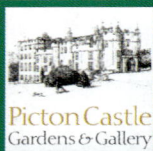

Picton Castle

Before you leave you should also visit the old courtyard. This was once the site of the Castle's carpentry shop, the laundry and bakery, but now you will find a Mediterranean style restaurant offering innovative cuisine, a garden nursery that sells many of Picton's rare plants, a gallery that is regularly used for national art exhibitions and a gift shop that stocks a range of individually crafted high quality gifts. The Castle and gardens are open from Easter to 30th September, every day except non Bank Holiday Mondays. You can visit Gardens 10.30am to 5pm and Castle tours run from 11.30am to 3.30pm. The Gardens remain open in October, 7 days a week, 10.30am to dusk.

for all information ring 01437 751326 or visit www.pictoncastle.co.uk

THE OLD SMITHY

Acquired by Janet & Dario Algieri in early 1998, The Old Smithy at Simpson Cross is one of the oldest stone buildings in the area and was in a poor state of repair. After renovation, it now boasts two well lit rooms full of genuine Welsh made crafts and gifts, plus a new purpose built gallery displaying the work of many local artists, including resident artists and woodturner. Gifts include Welsh Royal Crystal, Pembertons chocolates, Caldey Island products, Silver Scenes gifts and Celtic Jewellery and many other gifts and crafts sourced in Wales. There's a large car park shared with the Pembrokeshire Motor Museum. Opening hours 10am to 5.30pm 7 days a week, Easter to end of October, other times by arrangement.

for more information ring 01437 710628

SCOLTON HERITAGE PARK

Within the park's 60 acres of landscaped grounds and woodland stands Scolton House, which dates back to the 1840's and is furnished throughout in the style of the 1920's. New displays in the Victorian stable block illustrate what life was like on a Pembrokeshire country estate, including stabling, cart shed, carpenter's workshop and smithy. Other attractions include an animal enclosure, arboretum, nature trail and a new "green" visitor centre made entirely of local materials.

for more information ring 01437 731328

Rhos

Virtually on the doorstep of this quiet and attractive little village, situated about two miles to the south of the main A40 Haverfordwest to St. Clears road, is the stately Picton Castle. The road through the village also gives you access to the banks of the Eastern Cleddau, an ideal picnic site on a warm Summer's day. Facing you across the water here is the slipway at Landshipping and a few hundred yards to your right is Picton Point, the confluence of the Western and Eastern Cleddau rivers.

Little Haven

This is a tiny village resort of great charm and beauty, nestling between high cliffs. The beach, a sandy cove which at low tide connects with neighbouring Broad Haven, is popular with bathers and boaters and visitors to its welcoming pubs and restaurants. It is hard to imagine that coal from local pits was once exported from here.

Little Haven

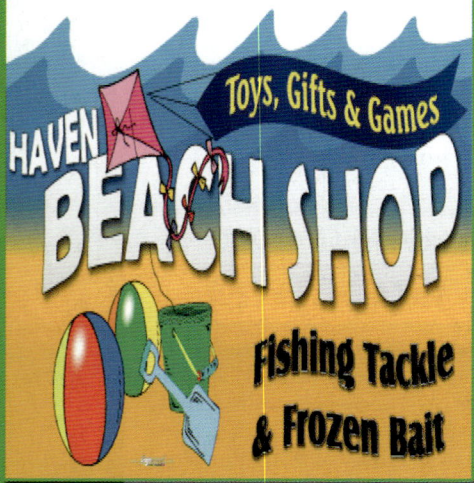

Broad Haven

A favourite beach for bathers since 1800, Broad Haven is the biggest and the most popular resort on Pembrokeshire's west coast. The village has good facilities, including a cafe, guesthouses, shops, watersports equipment hire, public toilets and plenty of self catering accommodation, from caravans to cottages. At the Northern end of the superb long sandy beach are a number of interesting geological features - folding stacks and natural arches.

Wolf's Castle

Wolf's Castle (also frequently referred to in print as Wolfscastle) is at the northern end of the Treffgarne Gorge, where, in the early part of the century, railwaymen toiled to blast an unlikely route through the very old and very hard rock bed in a bid to fulfil Brunel's dream. A motte and bailey castle stands near the centre of the village, which is popular with holidaymakers by virtue of its inn, hotel and pottery. Archaeological finds nearby include Roman tiles and slates, indicating the site of a fortified Roman-British villa. The village was the birthplace in 1773 of Joseph Harris, who in 1814 published Seren Gomer, the first all Welsh weekly newspaper.

Roch

Dominating the otherwise flat landscape for miles around, Roch Castle stands on an igneous rock outcrop. The origin of the castle and its large pele tower is unknown, but it is thought that it was built in the 13th century by Adam de Rupe. Legend says that he chose the site because of a prophecy that he would die from an adder's bite. Unluckily for him, an adder was brought into the castle in a bundle of firewood and duly fulfilled the prediction. The small village of Roch has a 19th century church with a circular churchyard.

Newgale

A popular surfing resort, newgale is a small village at the northeastern end of St. Bride's Bay, overlooking the impressive two mile stretch of Newgale Sands. The sands are separated from the road and village by a high ridge of pebbles. At exceptionally low tides the stumps of a drowned prehistoric forest are some-times exposed.

Nolton Haven

This compact coastal village, with its attractive cove, is virtually midway between little Haven and Newgale. In the 18th century, coal was exported from here, and the the line of the tramway which brought the anthracite and coal from the mines to the coast can still be seen. Alongside the old track bed is the Counting House, which recorded how many wagon-loads of coal were trans ported to the quay. The quay itself, built in 1769, no longer exists. Half a mile north of Nolton Haven was Trefran Cliff Colliery, which worked coal seams beneath St. Bride's Bay between 1850 and 1905. Part of an old chimney and other ruins are now the only evidence of this once thriving industry. The bellcoted church of St. Madoc's has a medieval carved stone bracket.

Nolton Haven

Newgale

Treffgarne

Treffgarne was the birthplace of the rebellious Welsh hero Owain Glyndwr. The village stands close to the wooded rocky gorge, through which runs the Western Cleddau river, railway line and main A40 trunk road. The Treffgarne Gorge was cut by meltwater rushing south towards Milford Haven during the retreat of the last Ice Age. The areas around the gorge are dotted with sites of early settlements and fortifications, and on the western side rises the igneous outcrop of Great Treffgarne Mountain and other striking rock formations.

NANT-Y-COY MILL

Restored Nant y Coy Mill dates back to 1332 and possibly even earlier. The last corn was ground here in the 1950's, but the mill wheel is still turning 150 years after it was built. The mill is an attractive Art gallery, cafe and craft shop, with a nature trail leading up to the Great Treffgarne Rocks, from where the views of the gorge are spectacular. You can also take a detour to Lion Rock and Bear Rock, two of the most distinctive features of the Pembrokeshire landscape.

visit www.nantycoy.co.uk

Rudbaxton

Rudbaxton is about 2 miles north of Haverfordwest and is the site of one of the regions most impressive earthworks, a motte and bailey fortress established in the 11th century. In a valley below the mound is the parish church of St. Michael. This dates from the 12th century and was restored in the 1870's.

Milford Haven

Distances: Fishguard 24m, Haverfordwest 7m, Narberth 15m, Pembroke 7m, St. Davids 21, Tenby 17m, Carmarthen 37m and London 253m

Since its development as a new town and whaling port in the late 18th century, Milford Haven has seen its economic fortunes seesaw. Sir William Hamilton, husband of Nelson's Emma, was granted an Act of Parliament to proceed with the development of the town and port, and from the beginning it was envisaged that new Milford would secure its share of the transatlantic shipping trade. Assisted by settlers from overseas, progress was rapid, with the early establishment of a quay, custom house, inn and naval dockyard. When Nelson visited in 1802 he was

Milford Haven

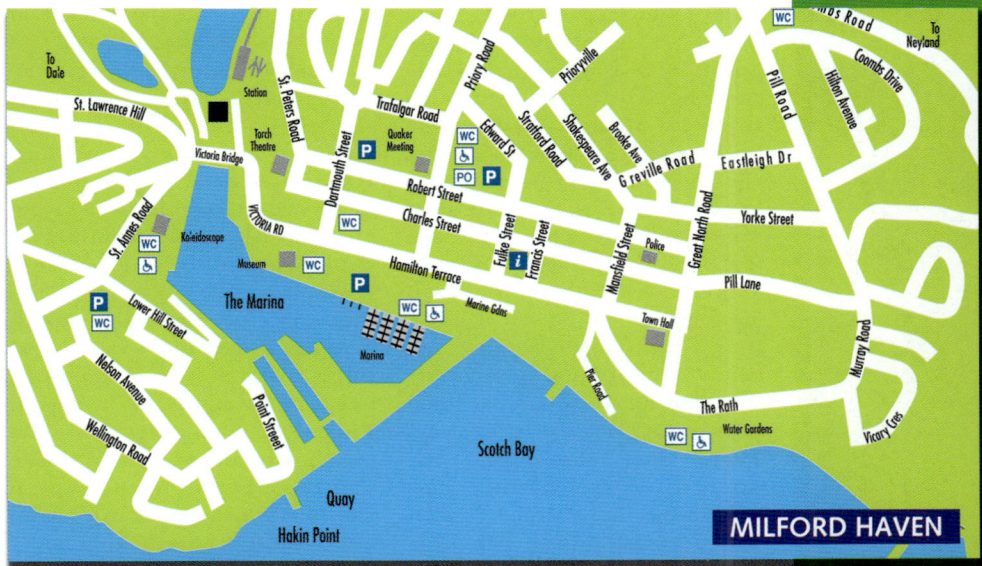

MILFORD HAVEN

Map labels: To Dale, St. Lawrence Hill, Station, St. Peters Road, Torch Theatre, Victoria Bridge, Quaker Meeting, Trafalgar Road, Priory Road, Prioryville, Edward St, Stratford Road, Shakespeare Ave, Brooke Ave, Greville Road, Eastleigh Dr, Coombs Drive, To Neyland, Pill Road, Hilton Avenue, WC, Robert Street, PO, Charles Street, Dartmouth Street, VICTORIA RD, St. Annes Road, Kaleidoscope, Museum, Hamilton Terrace, Fulke Street, Francis Street, Mansfield Street, Police, Great North Road, Yorke Street, Pill Lane, The Marina, Marina, Marine Gdns, Town Hall, Pier Road, P, Lower Hill Street, Nelson Avenue, Point Street, Wellington Road, Quay, Hakin Point, Scotch Bay, The Rath, Water Gardens, Murray Road, Vicary Cres, WC

suitably impressed with the development and the Haven waterway, which he described as "one of the worlds finest natural harbours". However it was not long before the town's development suffered major setbacks. Whaling at the port ceased, and in 1814 the Admiralty transferred the naval dockyard several miles east to Paterchurch, now Pembroke Dock, despite the fact that many fine ships had been built at Milford Haven in a very short space of time. Another setback followed when in 1836 the daily Irish Packet boat service was also moved from Milford to Paterchurch. During the mid 1800's, a renewed effort was made to re-establish Milford Haven as a transatlantic staging post, and ambitious plans were drawn up for the building of docks to rival those at Liverpool and Southampton. Although these never materialised, the far more modest Milford Haven docks opened in 1888. New life was breathed into the new docks, when the first vessel to enter was the steam trawler Sybil on the 27th September 1888. Her arrival marked the beginning of a prosperous new era for Milford Haven as the port turned its attention to deep-sea fishing.

Milford Haven

80

HAVERFORDWEST & THE WEST COAST

The combination of new docks, excellent fishing grounds and good rail links saw the enterprise reap rich rewards. Milford Haven thus became one of Britain's most successful fishing ports. In its heyday in the 1920's, the port was home to 130 deep sea trawlers which offered employment to around 4,000 men either afloat or ashore. By the 1950's the seesaw had tipped the other way again as the fishing industry slipped into an irretrievable decline. This time however, the promise of yet another new beginning for Milford Haven was already in the pipeline, the coming of the oil industry. The oil companies were attracted to West Wales for a number of reasons. Of major consideration was the sheltered deep water anchorage offered by the Haven waterway, which could accommodate crude oil tankers of ever increasing size. The local authorities also made it clear they welcomed the new industry, pointing out the availability of a large labour pool. In recent years this industry too has had its ups and downs. The rising cost of crude oil in the 1970's and 1980's saw many refineries in Europe close, and a subsequent slimming down of the oil business around Milford Haven, resulted in the closure of the Esso refinery in 1983 and the BP ocean terminal in 1985. Now only one refinery remains, but despite the industry's problems the wealth generated by oil has helped fund Milford Haven's massive new investment in tourism. This has seen the complete refurbishment of the old docks and the creation of the superb 150 berth marina. Many of the old buildings have been demolished, while others of historic significance have been renovated and now house such attractions as the museum. A thriving retail and business park has been developed which has attracted many new business to the docks area. The old shopping centre has been attractively remodelled and the town's gardens and esplanade upgraded and landscaped to reflect their Victorian heritage. In addition leisure facilities are first class.

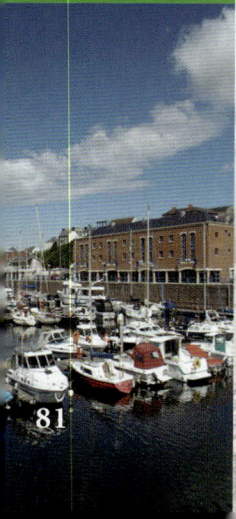

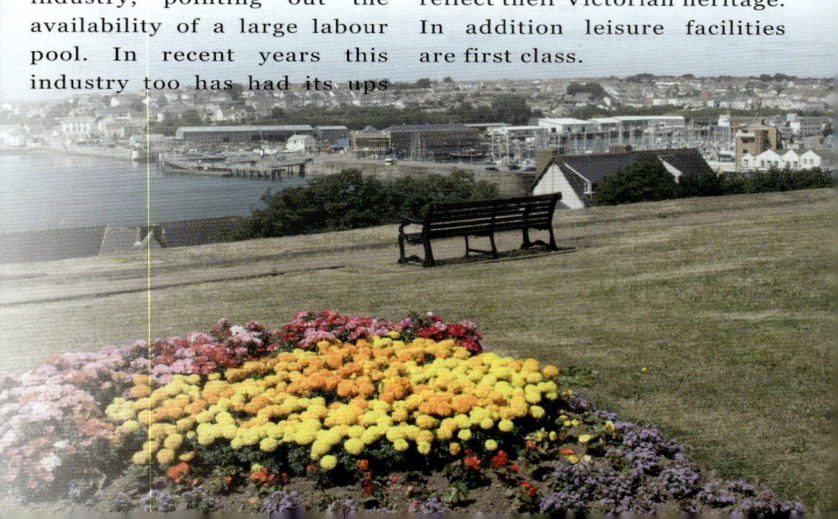

TORCH THEATRE

Milford Haven's Torch Theatre celebrated its 30th anniversary in 2007 with an ambitious refurbishment project which has transformed it into one of the most comfortable venues in the British Isles.

The Torch is a celebrated producing theatre company, and the striking new theatre was relaunched this Spring with a highly acclaimed version of the award-winning musical The Hired Man. The Torch Theatre Company boasts an impressive repertoire including One Flew Over The Cuckoo's Nest, Neville's Island, Abigail's Party, The Little Shop of Horrors, Of Mice and Men and Educating Rita. The Christmas show is always a firm family favourite.

The intimate main house offers a wonderful space to see professionals perform. With just under 300 comfortable seats, everyone feels close to the action. The multi-million pound makeover has also created a new studio theatre, which allows the Torch to offer a choice of films and live performances every night of the week. Between the two spaces, there's a tantalizing entertainment line-up for everyone to enjoy. As well as the Torch's own productions, you can catch first rate touring shows ranging from musical theatre, plays and comedy to dance, opera, lectures and the best in live music.

You can rely on the Torch to show the latest movie blockbusters too - alongside art house and off-beat films - so there will always be an option for those days when the sun forgets to put his hat on...

Visitors can also take pleasure in viewing paintings, photographs, ceramics, crafts and installations by local and national artists in the Joanna Field Gallery. The programme changes regularly, and entry is free.

Café Torch is the perfect place to enjoy a light lunch or a coffee in a relaxed and friendly setting, opening onto a cliff top terrace with panoramic views over Milford's marina and docks. The café allows you to make the most of your day by offering pre-show suppers and there's a bar to make you feel right at home.

To find out what's on call the Box Office on 01646 695267, visit the website at www.torchtheatre.co.uk, drop by and pick up a brochure or check the local press. Whatever you come to see, you'll always be assured of a warm Pembrokeshire welcome!

Connie Fisher in Aladdin 2005

Only A Matter Of Time 2006

**Brunel Statue
Neyland**

Neyland

MILFORD MARINA

Since it so successfully hosted the start of the 1991 Cutty Sark Tall Ships Race, Milford Marina has seen visitors returning in large numbers. There is an excellent variety of restaurants and cafes to suit all tastes and budgets, an adventure play-ground for younger visitors and a ten-pin bowling centre.

*for further information
ring 01646 692272*

MILFORD HAVEN MUSEUM

Housed in the Old Custom House of 1797, this fascinating museum tells the story of Charles Francis Greville, who supervised the development of Milford into a new town and port two centuries ago, and the American whalers from Nantucket who settled here. It also recalls the days in the port's history when trawlers and drifters filled the docks and "every day was pay day" and relates Milford's role in two world wars and the arrival of the oil industry with its multi million pound refineries.

*for more information ring
01646 694496*

Neyland

Like Milford Haven, Neyland has been revitalised by the building of an impressive new marina and waterfront develop-ment, Brunel Quay. Its name could only be a reference to the great railway engineer, whose aim was to establish Neyland as a prosperous transatlantic port by choosing it as the terminus of the South Wales Railway. An impressive statue of Brunel now stands at the entrance to Brunel Quay in recognition of his achievements. At one time or another during the 18th and 19th centuries, virtually every port and resort on the entire Welsh coast had designs on winning the battle for the highly lucrative transatlantic trade. Sadly none of them ever suc-ceeded. In the event, Neyland was not to realise this grand ambition, but until 1906 the town did become an important terminus for the Irish ferries. In that year the service was trans-ferred to Fishguard in the north of the county. The railway remained operational until 1964 when the town's depot was closed. The route of the old railway line now provides an enjoyable country walk between the marina and the village of Rosemarket. Mountain bikers can also tackle the 14m circular Brunel Cycle Route. The 380 berth marina itself occupies the site where Brunel's depot and quay once stood, and in the last few years has established Neyland as a major sailing and watersports centre. Alongside the marina are attractive new homes and a popular waterside bar and cafe. The redevelopment scheme has also created a fine promenade and picnic area, with superb views of the Cleddau Bridge and the busy waterway.

Herbrandston

Located approximately 3 miles north west of Milford Haven and just off the main road to Dale/Marloes, Herbrandston is a pretty village with post office/store, village pub and church. The vilage derives its name from one of the Norman or Flemish settlers in Pembrokeshire named Herbrand who, soon after the Conquest, made his home here. The nearest beach is Sandy Haven, where there is free parking, and sea angling and sailing can be done from here.

St. Ishmaels

Located between Milford Haven and Dale, the village of St. Ishmaels lies in a deep sheltered valley. Nearby are important historical sites, a Norman motte and bailey to the north and the Iron Age forts of Great and Little Castle Heads to the east. The 12th century church stands away from the village, on the site where St. Ishmael is believed to have founded his principle church in the 6th century. A stream divides the churchyard.

Dale

The seaside village of Dale enjoys a sheltered position on the northern shoreline of the Haven waterway, close to the entrance at St Ann's Head. This one time shipbuilding and trading port is now one of the most popular sailing centres in Pembrokeshire and has good facilities for visitors. Races are held on most days during the summer and in August there is a regatta. Close to the village is Dale Fort, one of the Victorian defences built to protect the waterway and is now used as a geographi cal field study centre. At the western end of the village, the road leads to the magnificent St Ann's Head, with its lighthouse and coastguard station from where there are stunning views of the Haven waterway and its busy shipping lanes.

Marloes

This pretty little village with its attractive cottages and church lies en-route to Marloes Sands, off the B4327. Marloes Sands can be reached from the village or from Dale. The panoramic views above the beach take in the islands of Skomer, Skokholm and the much smaller Grassholm, which at low tide can be reached from the northern end of the beach. The road through Marloes village also gives you access to the peaceful cove of Martin's Haven, the departure point for Skomer Island and other island boat trips.

84

SPORT AND ACTIVITIES

Health and fitness are increasingly important facets of modern lifestyles, and this is reflected in the growing number of visitors who come in great numbers to Pembrokeshire in search of sporting and activity holidays Certainly there is no better place to choose, with the only coastline in Britain designated a National Park, Pembrokeshire combines the best of the great outdoors with the very best in indoor leisure facilities. The variety and quality of activities are second to none, whether visitors want to enjoy the sedate pleasure of bird watching or tackle the more taxing pursuits of surfing, canoeing or climbing. Whatever you favour, it's all here in Pembrokeshire as the following guide illustrates.

EXPLORING PEMBROKESHIRE'S MAGICAL COASTLINE

A holiday in Pembrokeshire presents you with dozens of choices. Trying to make decisions about where to go, what to do and keeping the whole family happy can interfere with actually getting on and doing!. Some days you just need to get away, find somewhere new and leave the everyday world behind. If simply sitting on the beach is not an option, or the kids are demanding more things to keep them busy then TYF Coastal Explorer days fit the bill. Rachel Allan from Cardiff, came exploring with her family in the summer. "We have coasteered several times before and the Explorer days are a great extension to that, it is the perfect answer of packing the fun in whilst keeping the holiday stress down". Coastal Explorer days are just that - there is no fixed script to follow. The three elements to the day, Kayaking, Coasteering® and Snorkelling, all come with specialist equipment; you simply choose how wet to get and how far you want or need to go. Your TYF Adventure Guide will be with you, showing, helping and teaching you about the most beautiful coastline in Britain, as you paddle, dabble and scrabble your way along.

Scaling the heights

86

SPORT & ACTIVITIES

Sit on top Kayaks are your chariot for the day and are a great way of covering the distance between launch and lunch. They are highly stable and run in a straight line so no need for exhaustive lessons or frustrating circles. If you jump off for a swim you simply climb back on and get going again. You will already have the kit with you for Coasteering© TYF's premier adventure, so you can stretch your legs while playing in "Hogwart's" wave machine or running the gauntlet of "Judgement Day". Cliff jumping is close by too, for those who want a quick adrenaline rush. This coastal national park is as impressive under the water as it is above. Wearing a diving mask and swimming or paddling around gives the feeling of flying across canyons and seaweed forests, with all sorts of weird and wonderful things not normally seen. Lunch in a remote place all part of the deal and you'll certainly have raised an appetite by the time you pull your Kayak from the water. The stories will start to flow between mouthfuls of sandwich, everyone with a special moment.

For those that would rather sit on the grass and watch, you may be tempted to wave goodbye to you adventurers at the TYF Eco Hotel, which is the first 100% organic hotel in Wales, and then spoil yourself with a quick snack in the bar, before strolling down to the cliffs with your camera to capture the action. At the end of the day as the fisherman stories get bigger, you'll be sharing a glow and buzz coming from spending a day out of doors being active and sharing great times. Finish with a celebratory meal or just an ice-cream and then back to planning the rest of your week.

details of the Coastal Explorer and all TYF Adventure breaks are available at their shop in St. Davids visit www.tyf.com call 01437 721611

Activity Centres

ACTIVITY WALES
Coastal House, Narberth Road
Haverfordwest, Pembrokeshire
SA61 2XG
Tel: 01437 765777
Holidays@activitywales.com

BASE CAMP OUTDOOR CENTRE
Llawhaden, Narberth
Offers canoeing and kayaking, climbing and abseiling, walking and hillwalking.
tel: 01437 541318

CELTIC DIVING
The Parrog, Goodwick.
Offers diving, snorkelling courses, refresher dives and boat trips.
tel: 01348 871938

DIVE PEMBROKESHIRE
The Dive Lodge, Old School House, Walton West, Little Haven.
RYA powerboat courses, diving, windsurfing, surfing and sailing.
tel: 01437 781117

FFOREST OUTDOOR
Bridge Warehouse, Teifi Wharf, Cardigan, SA43 3AA
Clothing and accessories for a range of outdoor sports including climbing, walking, kayaking and canoeing
tel: 01239 62 36 33
www.fforestoutdoor.co.uk

PEMBROKESHIRE DIVE CHARTERS
Brunel Quay, Neyland.
Dive training centre aimed at recreational divers.
tel:08081 445529

PEMBROKESHIRE WATER SPORTS
Cleddau River Centre, Pembroke Dock.
tel:01646 622013
The Parrog, Fishguard
tel: 01348 874803
The centre offers dinghy sailing, windsurfing, powerboating, canoeing, kayaking, coasteering and caters for wheelchair students.

THE PRINCE'S TRUST
Dolphin Court, Brunel Quay, Neyland.
Here you can enjoy canoeing and kayaking, caving, coasteering, orienteering, climbing, abseiling, walking and hillwalking, caters for wheelchair users.
tel: 01646 603130

WEST WALES WIND, SURF AND SAILING
Dale
Canoeing, kayaking, surfing, sailing, windsurfing and powerboats. Caters for wheelchair users.
tel: 01646 636642

Puffins

Birdwatching

Ardent twitchers or those who just enjoy watching birds can have the time of their lives whatever the season. In winter the rivers Teifi, Cleddau and Nevern are home to Little Egrets, Slovonian Grebes and Great Northern Divers, together with Wildfowl Waders. Spring sees the arrival of swallows, warblers and many varieties of seabirds, while inland Peregrine falcons, Merlins, together with Lapwings, Golden Plovers and Buzzards take to the sky. The islands of Ramsey, Skomer and Grassholm offer the widest selection of birds including Fulmars, Kittiwakes, Guillemots, Razorbills and Puffins to name but a few. Skomer has the distinction of being home to the largest colony of Manx Shearwaters in the world, while Grassholm has the second largest colony of Gannets in the North Atlantic. Elegug Stacks near Castlemartin also has large colonies of Guillemots, Razorbills and Kittiwakes, while the Welsh Wildlife Centre at Cilgerran near Cardigan is home to countless varieties of birds and wildfowl. Both Skomer and Ramsey can be visited by boat. Skomer boats run daily (except Monday) from Martins Haven between April 1st or Easter, which ever is sooner, until October 31st. *Contact Dale Sailing Company tel: 01646 603123*

There are a number of boat operators who visit Ramsey, *contact Voyages of Discovery on 0800 854367 and 01437 721911 or Thousand Islands on 01437 721721, or pick up leaflets locally.*

A number of the boat operators also visit Grassholm, where you can't go ashore.

Vantage points for bird watching include Amroth, Strumble Head, Nevern Estuary, Cleddau Estuary, Carew Mill Pond, Fishguard Harbour, Westfield Pill at Neyland and Bosherston Lily Ponds near Pembroke.

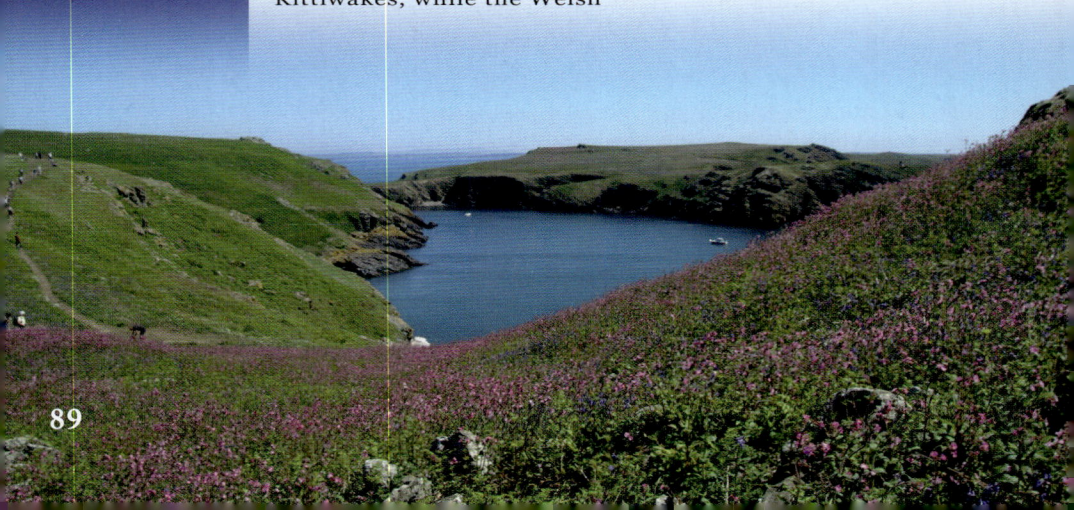

Canoeing & Kayaking

North Pembrokeshire's dramatic coastline offers just the sort of conditions ideal for canoeing and kayaking. For beginners there are quiet sheltered bays where even the complete novice soon feels at home, while the more expert can take up the challenge of tide races and overfalls. Beginners are often surprised to discover that even on their first trip, under the guidance of an experienced and quali fied instructor, they begin to master the basic skills and are able to enjoy the thrills of exploring cliffs and sea caves and negotiating rocks and waves.

TYF ADVENTURE
1, High Street, St. Davids.
tel:01437 721611
Freshwater East.
tel:01646 672764
freephone 0800 132588

**PEMBROKESHIRE
WATERSPORTS**
The Cleddau River Centre,
Pembroke Dock.
tel: 01646 622013
The Parrog, Fishguard.
tel: 01348 874803

FFOREST OUTDOOR
Bridge Warehouse, Teifi
Wharf, Cardigan, SA43 3AA
tel: 01239 62 36 33
www.fforestoutdoor.co.uk

Climbing

Pembrokeshire offers climbers of all abilities the opportunity to experience some of the finest sea cliff climbing in the British Isles. The county's geographical location and mild winters mean all year round climbing on dry, warm rock, a treat rarely available in mountainous areas. So the area is very popular, especially during early bank holidays, and there may well be queues for some of the plum 3 star routes. The sea cliffs are the home of many nesting birds, some of them rare and because of this very necessary restrictions have been imposed in certain areas from early February until mid August. So climbers are advised to choose their routes carefully as it cannot be stressed too strongly that if climbers and wildlife are to co-exist successfully in this environmentally sensitive corner of Britain, the restrictions imposed must be adhered to. Further details of these restrictions are available from all National Park Information Centres and in the Climbers Guide to Pembrokeshire. You should also remember that this hazardous coastline keeps the rescue services fully occupied without help from stranded climbers, so take every possible precaution. including the use of safety helmets because of loose rock.

FFOREST OUTDOOR

Bridge Warehouse, Teifi
Wharf, Cardigan, SA43 3AA
tel: 01239 62 36 33
www.fforestoutdoor.co.uk

Fforest Outdoor has West Wales' largest selection of equipment, clothing and accessories for a range of outdoor sports including climbing, walking, kayaking and canoeing, with over 35 boats of all shapes and sizes in stock. From our waterside location you can try before you buy on our entire range, book on a variety of activities, hire a mountain bike or just take a quiet coffee and cake in our dedicated adventure café! Find us by the old bridge in the centre of Cardigan.

Cycling & Mountain Biking

There is no better way to enjoy the magnificence of the Pembrokeshire coastline and the beauty and tranquillity of the countryside than on a bike, especially as the whole of the National Park is crisscrossed with a network of hidden tracks, bridle ways and sunken lanes. When cycling in Pembrokeshire it is very important to remember that the coast path is for walkers only, a law strictly enforced by the National Park Authority, who are responsible for maintaining this long distance footpath Furthermore, off road cyclists should give way at all times to walkers and horse

riders, and be courteous and considerate to the farmers and landowners whose land they are crossing. For cyclists who prefer to be on the road than off it Pembrokeshire has more quiet lanes than most people could cycle round in a lifetime. Touring in the county could hardly be easier, with bed and breakfast available round every corner and plenty of youth hostels within easy reach.

Coasteering

Another growing sport is Coasteering, which is definitely an activity for the more daring. It involves a combination of climbing and scrambling along the rocky coastline, swimming and cliff jumping into the sea.

Diving

The natural beauty of Pembrokeshire with its picturesque countryside and dramatic scenery is mirrored in its underwater landscape. Diving is a very popular pastime with clubs from all over Britain visiting the clear water where hundreds of wrecks abound, and reefs offer a variety of fish life. Some of the dive sites are marine reserves so their inhabitants remain untouched. Seals often accompany divers as they explore the underwater world and if you're lucky enough, dolphins, porpoises and even sea horses have been known to swim in certain areas, particularly around Cardigan Bay where a pod of dolphins are resident to the area. There are dive sites to suit all abilities, from novice to the more experienced diver.

DIVE PEMBROKESHIRE

The Dive Lodge, Little Haven, Haverfordwest
tel: 01437 781117

PEMBROKESHIRE DIVE CHARTERS

Brunel Quay, Neyland
tel: 08081 445529

WEST WALES DIVING CENTRE

Hasguard Cross, Broad Haven
tel:01437 781457

WEST WALES DIVING SCHOOL

Sessions Hall, Mathry near Haverfordwest
tel/fax: 01348 831526

Fishing

Whether you are looking for an out and out fishing holiday or you simply want to enjoy a bit of fishing while you're here, Pembrokeshire and West Wales provide wonderful opportunities for sea, game and coarse fishing. The coastlines of Pembrokshire, Cardigan Bay and Carmarthen Bay are excellent venues for summer sea angling, either from the beach or from established rock marks. Bass, pollack, garfish, mackerel, conger eel and even tope are all here for the taking, while if you want to fish offshore, there is no shortage of charter boats offering fishing trips from local harbours. West Wales has long been renowned for the quality of its game fishing, with most of the area's rivers and their tributaries experiencing good runs of salmon and sea trout during the summer months. Indeed, the region boasts three of Britain's premier salmon rivers, the Towy, Teifi and Taf, and many others provide terrific sport when conditions are favourable. These include the Nevern, Aeron, Eastern Cleddau, Western Cleddau, Rheidol and Ystwyth. Wales also has an abundance of lakes and reservoirs that are well stocked with brown and rainbow trout. Venues popular with visitors are the reservoirs at Llys-y-fran Country Park and Rosebush, both close to the B4329 about six miles from Haverfordwest; White House Mill and Latch y Goroff, (near Whitland) and the fisheries of Llwyndrissi, Llanllawddog and Garnffrwd, (near Carmarthen). For coarse anglers there are exciting prospects at a variety of locations. Bosherston Lakes offer excellent pike fishing and Llyn Carfan Lake at Tavernspite boasts top class carp fishing and a good head of tench and roach. Glas Llyn fishery near Blaenwaen is also stoked with carp and tench. But remember, anyone over 12 years old who fishes for salmon, trout, freshwater fish or eels in England and Wales must have an Environmental Agency rod fishing licence, available from the Post Office or Environment Agency offices. In addition, you must have permission from the fishery owner before you may fish on waters under their control, and remember to take your litter home, as discarded tackle can injure wildlife.

PENRALLT NURSERY MOYLEGROVE

Small lake well stocked with Rainbow Trout and situated in a peaceful setting with spectacular views. There is also a picnic area, children's play area and plant nursery and garden centre. Dogs welcome.

tel: 01239 881295

LLYS-Y-FRAN RESERVOIR & COUNTRY PARK
tel: 01427 532273/532694

94

Pembrokeshire Coast
NATIONAL PARK

The Pembrokeshire Coast National Park, one of Britain's breathing spaces, takes in about a third of the county including the entire coastal strip, the upper reaches of the Daugleddau (two swords) and the Preseli's. Its the only National Park that is almost all coastal. The National Park run an extensive programme of activities and events for both adults and children: rockpool safaris, crab catching, bat walks and even time travel.

The National Trust owns and protects many of the most important sections of the coast especially around Barafundle beach, Marloes, St Davids, Porthgain & Dinas. The trust also runs the superb Colby Woodland Gardens at Amroth and the Tudor Merchants house near the harbour in Tenby.

✴ *Britain's Only Coastal National Park, The Pembrokeshire Coast National Park is the only one of Britain's 14 National Parks to be entirely coastal in nature.*

✴ *It covers a third of Pembrokeshire including the Preseli Mountains and the upper reaches of the Daugleddau Estuary.*

✴ *Tenby, St Davids, Saundersfoot, Newport and Manorbier are all in the National Park.*

✴ *So are Skomer, Skokholm, Caldey and Ramsey Islands Two inland areas are also in the National Park, The Preseli Mountains and the upper reaches of the Daugleddau Estuary.*

✴ *The Preseli Mountains are where the Stonehenge bluestones are supposed to have come from.*

✴ *The Daugleddau Estuary is known, locally, as the secret waterway.*

WALKING ROUTES

Pembrokeshire's best known footpath is the **PEMBROKESHIRE COAST PATH**, which winds its way around the magnificent bays and spectacular headlands and is one of only 18 National Trails in the UK and Europe's premier coastal walking experience. The 186 mile, 299km trek is a strenuous undertaking if you want to complete the route from start to finish.

CEMAES HEAD is a rugged and wild section of intensely folded high cliffs. Start at the car park at Poppit near St. Dogmael's and walk up the road past the Youth hostel. Follow the coast path to Ceibwr Bay, a distance of 5.5m/7km. By the time you've returned, across country, you'll have covered 9½ miles or 16km. Catch the Poppit Rocket the walker's bus.

DINAS ISLAND is a rocky headland near Fishguard. Start at either Cwm yr Eglwys or Pwllgwaelod and take the coast path around the island, returning to your start point via the low lying valley that connects it to the mainland. Total distance covered is about 3 miles or 5km. Catch the Poppit Rocket the walker's bus.

CARREGWASTAD POINT is famous for being the landing point for the last invasion of mainland Britain in 1797, when 1500 French troops came ashore on a disastrous and futile attempt to raise a peasants revolt. Start in the pretty village of Llanwnda, near Fishguard and backtrack along the road for ¼ mile before cutting across country towards the ferry terminal at Goodwick. Pick up the coast path and follow it round to Carregwastad Point. If you want to turn back here the distance is about 5½ miles or 9km. To carry on to Strumble Head will double the distance. Catch the Strumble Shuttle the walker's bus.

STRUMBLE HEAD is a wild and unpopulated stretch of the path with some spectacular cliffs. Start at the car park at Garn Fawr, 2 miles south of Strumble Head and follow winding country lanes all the way to Strumble lighthouse. Continue along the coast path to the Youth Hostel at Pwll Deri and return to the car park via the hilltop where you get magnificent views of the Pen Caer peninsula you've just walked around. Total distance 5½ miles, 9km. Catch the Strumble Shuttle the walker's bus.

Either start at **ABEREIDDY** or at **PORTHGAIN**, a safe-haven harbour with a good pub and restaurant. There's plenty of interest on the way including old stone quarries, the Blue Lagoon - a flooded slate quarry and the secret beach of Traeth Llyfn. Returning to your starting point via Barry Island Farm and Felindre House. Total distance is 4 miles/6km. Catch the Strumble Shuttle the walkers bus.

ST. DAVIDS PENINSULA Start behind the Cathedral and follow the lanes north along the valley. When you reach Treleddyd Fawr continue across country until you reach the coast path which you can then follow all the way round the peninsular to Caerfai before returning to St. Davids. This route cover 15miles, 23km or it can be tackled in smaller sections: Whitesands to St. Davids Head and back via Carn Llidi 4 miles/6km Porthstinian to Porthclais and return on the country roads 6miles/10km St. Davids to Porthclais and return via Caerfai 2miles/3km. Catch the Celtic Coaster the walker's bus.

Thanks to the introduction of the **PUFFIN SHUTTLE** between St. Davids and Milford Haven, some excellent stretches of the coast path can now be tackled without the need to do a circular route. Use the shuttle to travel to the far end of your day's walk and walk back to where you started. Good sections to tackle in this fashion include:

Solva to St Davids
Newgale to Solva
Little Haven to Nolton Haven
St Brides Haven to Little Haven
Dale to Martins Haven

97

Take a circular route around the **MARLOES PENINSULA**, starting at either Marloes beacon or the National Trust car park for Marloes beach. It covers a distance of 6.5miles/11km

Another good circular route is around the **DALE PENINSULA**, starting from the car park near St. Ann's head. The path follows some dramatic cliff tops, dropping down to several lovely sandy coves on the way. Total distance is about 6miles/10km.

SOUTH OF MILFORD HAVEN, another circular route is possible around the Angle Peninsula, starting from either Freshwater West or from West Angle Bay. Travelling in a clockwise direction, you are treated to one of the most dramatic views in Britain as you come over the ridge and see the magnificent beach at Freshwater West stretching away into the distance. Total distance is around 9miles/15km.
Catch the Coastal Cruiser bus

The coast path between **STACK ROCKS** and **BROAD HAVEN SOUTH** is only accessible when the army ranges are open. It's a fascinating stretch of coast but can't be easily incorporated into a circular route because the ranges get in the way. Some unusual rock features, arches, stacks, caves and hidden beaches as well as a visit to St. Govan's Chapel make the walk interesting. Distance one way is 4½ miles/7½ km.
Catch the Coastal Cruiser bus

STACKPOLE QUAY is the start point for a good walk that takes in dramatic cliffs, the lily ponds at Bosherston and one of the most remarkably unspoilt beaches in Britain, Barafundle. As with the previous walk, there isn't a circular option, merely retrace your steps. With teashops at both ends, Stackpole Quay and Bosherston Village, dehydration shouldn't be a problem. Total distance 4½ miles/7km.
Catch the Coastal Cruiser bus

From the National Park car park at **MANORBIER BEACH**, below the castle, two walks are available, one going west to the secluded Swanlake Bay a distance of 3miles/5km. The path to the east provides a short circular walk returning through the village. Local Bus Service 349/359

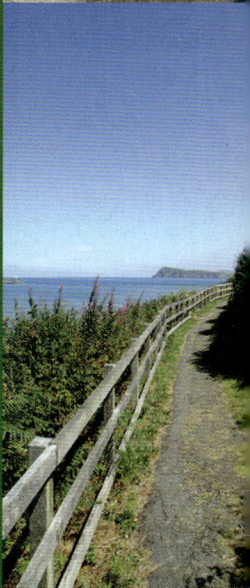

The coast path from **TENBY** to
SAUNDERSFOOT passes some of the best
beaches you're likely to find in Britain including
Glen beach, Monkstone and Waterwynch. There's
a regular bus service between the towns, the best
way to organise a circular route. To walk the
route from one direction from harbour to harbour
is around 4 miles/6km. Local Bus Service 350/351

From **SAUNDERSFOOT** to **AMROTH**, the coast
path follows an old tramway, which takes in a
series of tunnels for the first mile. The route
there and back is approx 5miles/8km. Local bus
service 350/351

WITHYBUSH WOODS A gentle one mile trail
near the centre of Haverfordwest, yet a haven for
peace and tranquillity, except for bird song. The
trail is especially suitable for physically and
visually handicapped people - it has its own audio
trail for enhanced enjoyment.

LLYS-Y-FRAN COUNTRY PARK.
Approximately 7.5 miles, 11km around the reservoir, focal point of the Country Park which has
car parks on each side of the lake. Picnic sites,
visitor centre, licensed restaurant, toilets,
exhibitions area and shops available.
Special events and guided walks are also
arranged. These include a tour of the reservoir,
woodland bird spotting, the chance to try fly
fishing and children activities days (including a
boat trip)
Tel- 01437 532273/532694 for details.

A walk in **SLEBECH FOREST**, approx 1½
miles/2½ km starts and finishes at the National
Park picnic site overlooking Canaston Bridge on
the minor road from Minwear to Blackpool Mill.

TENBY GHOST WALKS and **GUIDED WALKS**,
regular guided walks from Tudor Square detailing
Tenby's fascinating and sometimes chilling past.
Tel - 01834 845841 for details.

Flying

f taking to the skies is more to your fancy, the Haverfordwest Airport is the place to head for. There they have a Flying School for both aeroplanes and helicopters together with a Microlight Centre.

for more information
tel: 01437 760822

Golf
TENBY GOLF CLUB

Tenby hosts the oldest golf club in Wales where the Burrows offers a superb 18 hole links course that regularly hosts events. In 2006 it hosted the Welsh PGA Championship. Overlooking Caldey Island, the clubhouse has a restaurant together with bar, lounge and snooker room.

tel: 01834 842978

TREFLOYNE GOLF COURSE

Trefloyne is a family owned golf course, located in the small village of Penally just outside Tenby. Trefloyne offers guests an 18 hole challenging parkland course set in mixed woodlands, with breathtaking views over Carmarthen Bay and Caldey Island. The focus of Trefloyneis pure and simple, a relaxed atmosphere with a warm and friendly welcome. You don't have to be a golfer to enjoy the bar and restaurant. Whether you have been out for the full 18, enjoyed a long walk through the woods or just wanted a lazy lunch with friends, Treflyone really can cater for everyone.

visit us at
www.trefloyne.com

100

DERLLYS COURT GOLF CLUB

A delightful 9 hole treelined course of parkland nature, set in beautiful Carmarthenshire countryside with easy access off the bypass between Carmarthen and St. Clears. The two lakes on the course afford a natural haven for an abundance of wildlife. The par 35 is of average length and the subtle nature of the course demands a great deal of driving accuracy. The clubhouse provides changing and shower facilities and easy access for the handicapped. Along with a licensed bar, snacks and meals are available during opening hours. 2004 saw the opening of a new 9 holes.

for more information call 01267 211575

ST. DAVIDS CITY GOLF CLUB

Established in 1902, this is one of the oldest golf clubs in Wales, and certainly the most westerly. The all weather links course is playable all year round, and with the added attraction of stunning views over the bay and St. Davids Head, it is not surprising that this 6000 yard par 70 course is so popular visitors.

for more information ring the clubhouse tel: 01437 721751 or ring the secretary tel: 01437 720058

SOUTH PEMBROKESHIRE GOLF CLUB

This 18 hole hillside course is located at Pembroke Dock, on an elevated site overlooking the River Cleddau and the beautiful Haven Waterway. There is always a warm welcome in the clubhouse, with an excellent restaurant and bar, which also have panoramic views of the Haven. The club is only five minutes from the Irish Ferries Terminal at Pembroke Dock.

for more information call tel: 01646 682442

Derllys Court Golf Club

101

HAVERFORDWEST GOLF CLUB

Haverfordwest Golf Club, formed in 1904, is situated on the outskirts of the town. The 18 hole course is a challenging one offering fabulous views of the Preseli Hills.

for more information
tel: 01437 764523

MILFORD HAVEN GOLF CLUB

A superb 18 hole par 71 meadowland course, with panoramic views of the Haven Waterway.

tel: 01646 697762

PRISKILLY FOREST GOLF CLUB

Priskilly Forest near Letterston is a nine hole course set in mature parkland and only a ten minute drive from the Stena Ferry terminal at Fishguard.

tel: 01348 840276

ROSEMARKET GOLF COURSE

Rosemarket offers a challenging and very long nine hole parkland course cursed with numerous sand and water hazards to test players. An added unusual feature is a bookable grass landing strip offering a fly-drive with a difference.

HEATHERON & HERONS BROOK GOLF COURSES

Other golf courses include one at St. Florence, an 18 hole pitch and putt course situated at the Heatherton Sports Park, *tel: 01646 651025,* and the 18 and 9 hole courses at the Heron's Brook in Narberth

tel: 01834 860723 or
860023

NEWPORT GOLF CLUB

Newport Golf Club & Dormy House Holiday Flats: here you have a golf course which overlooks the magnificent coastline of Newport Bay, and the superbly appointed holiday flats which overlook both. Opening in Spring 2008 will be an additional 9 holes extending the current course to a full 18. The clubhouse offers full catering facilities, and accomodation, including twelve twin bedrooms and three luxury suites.

tel: 01239 820244
or visit
www.newportlinks.co.uk

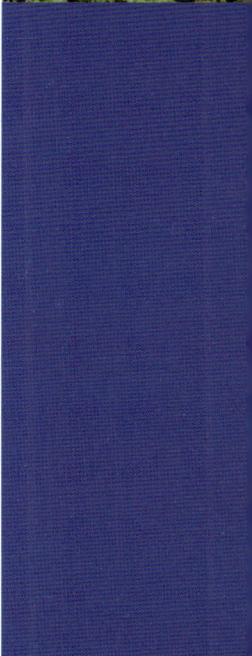

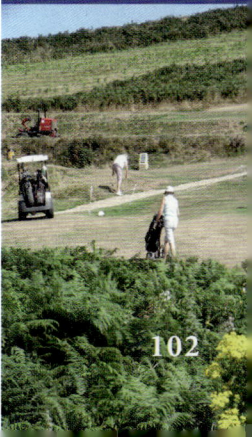

SPORT & ACTIVITIES

SYCAMORES RANCH WESTERN RIDING CENTRE
Near Llawhaden, Narberth

Have you ever dreamed of riding a western horse on the American plains but thought it was either too expensive or too far to travel?. Well Sycamores Ranch in Llawhaden near Narberth can offer you this experience here in beautiful Wales. The comfortable saddles, well behaved horses, idyllic scenery all add up to an opportunity not to be missed. The Ranch caters for people from the average to the more experienced rider and offer from one hour to whole day trails with barbeque. The trails include riding along quiet offroad bridle paths to crossing rivers, streams and fords. Passing through the delightful Pembrokeshire countryside you will also come across many historical monuments, ranging from ancient castles to traditional Welsh farmhouses and picturesque churches. They also arrange night rides in the summer months. These consist of leaving the Ranch early evening and riding out to a stop off point where a meal is provided, and then riding back to the Ranch in time to put the horses to bed. As well as the trail side they also teach people western riding for those who want to take it a bit more seriously and they also take in horses for backing and schooling in western. The Ranch also has its beautiful American Quarter Horse stallion standing at stud and a Western Tack Shop, which has possibly the largest selection of Western Tack from saddles to Stetsons in Wales.

for more information visit
www.sycamoresranch.com

Karting

BP KARTING
County Showground,
Withybush,
Haverfordwest
tel: 01437 769555

CAREW KARTING
Carew Airfield,
Sageston, Nr Tenby
tel: 01559 384078
or
07974 540689

KARTRAX
St. Davids Road,
Letterston
tel: 01348 840447

Quad Biking

RITEC VALLEY BUGGIES
Penally, Nr Tenby
tel: 01834 843390
see our advert on page 28

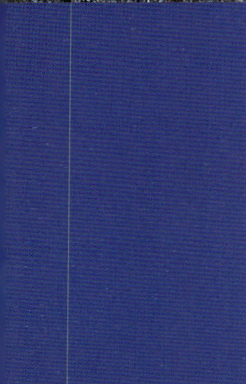

THE DUNES RIDING CENTRE
Martletwy, Narberth

A visit to Pembrokeshire wouldn't be complete without sampling the horse riding at the Dunes Riding Centre. A friendly, family run stables offering riding for all abilities from complete beginners to those wanting a more adventurous ride. Their fit, forward going horses and ponies will take you through woodland and forestry at a pace to suit your ability, ranging from an hour for the experienced, to a half day for the competent rider who can walk, trot and canter. Nervous riders and children can be led on the one hour ride which is suitable for novices from 5 to 75! All prices include the use of approved riding hats and jodphur boots, and it is essential to book in advance. All rides are accompanied by cheerful competent escorts who will make this an experience to remember and cherish.

for more information or to book a visit tel: 01834 891398

104

Sailing

Traditionally, dinghy sailing is very popular all over Pembrokeshire and southwest Wales. Yacht clubs such as Newport, Fishguard and Solva in the north of the county and Tenby and Saundersfoot in the South, offer a friendly club atmosphere and a variety of facilities and racing programmes. Along the Milford Haven waterway, perhaps the most popular sailing location because it is sheltered from the open sea, you will find some of the larger and more active clubs, such as Neyland, Pembroke Haven Pembrokeshire (Gelliswick, Milford Haven) and Dale. For yachtsmen, the Haven has 22 miles of navigable inland waterway, with the additional challenge of exciting offshore sailing to the nearby islands of Skomer, Skokholm and Grassholm. There are marinas at Milford Haven and Neyland, pontoons at Dale, Angle, Burton and Neyland and various mooring sites all along the waterway.

DALE YACHT CLUB
tel: 01646 636362

MILFORD MARINA
tel: 01646 692272

NEYLAND MARINA
tel: 01646 601601

PEMBROKESHIRE YACHT CLUB
Gelliswick,
Milford Haven
tel:01646 692799

PEMBROKESHIRE CRUISING
Neyland Marina,
Brunel Quay, Neyland
tel: 01646 602500

PEMBROKESHIRE WATERSPORTS
The Cleddau River Centre,
Pembroke Dock
tel: 01646 622013
The Parrog,
Fishguard
tel: 01348 874803

SOLVA SAILBOATS
Trinity Quay,
Solva
tel: 01437 720972

WEST WALES WIND, SURF & SAILING
Dale, Nr Haverfordwest
tel: 01646 636642

Surfing & Windsurfing

Big waves, clear blue unpolluted waters, no crowds and relatively mild air and water temperatures - the tempting combination which Pembrokshire offers to surfers who are willing to travel that bit further in order to stand out from the rest. Late summer and early autumn are particularly good times to take advantage of the county's superb beaches and surfing conditions. Freshwater West, in South Pembrokeshire boasts the biggest and most consistent waves in the whole of Wales, with a variety of breaks to choose from. However there are strong currents and no lifeguards, so beginners should not surf here. Other beaches worth checking out nearby include Broad Haven (south), Freshwater East and Manorbier. In North Pembrokeshire, good surfing can be enjoyed at Whitesands Bay, Newgale, Broad Haven and West Dale. Age is no barrier to windsurfing which attracts enthusiasts from 8 to 80. Some enjoy setting sail in light winds for a tranquil afternoons cruise, whilst others like to display their competitive streak by racing, and for the most adventurous there are the strong winds and wave jumping.

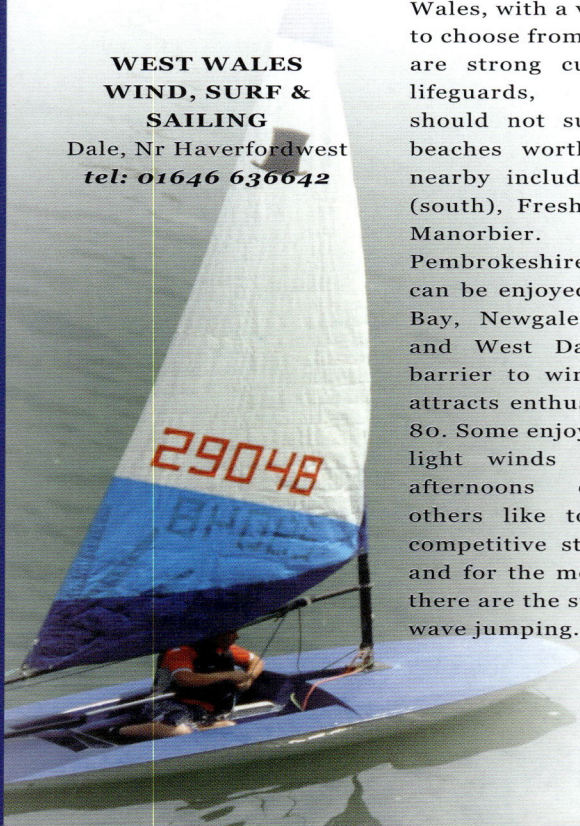

Another big attraction of windsurfing is that it's easy to learn, provided you have the right equipment and and tuition. One of Britain's top windsurfing and sailing venues is Dale. Its mile wide bay promises superb sea sailing on flat water, with no strong tidal currents, and is ideal for beginners and experts alike. West Wales Windsurfing, Sailing and Canoeing, is based on Dale waterfront and is a specialist watersports centre approved by the Royal Yachting Association. The expert tuition available here caters for everyone, from beginner to advanced windsurfers. All equipment is provided including wet-suits and buoyancy aids, and every instructor holds a nationally recognised qualification. As for recommending the best beaches , Broad Haven, (St. Brides Bay) and Newgale are ideal for more experienced windsurfers, except in particularly calm conditions, where as beginners and intermediates will breeze along more easily at Tenby, Saundersfoot, Newport and Fishguard.

SURF SHOPS & HIRE

HAVEN SPORTS
Broad Haven
tel: 01437 781354

MA SIME'S SURF HUT
St. Davids
tel: 01437 720433

NEWSURF
Newgale
tel: 01437 721398

TYF
ADVENTURE
St. Davids
tel: 01437 721611
freephone 0800 132588

WAVES "N" WHEELS
Pembroke
01646 622066

CYCLING ROUTES

Pembrokeshire is the perfect county to see from the comfort of a bicycle. Long flat coastal roads, fantastic scenery and views to be enjoyed at a slow and relaxed pace. There are plenty of more exciting and difficult woodland routes if you are adventurously inclined.

The following are a mixture of difficulty level routes for you to try and enjoy, or you are always most welcome to use the maps published in this guide book or purchase our sister map, and discover Pembrokeshire yourself

Newgale to Broad Haven 6 miles (hilly)

The miles of golden sands and sweeping cliff landscapes at Newgale have to be seen to be loved. Head out of the village southwards along the back of this sea wall until a right turn takes you to a smaller lane. This takes you up a climb to the top of the cliffs from where you can see the whole of St. Bride's Bay from Ramsey Island in the north to Skomer Island in the south. From here you head down into Nolton Haven, past the pub and turn right up a steep hill onto a lane that runs along the cliffs until you turn inland to a T junction. Turn right here to Haroldston West and then straight down the hill into Broad Haven, a sandy beach that is popular with surfers, windsurfers and sun worshippers alike. You can also continue along the coast to Little Haven, a cosy little fishing village.

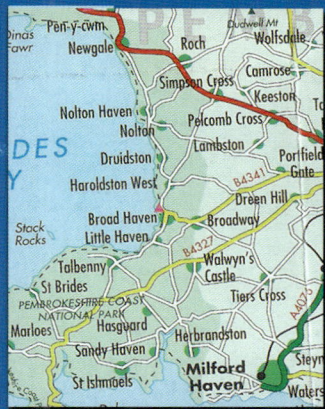

Pembroke to Tenby 11 miles (easy)

Pembroke town is built around the spectacular Tudor castle, with a large round central keep and complete set of castle walls. The route towards Tenby takes you along the busy high street, a one way street with plenty of room for bikes, to the roundabout. Ignore the turn to Tenby and take the next exit down Well Hill. Within fifty metres you take a left turn to Lamphey, a quiet, high banked lane that runs parallel to the busy A4139. Once in Lamphey turn left along the main road to cross the railway bridge and immediately right on a lane marked "The Ridgeway". There is a left turn straight away that takes you to a picnic place and the site of the Bishops Palace, while the road ahead climbs steadily to the top of the Ridgeway. Once on top of the ridge this long straight road gives you splendid views to the distant Preseli Hills on one side and the coast on the other. About four miles out of Lamphey turn left up Coal Lane and then right and right again into the old village of St. Florence. Go straight over the crossroads in the village and continue down the lane to a left at a T-junction that brings you out onto the A4139 for the last mile into Tenby.

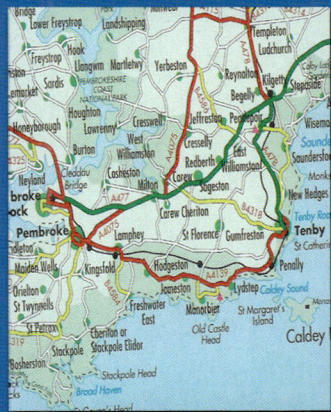

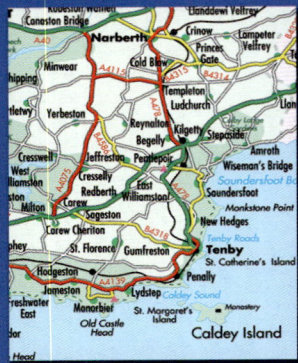

Tenby to Amroth 6 miles (easy)

Start from the entrance to the harbour beside the Caldey Island Ticket Office. Head up hill and immediately turn right on to Crackwell Street overlooking the harbour. At Junction turn right and over mini roundabout, down the hill past the entrance to the car park and follow the Celtic Trail signs right up Slippery Back, an old cobbled lane that, two hundred years ago, was the main road into Tenby. At the top of the path follow the Celtic Trail signs and cycle paths through New Hedges and down into Saundersfoot with its long sweep of sand and rock pools. From the harbour in the centre of the town follow the one way system and Celtic Trail signs until you reach a large car park. From here push your bike through the tunnels and along the footpath on the old railway line that runs along the seafront to Wiseman's Bridge. As you climb away from the seafront look for a right hand turn to Summerhill, then take the next right that takes you to an old greenway that follows the cliff top into Amroth

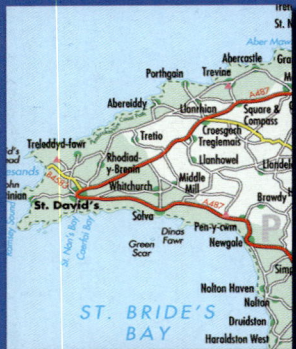

Porthgain to Middle Mill 12 miles (easy)

Porthgain is a small picturesque little fishing village on the north coast where a small enclosed harbour was constructed in the nineteenth century for the stone quarry west of the village. There is only one road into and out of Porthgain and this takes you to the crossroads at Llanrhian where you turn right for the back road into St. Davids. Follow lane for about 4 miles past the two right turns to Abereiddy. Take the next right until you reach the B4583. Go straight across and look for the first right that takes you past the ruined Bishops Palace to a ford right in front of St. Davids cathedral. Through the ford the road takes you under an impressive stone gateway to the centre of St. Davids, Britain's smallest City. Cross the square and take the A487 Haverfordwest road, Turn left by the secondary school onto a lane that takes you to Whitchurch and on to Middle Mill, a small village with a working weaving mill that is open to the public. From the mill a lovely lane, with woods to your right and a stream to your left, takes you down to Solva, one of the gems of Pembrokeshire. The fishing village has a variety of shops, pubs and eateries with which to replenish.

111

Fishguard to Trefin 10 Miles (hilly)

Starting from the car park on the Parrog, the seafront between Fishguard and Goodwick, follow the path in front of the Ocean Lab along the seafront heading towards Fishguard. Next follow the Celtic Trail signs along a path which is traffic free to the top of the hill. At the end of the cycle path follow the lane down and over the railway line before turning left along the St. Davids road. After less than half a mile turn right, again following the Celtic Trail signs, up a quiet lane until you take a left turn at the top of the hill. The lane continues for about 3 miles, there are some spectacular views of the Preseli Hills to enjoy, until you reach a wooded area. Take a right turn through the woods and round a sharp left up a narrow, steep wooded lane, which is just as pleasant to walk up as to ride. Out of the woods you take a right at the next crossroads to take you down into Abercastle, with public toilets and sheltered cove. You have a stiff climb out of Abercastle, but once at the top it is only a mile into the village of Trefin. Three attractions can be visited en-route, Ocean Lab at Goodwick, Melin Tregwynt woollen mill at mid route and a hand weaving centre in Trefin.

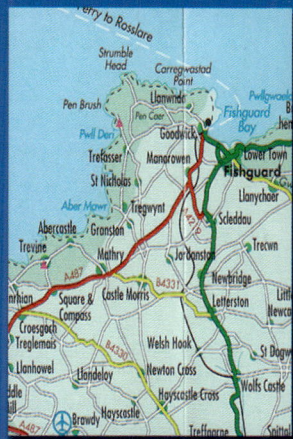

Newport to Rosebush 12miles (hilly)

This route takes you from the sea at Newport by way of the delightful Gwaun Valley to Rosebush, the highest village in the Preseli Hills. As you might expect this is a much easier ride on the return trip, but having said that, the first mile out of Newport is the steepest climb of the whole route. From the top of Market Street turn left and follow the road past the church to the top of the hill before descending to a steep sharp bend by the candle workshop at Cilgwyn. Ignore the turn to Nevern and take the right at the next junction to ride down the historic and beautiful Gwaun Valley until you reach The Dyffryn Arms, the renowned "Bessie's", one of the last traditional pubs still serving ale from the jug. Turn left over the bridge and up the hill, past the old church and a turn to the right, until you reach the B4313. Turn left here, and go straight across to Rosebush when you reach the crossroads, where a left turn takes you into the village with its disused, but preserved railway station, and Pembrokeshire's only corrugated tin pub,
Tafarn Sinc.

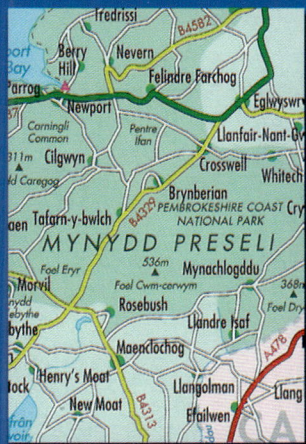

ST DAVIDS & THE NORTH COAST

Compared with Tenby and the more developed south, North Pembrokeshire is better known for its rugged beauty and ancient landscape than its leisure attractions and amusements. Yet many of the features which annually bring hundreds of thousands of visitors to the area can be described truthfully as man made - some as long ago as 5000 years. The sights awaiting those visitors with a will to explore are as fascinating as they are varied. They include such delights as the cathedral and city of St. Davids, the superb beach of Whitesands, the picturesque village and harbour of Solva, small coastal resorts such as Abereiddy and Porthgain and the golden sands of Newport. There are also traditional crafts and Welsh industries such as cheese making as well as working woollen mills, together with the historic port of Fishguard.

Inland, the beautiful Gwaun Valley and rolling Preseli Hills add their own mystique to a landscape liberally endowed with prehistoric sites and ancient burial chambers. To the Welsh, the greatest saint of all was St. David, the patron saint of Wales. The spectacularly beautiful peninsula which bears his name is the most hallowed spot in the country, for this was his reputed birth place. It was here that he established a semi-monastic religious settlement in around 550. This site is now occupied by the famous 12th century cathedral which gives the village of St Davids its entitle ment to city status. It is the smallest city in Britain, some sources claim it to be the smallest in the world. The skyline is dominated not by the tower of St Davids Cathedral, as you might think, but by the stark hills of igneous rock such as Carn Llidi. If anything the cathe dral is conspicuous by its absence, because until you are in its immediate vicinity it is very effectively hidden in the vale of the tiny River Alun.

Carn Llidi is deceptive to the eye. It rises a modest 600ft above sea level, but looks much higher. It was because of the unprecedented views to the west and north that Carn Llidi proved useful strategi cally in both world wars. In the first it bore a hydrophone station for detecting subma rines, in the second it was the site for a lookout and radar installation. Near Carn Llidi, and overlooked by St Davids Head, is Whitesands Bay. This superb beach, very popular in summer, is the best in North Pembrokeshire and has been described as the best in Wales. South of Whitesands Bay is an expanse of countryside, an ancient agricultural landscape of fertile soils and arable fields. Further south still, the ruins of St Justinian's Chapel stand near the little cove of Porthstinian, which is also home to the St Davids lifeboat Station. This was built in 1869.

The Bell Tower St Davids

114

St. Davids

Distances: Fishguard 16m
Haverfordwest 16m,
Milford Haven 21m,
Narberth 25m, Pembroke
26m, Tenby 35m,
Carmarthen 46m and
London 266m

St. Davids is living proof that size is not important. As any visitor will quickly discover, the cathedral city is in reality a modest but very charming village. People still flock here in their thousands as they did throughout the Middle Ages when this was a place of pilgrimage, and the cathedral remains the major object of attention. Yet impressive and hugely significant though it is, the cathedral is small by English standards, and because it is hidden in a sheltered valley you could pass through St. Davids without even noticing that Wales' greatest religious monument is here. The village-cum-city dates back to the 6th century and stands about a mile from the sea, on a wide plateau overlooking the diminutive River Alun. The centre of St. Davids is marked by Cross Square, so called because of its restored ancient cross. High Street is something of a misnomer, for the road runs in from Solva and Haverfordwest but does not contain City Hall. Inevitably all roads lead to the 12th century cathedral. Less well known, but no less impressive, are the ruins of the once magnificent Bishop's Palace, which stands opposite the cathedral in Cathedral Close. The close is an area of 18 acres, lying below the city in the vale of the River Alun. It is believed that this secluded site was chosen for the

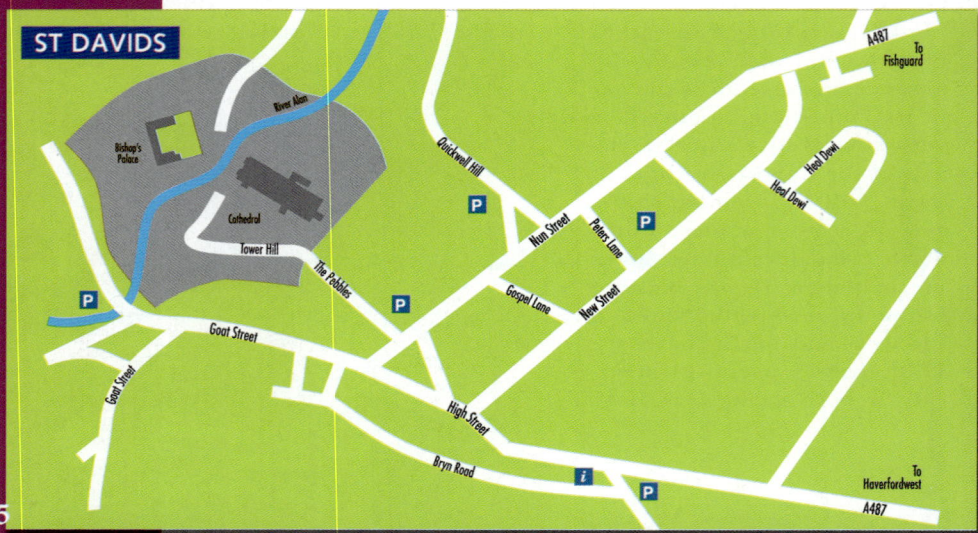

original 6th century church so that it would not be visible from the sea to passing pirates and raiders, who frequently made it their business to ransack western coastal communities and pilfer whatever treasures the churches and chapels might contain. However, the ploy failed, Vikings burnt the church no less than eight times during the centuries leading up to the Norman Conquest. The path from the city down to Cathedral Close takes you through the 13th century Tower Gate, one of four gatehouses which formed part of the close's precinct wall. Within the Close stands the cathedral, the Bishop's Palace and various other ecclesiatical buildings, including the houses of church dignitaries. At this point you are still above the level of the cathedral and to reach it requires a further descent of a flight of thirty nine steps known as the Thirty-Nine Articles. The Cathedral and Bishop's Palace are marvels of medieval architecture, all the more striking for the remarkable tranquillity of this remote setting.

ST. DAVIDS CATHEDRAL

The cathedral as it stands today was begun in 1180 by Peter de Leia, the third Norman bishop, and completed in 1522. In 1220 thecentral tower collapsed, an occurrence apparently not unknown in medieval churches, and further damage was inflicted by a severe earthquake in 1248. Early in the 14th century, Bishop Gower, nick

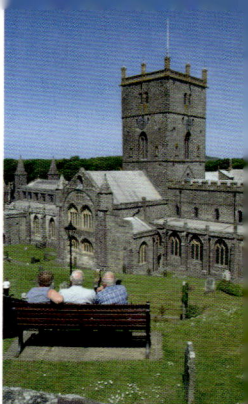

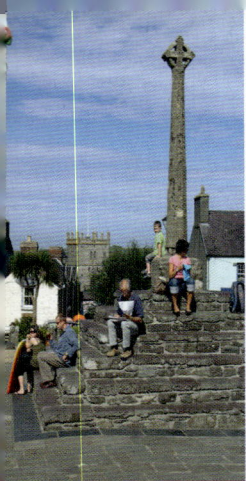

**Cross Square
St. Davids**

named "The Building Bishop" because of his love of creating great buildings, carried out many changes and improvements to the cathedral. He raised the walls of the aisles, inserted the decorated and much larger windows, built the south porch and transept chapels and vaulted the Lady Chapel. In around 1340 he also built the Bishop's Palace to accommodate the large numbers of pilgrims visiting the cathedral. The Palace, a structure of such spendour that even the ruins are impressive, stands opposite the cathedral. As the cathedral expanded, an increasing number of clerical residences and other ecclesiastical buildings grew up around it, and a wall with gatehouses was built to protect the community. The last of the great builders to contribute to the cathedral was Bishop Vaughan, who in the early 16th century raised the tower to its present height and built the perpendicular chapel dedicated to the Holy Trinity. Following the Reformation the cathedral was neglected. The roof was stripped of its lead and subsequently, though much later, collapsed. Severe damage was also inflicted in the Civil War. In 1862 Sir George Gilbert Scott was commissioned to begin a complete restoration of the cathedral, and not surprisingly the work continued into this century. In 1866, during the restoration, the bones of two men were found in a recess which had been walled up. It is believed that these were the remains of St. David and his friend and teacher St. Justinian. They are now contained in an oak chest in the Holy Trinity Chapel. Other tombs in the cathedral include those of Bishop Gower, Edmund Tudor, father of Henry VII, and Giraldus Cambrensis. St. Davids Cathedral which is open to visitors every day, is the largest church in Wales and is certainly the most interesting. The total interior length is nearly 300ft and the tower is 125ft high, small by comparison with cathedrals on the grand scale of York Minster, but a mighty inspiration to the Welsh for centuries past and, no doubt, for centuries to come.

BISHOP'S PALACE

This grand and richly decorated palace was largely the work of Bishop Henry de Gower, who also left his very distinctive mark on Lamphey Bishops Palace and Swansea Castle. It was built mainly between 1328 and 1347, and stands opposite the cathedral in Cathedral Close, amongst a group of medieval buildings unique in Wales. The palace played host to many pilgrims whose number included monks, bishops and kings. Even in ruin the battlements, curtain walls, gatehouse and entrance to the great hall are impressive, and of particular interest are Bishop Gower's arcaded parapets, which are decorated with some of the finest examples of medieval sculptured heads and animals to be found in Wales. The Bishop's Palace will hold a conservation exhibition in July and August 2008. It is also the venue for a number of special events. These include performances of Shakespeare plays and a December carol service. The palace is in the care of CADW (Welsh Historic Monuments).

for more information ring 01437 720517 or 01443 336000

118

ST. DAVIDS CATHEDRAL FESTIVAL

Founded in 1979, the St Davids Cathedral Festival is an annual event; a week of classical and contemporary music concerts set in the stunning surroundings of St. Davids Cathedral. The Festival aims to offer a wide variety of music to as many people as possible. It offers top-class professional concerts at reasonable prices, with free admission for children under 16 at most concerts, and concessions for the disabled and unwaged. The style of the concerts is varied; in addition to both early and late evening concerts (featuring soloists, chamber music ensembles, choral, jazz and orchestral groups) there are also a series of afternoon recitals. The Festival has expanded its activities in the community with a masterclass for young musicians. The Cathedral has always had a long tradition of musical excellence. It is remarkable that Britain's smallest city with a population of less than 1,700 and no choir-school has three cathedral choirs. The choral services of the cathedral form part of the Festival celebrations.The Festival has made a substantial contribution to the cultural life of West Wales.

01437 721854
cathedralfestival@onetel.com

St. Non's Chapel

Non was the mother of David, the man destined to become the patron saint of Wales. Standing in a field above St. Non's Bay, just south of St. Davids, the original ruined chapel is reputedly the oldest Christian monument in Wales. It is also said to mark the exact spot where St. David was born in the 6th century, during a thunderstorm. Near the chapel is a holy well that miraculously appeared at the moment of birth. In the Middle Ages the well attracted many people who came to cure their ailments. The present St. Non's Chapel was built in 1934.

Porthclais

In centuries past, this picturesque inlet was a busy little harbour, the port of the monastic community at St. Davids. Its sheltered anchorage saw the comings and goings of countless monks, priests, pilgrims, Norman soldiers, pirates and even Kings. Purple stone from nearby Caerfai and Caerbwdy was landed here to help build the cathedral, along with Irish oak for the roof of the nave.

Trade thrived here in the Tudor and Stuart periods, with exports of cereal to the West Country. Later years saw the import of limestone to feed the four kilns on the quayside, two of which have been restored.

St. Justinian's

The name actually refers to the remains of St. Justinian's Chapel, but over time it has become synonymous with the little creek and harbour of Porthstinian. The presence of the chapel recalls the legend of St. Justinian, who founded a small religious community on nearby Ramsey Island. The discipline he imposed on his followers was so strict that they rebelled and cut off his head, whereupon St. Justinian picked it up, walked over the sea to the mainland, laid down on his head and died.

Porthstinian

Porthstinian is well known as the home of the St. Davids lifeboat station. This was founded in 1868, though it was 1912 before the building and slipway were built. The rocky coastline and dangerous offshore reefs, such as the Smalls and the Bishops and Clerks, make this an extremely treacherous area for seaborne traffic, and the lifeboats which have seen service here have been involved in many dramatic rescues. Porthstinian has a beach but is unsuitable for bathing. Just across the water is Ramsey Island separated from the mainland by hazardous Ramsey Sound.

Solva

Without question this must be one of the most charming and attractive coastal villages in Britain. Just east of St. Davids on the A487 Haverfordwest road, Solva is a beautiful rocky inlet which floods at low tide providing a sheltered, safe anchorage for yachts and pleasure craft. Not surprisingly, this fine natural harbour has given the village a long seafaring tradition. Shipbuilding and maritime trade flourished here until the railway arrived in Pembrokeshire in the middle of the 19th century. In its heyday the busy port had a thriving import and export business, nine warehouses, twelve lime-kilns, a direct passenger service to New York and also played an important role in the construction of the two remote light-houses erected at different times on the smalls, a treacherous cluster of jagged rocks lurking 21 miles off Pembrokeshire's west coast. The facts relating to the passenger service to New York are a particularly fascinating slice of Solva's history. In 1848 the one way fare for an adult was £3. For this you were sure of a bed space, but had to take your own food, and the voyage could take anything from 7 to 17 weeks. The most popular part of this favourite holiday village, which is split into two, is Lower Solva with its harbour, surviving limekilns and a charming selection of shops, pubs and restaurants. Solva is an excellent place to join the Pembrokeshire Coastal Path, as the cliff scenery on either side of the inlet is magnificent. If you fancy an easy stroll you can walk along the harbour or take the footpath above the opposite (eastern) side of the inlet. This takes you to the top of the Gribin - a strip of land between two valleys - where you can see the site of an Iron Age settlement and superb views of the village and harbour.

Abereiddy

The Blue Lagoon

Middle Mill

Just north of Solva, a mile up the valley of the river of the same name, nestles the attractive little waterside hamlet of Middle Mill. Here you will find a working woollen mill, which opened in 1907 and has been in production ever since. This family run business invites you to watch the process that turns the finest Welsh wool into a range of high quality rugs, tweeds, carpets and clothes, all of which are for sale on the premises.

Abereiddy

An attractive west facing bay on the north coast of the St. Davids Peninsula, Abereiddy is famous locally for its striking Blue Lagoon once a slate quarry linked to the sea by a narrow channel, but closed in 1904 after it was flooded during a storm. The lagoon is mow considered an important geological feature, and the quarry yields many fossils. The coastal scenery between here and St. Davids Head is outstanding. To the north there are traces of the old narrow gauge railway track which once took the quarried slate and shale to the harbour at nearby Porthgain for export. Abereiddy is about two miles east of Croesgoch, on the A487 St. Davids to Fishguard road.

PEMBROKESHIRE SHEEPDOGS

On the beautiful north coast of Pembrokeshire, close to St. Davids is Tremynydd Fach Farm, home of Pembrokeshire Sheepdogs Training Centre. The centre runs courses for owners, handlers and their dogs from novice right up to " One Man and His Dog" standard. However, for the casual visitor they also run demonstrations throughout the season, which allow everyone to watch a wonderful exhibition of the skills of the working dogs. From the youngest pups just beginning to show the natural instincts for their work, through all stages of training, to dogs of three or four years at the height of their skills. All can be seen working sheep, and other animals, and clearly having a great time doing it. There is also a surprise finale. Teas and home baked cakes at extremely reasonable prices, plus the opportunity to talk to the handlers, make this a wonderful insight into working dogs. You can even bring your own dog to watch but keep them on a lead please.

for further information call 01437 721677

Llanrhian

lanrhian is a hamlet standing at a crossroads on the road between Croesgoch and Porthgain. It is notable because of the unusual parish church, dedicated to St. Rhian, which is cruciform in shape, and has a number of interesting features including a 15th century ten sided font. Also striking is the tall tower, built in the 13th century. The rest of the church was completely rebuilt in 1836 and restored in 1891.

Porthgain

A small hamlet in the parish of Llanrhian, Porthgain is one of the most individual places in Pembrokeshire, with superbcoastal scenery and an unpretentious mixture of traditional, Victorian and later style houses and a man made 19th century harbour. The harbour was once a hive of activity and its reconstruction between 1902 and 1904 to make way for larger quays reflected its significant shipping activities. These included the exportation of slate and shale from the quarry at Abereiddy and bricks made from local clay, mainly for local use. The main export however was the medium to fine granite stone; exceptionally hard and used for the construction of buildings and roads as far apart as Liverpool, Dublin and London.

124

Porthgain was a village whose employment was entirely dependant on the prosperity of the quarry and by the turn of the century, the company known as Porthgain Village Industries Ltd. boasted a fleet of nearly 100 vessels including six steam coasters of 350 tons each. Even as late as 1931, the harbour was improved for a hoped for 170ft 650 ton ship to enter, but after the First World War this maritime trade went into decline and by 1931 had ceased production entirely. In 1983 the Pembrokeshire Coast National Park Authority acquired the attractive harbour and the remains of the buildings bear testimony to Porthgain's industrial past. Porthgain remains a very lively community with a flourishing tourism trade due to its magnificent stretch of coastline and many significant antiquarian remains, making it a must see for those interested in either industrial archaeology or ancient history. A couple of miles north east of Porthgain lies a fine Iron Age fort called Castell Coch. Porthgain is well worth a visit for its diversity of interest. One of Britain's finest geographers described the coast between Porthgain and Abereiddy as the finest in Britain. Today fish are still regularly landed at Porthgain harbour. The Sloop Inn at Porthgain is probably one of the best known pubs in the area. The pub dates back to 1743, when it was more a workers than walkers pub. Nowadays, the Sloop makes a welcome stop for those walking along the coastal path. The premises offer good parking and space for children to play together with a large picnic area.

Mathry

The village of Mathry stands on a hill just off the A487 between St. Davids and Fishguard, a few miles east of Trefin. Its elevated position gives superb coastal views and of particular interest here is the parish church. This unusual squat building and circular churchyard occupy a prehistoric site, possibly dating from the Iron Age. At one time the church had a steeple that served as a landmark for mariners. Like Trefin, the village is a popular watering hole for visitors passing through. Just west of Mathry is the ancient site of a burial chamber.

Trefin

Just to the east of Porthgain and its attractive harbour, Trefin is the largest coastal village between St. Davids and Fishguard. It is close to a shingle and sand beach known as Aber Felin and the proximity of the coast path makes this a popular watering hole for walkers. It is worth noting that disabled visitors can gain easy access to this section of the coast path. There is also a youth hostel in the village. Near the shoreline stands the ruin of Trefin Mill, which closed in 1918 and has been partly restored by the National Park Authority. The mill was immortalised in the famous Welsh poem, Melin Trefin.

126

Abercastle

Abercastle stands on Pembrokeshire's rocky northern coastline, southwest of Strumble Head and close to the villages of Trefin and Mathry. From the 16th century onwards this was a busy little coastal port, at various times in its history involved in the export of corn, butter and oats and the import of general goods, anthracite, culm and limestone. The limekiln still survives on the attractive harbour. Abercastle can claim a small piece of important maritime history; in 1876 the first man to sail solo across the Atlantic landed here. Half a mile west of the village, standing just off the coast path, is Carreg Samson, an excellent example of a Bronze Age burial chamber. The capstone is 15ft long and 9ft wide, and according to legend Samson placed it in position using only his little finger.

Goodwick

Goodwick

Until the harbour was completed in 1906, Goodwick was nothing more than a cluster of fisherman cottages. As the new terminus for the main railway line from London, this one time village quickly adopted the status of a major ferry port and today is still the link between Fishguard and Rosslare in Ireland. Inevitably Goodwick has grown so close, in every sense, to its very near neighbour Fishguard that it is now virtually a suburb of the larger town and the two are synonymous.

Fishguard

Distances: Haverforwest 16m, Milford Haven 22m, Narberth 24m, Pembroke 26m, Tenby 35m, Carmarthen 46m and London 272m

Fishguard and Goodwick, 16 miles northeast of St. Davids are the only parts of Pembrokeshire's outer coastline which are not within the National Park. But they are are certainly no less attractive for that. Offering a good choice of accommodation and an ideal base for discovering all that this part of the county has to show you. The harbour is in fact the main sailing centre of the North Pembrokeshire coast. Before the harbour, Fishguard had established itself as a very busy port, with slate, corn, butter and cured pilchards and herrings representing the main exports. During the 18th century only Haverfordwest was handling a greater volume of trade. Shipbuilding was important too; the shipyard was renowned for its schooners and square-rigged vessels. The harbour and impressive breakwaters on the Goodwick side of the bay were built in 1906 to attract the transatlantic liners away from Liverpool and Southampton. But as was the reality for Milford Haven, Cardigan, New Quay and other hopeful West Wales ports, the big dream did not materialise. However, there was compensation in successfully establishing the ferry links with Ireland – a lasting and positive return on the massive task of constructing the breakwater, which consumed 800 tones of rock along every foot of its half a mile length. Fishguard has remained a major British ferry port with excellent port facilities. However, its biggest contribution to the history books occurred on 22nd February 1797, when the town was the scene of an extraordinary invasion which has the dis tinction of being the last invasion on British soil. The uninvited guests were members of a French expeditionary force under the command of an American-Irish adventurer, Colonel William Tate, who had a commission in the French army. His mission was to seize Bristol, at the time Britain's second city, but bad weather forced the ships to land at Carreg Wastad Point, northwest of Fishguard. Once ashore, Tate's troops set about pilfering farms and homesteads, gorging themselves with as much food as they could lay their hands on, washed down with barrels of spirits which local people

The Marine walk, Fishguard

Fishguard

had salvaged from a recent shipwreck. In this somewhat unfit condition the soldiers approached the town and, according to local tradition, mistook a crowd of women in red shawls and tall hats for guardsmen. The leader of these women, Jemima Nicholas, a local cobbler-woman, is said to have captured a dozen Frenchmen single handed, armed with only a pitchfork. Her heroism is remembered in the form of a monument in the church-yard at St. Mary's, where she is buried. Within 48hrs of landing the French had sur-rendered. The heroism of the women has been painstak ingly recorded in a vivid

and carefully researched tapestry measuring 30 metres which superbly char-acterises the event. Fishguard is split into two distinct parts. The busy upper part is much like any small town, with many shops, pubs and places to eat. The Lower Town is much older and very attractive, its pretty cottage clustered around the old harbour, where the River Gwaun reaches the sea. In 1971 Lower Fishguard tem-porarily changed its identity to the fictional town of Llareggub when this pictur-esque location was chosen for the the film version of Dylan Thomas's famous radio play "Under Milk Wood", and

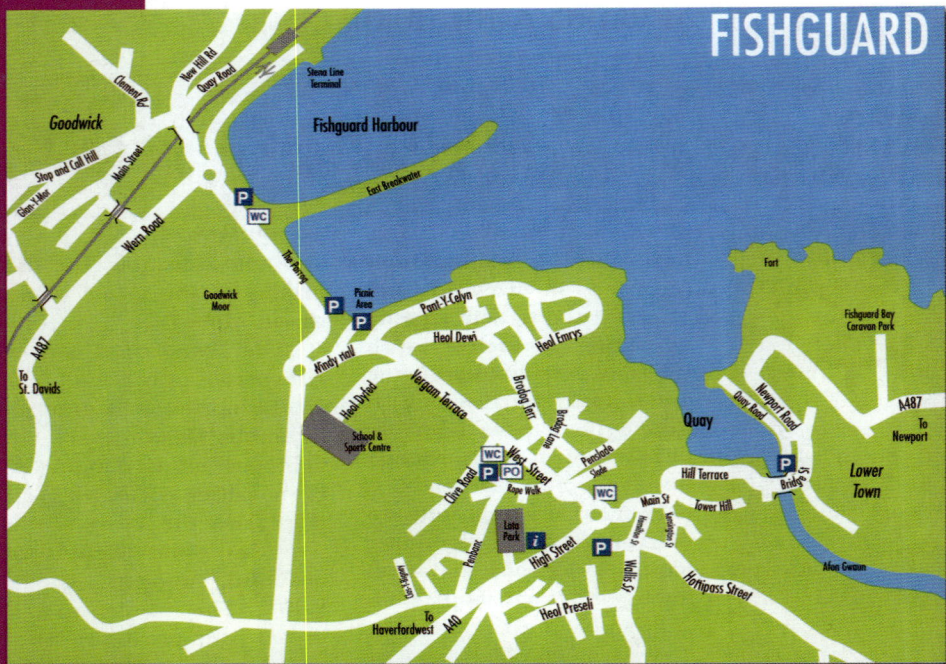

Lower Town Fishguard

FISHGUARD

Goodwick

New Hill Rd.
Quay Road
Clement Rd.
Stena Line Terminal

Fishguard Harbour

Stop and Call Hill
Main Street
Glan-Y-Mor
Wern Road

East Breakwater

Fort

WC
P

The Parsog

A487
To St. Davids

Goodwick Moor

Picnic Area
P
P

Pant-Y-Celyn
Heol Devi
Heol Emrys

Windy Hall

Heol Dyfed
Vergam Terrace

School & Sports Centre

Brodog Terr.
Glyn Brochan

Fishguard Bay Caravan Park

Newport Road
Quay Road
A487
To Newport

Quay

Lower Town

West Street
Clive Road
WC
PO
P
Rope Walk

Penslade Stdo
Pen y Bryd

Hill Terrace
Bridge St.
P

Main St
Tower Hill
Aberystwyth

Llanfihangel

Love Park
i
High Street
P

WC

Tower Hill

To Haverfordwest
A40
Wallis St.
Heol Preseli
Hamilton Street
Vergam Terr.

Hompass Street

Afon Gwaun

was also the location for the making of the Orson Welles classic "Moby Dick". The landscape around Fishguard is truly magnificent. To the northwest is the dramatic Stumble Head, where the lighthouse is linked to the cliff by a causeway. Dinas Head dominates the coast to the northeast, while inland is the beautiful wooded Gwaun Valley. The whole area is dotted with prehistoric sites.

**MELIN TREGWYNT
WOOLEN MILL**
Abermawr, Fishguard
*for more information
tel: 01348 891225*

FISHGUARD INTERNATIONAL MUSIC FESTIVAL

FISHGUARD International Music Festival
founded sefydluyd 1970
ABERGWAUN Gŵyl Gerdd Rynawladol

The 39th Fishguard International Music Festival
Music and events in Fishguard,Goodwick , St Davids
Cathedral and Rhos-y-gilwen Mansion
July 25th – 2nd August, 2008
Programme in Preparation
to include
National Youth Brass Band of Wales
John.S.Davies Singers with Alexander Mason (organ)
Mozart's Letters – E.S.O. winds – narrator Janet Suzman
Innovation Chamber Ensemble (CBSO Strings)
St. Petersburg String Quartet
Peter Donohoe
Phillip Dyson
Young Musicians' Platform
Sian James
Purbayan Chatterjee
Dennis O' Neil's Cardiff Academy Singers
Red Priest
BBC National Orchestra of Wales and Grant Llewellyn
With a Celebration of the music of Ralph Vaughan
Williams and Olivier Messiaen

Enquiries: 01348 891345
Festival Box Office available mid June
Tel: 01348 875538

The Gwaun Valley

The Gwuan Valley is exceptionally beautiful and runs inland from Lower Fishguard to its source high on the slopes of Foel Eryr in the Preseli Hills. It is one of several inland areas of Pembrokeshire which fall within the National Park, and is regarded by geologists as the best example in the British Isles, if not the world, of a sub-glacial meltwater channel. What this means is that about 200,000 years ago, towards the end off one of several recurring Ice Ages which have gripped the planet, the climate became progressively warmer and water began to tunnel beneath the melting ice. This meltwater was under intense pressure, the ice acting as a sort of geological pipe and moved with such tremendous force that it flowed uphill for long stretches. As this unstoppable water eventually crashed into the sea, taking with it huge bolders and blocks of ice, it created deep, steep sided gorges in the landscape. Such are the awesome forces of nature which have given us the spectacular Gwaun Valley. The valley is narrow and sheltered, with heavily wooded sides stretching up to 200ft high. It is rich in wildlife and prehistoric remains, with an abundance of wild flowers and such birds as the buzzard, kestrel, owl, kingfisher, warbler and dipper. The river Gwaun, low and gentle in the summer, becomes a roaring torrent in winter as it rushes down from the Preseli Hills rising behind the valley. Most of the valley's small communities are centred around the hamlets of Llanychaer and Pontfaen. These are largely farming communities, as much of the valley floor is farmed and several farmhouses boast interesting architectural features such as distinctive Flemish style chimneys. The people of the valley are distinctive too, not in appearance, but in the fact that they are sticklers for local tradition. They still celebrate New Years Day on the 13th January according to the old Gregorian calendar - despite the fact that the change to the Julian calendar was made legal in 1752. Other interesting stones can be seen at the restored church in picturesque Pontfaen, where memorial stones dating from the 9th century stand in the church-yard. The ancient woodland of the Gwaun Valley is very precious, and parts of it have been designated as SSSI's (Sites of Special Scientific Interest). The species to be found here include oak, ash,

Newport

sycamore, alder, blackthorn, hazel, hornbeam, wild cherry and wych elm. The National Park Authority has established the Cilrhedyn Woodland Centre to promote good woodland management in the valley. Though very much a working centre for the Park Authority's woodland experts and rangers, it is planned to encourage visitors to the centre on a limited number of special open days during the main holiday season. More details of this can be obtained from any National Park Centre. The National Park Authority has also made the valley more accessible on foot by creating the Golden Road Path. This takes you from Lower Fishguard to Crymych via the ridge of the Preseli Hills, passing such fascinating features as Bronze Age burial mounds, a Neolithic burial chamber, a particularly fine example of an Iron Age fort and Carn Meini - the source of the bluestone which thousands of years ago mysteriously found its way to Stonehenge for the construction of the monument's inner circle.

Newport

Newport is a very popular resort. The charming little town sits on the lower slopes of the Carn Ingli, which rises to more than 1100ft above sea level, and the superb stretch of sands on the east side of the Nevern estuary is rivalled only by Whitesands Bay as the best

beach in North Pembrokeshire. On the opposite shore of the estuary mouth is Parrog. It was here that Newport developed as a thriving port engaged in fishing, coastal trading and shipbuilding. Herrings were exported to Ireland, France and Spain and by 1566 Newport was an important wool centre. However, this industry faltered when an outbreak of plague hit the town during the reign of Elizabeth I and much business was lost to Fishguard. Later in the port's development slates were quarried from local cliffs went by sea to Haverfordwest, Pembroke, Tenby and parts of Ireland. In 1825 maritime trade received a boost when the quay was built, and come the end of the 19th century Newport boasted five warehouses, several limekilns, coal yards and a shipyard. Today the estuary is silted up and pleasure craft occupy the moorings. As far as the town itself, one of the main features is Newport Castle. This over-looks the estuary and was built in the early 13th century by William FitzMartin. It has had an eventful history: captured by Llewelyn the Great in 1215, then by Llewelyn the Last in 1257, and attacked and damaged in Owain Glyndwr's revolt in 1408, after which it fell into decline. It remained a ruin until 1859, when the gatehouse and one of its towers were converted into a residence. Today the castle is in private ownership and not open to

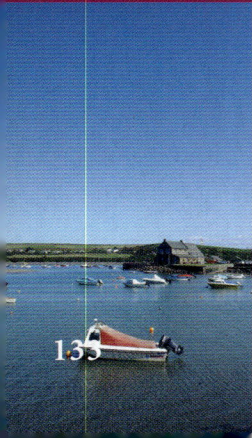

visitors. You can, however, see William FitzMartin's other contribution to Newport. He established St. Mary's, a huge church which is cruciform in plan and features a 13th century Norman tower. Other attractions in Newport include a 9 hole golf course (extending to 18 holes in 2008) alongside the sands and the prehistoric cromlech known as Carreg Goetan Arthur, which stands in a field by the bridge. There are many other such sites in the area. On Carn Ingli Common there are prehistoric hut circles and stones and the most famous and striking site of all is Pentre Ifan, 3 miles southeast of Newport. This Neolithic chambered tomb is one of the finest in Britain, with three upright stones over 6ft in height supporting a huge capstone.

Angel House *Newport*

A long established gift shop and newsagent in the centre of this busy community. Recently refurbished and re-stocked by Ron and Helen, a friendly welcome awaits all visitors. With a range of Welsh and UK made unusual gifts, including gemstone & silver jewellery, quality glassware and ceramics, local-scene greeting cards, toys, beachware, walking guides & maps. On a practical level, there is a watch battery fitting service, photocopying, laminating and fax service. The shelves of old-fashioned 'sweetie-jars' and delicious home-made cakes make Angel House a shop for 'all occasions', popular with locals and visitors alike.

Find us off the A487 on Long Street towards the public car park.

Newport
Sands

Dinas Cross

Dinas Cross and its surrounding area is notable for its prehistoric monuments, especially the Bronze Age cairns. Cairns and barrows - mounds of earth or stone and earth - were built throughout the Bronze Age (2000 - 600BC) and often mark the sites of burials. Stone cists at the centre of the mound often contain cremations and pottery vessels and it is thought that the cairns themselves acted as burial sites. The stones for the first stone phase of Stonehenge came from Carn Meini, high in the Preselis. The whole area is littered with prehistoric sites including Iron Age hillforts (600BC - 43AD) and earlier cairns and standing stones.

Sites like the spectacular hillfort at the summit of Carningli were clearly used over a long period of time and must have been important spiritual or religious places.

Mynydd Melyn, a short distance southeast of Dinas Mountain, contains abundant evidence of prehistoric activity including hut circles (the foundations of prehistoric dwellings) parts of a field system and several cairns.

The Teifi Estuary

The River Teifi is a natural boundary that lies between Pembrokeshire and Ceredigion and its wide estuary is of great interest. The large and popular beach of Poppit Sands is backed by extensive dunes and has good visitor facilities. The area is also excellent walking and watersports country, and the estuary is a favourite haunt for birdwatchers. The many species to be observed here include gulls, oystercatchers, curlews, cormorants and shelduck. The Teifi is also well known for its salmon and sea trout and the ancient Teifi coracle was used by fishermen long before the Romans arrived. The valley of the Teifi, which is a little further inland separates the counties of Ceredigion and Carmarthenshire, is said to be one of the most beautiful river valleys in Britain. It is certainly very scenic, with several picturesque towns and villages along its banks and for visitors to North Pembrokeshire is well worth exploring.

Nevern

Nevern is an ancient parish on the River Nyfer, close to Newport. Its imposing Norman church, dedicated to the Celtic saint Brynach, has a definite mystique and atmosphere that is com pounded by the famous bleeding yew in the church-yard, a broken branch that constantly drips blood red sap. The church features a magnificent 11th century wheel, headed Celtic cross which stands 13ft high and rivals the cross at Carew. Above the church, topping a deep ravine, is Nevern Castle, a motte and baily earthwork.

Moylegrove

This attractive coastal village stands on the Newport to St Dogmael's road, a mile from Ceibwr Bay. It dates back to Norman times and nearby are two burial chambers. Small cargo ships once used the bay and high cliffs and secluded coves mark the coast here, where Atlantic grey seals often bask.

St. Dogmaels

Facing Cardigan across the Teifi estuary is the picturesque hillside of the village St Dogmaels. It lies close to Poppit Sands, the most northerly beach in the National Park and also at the northern end of the Pembrokeshire Coastal Path. In St Dogmaels you will find the remains of a 12th century abbey built in 1115 by Benedictine monks from France - as a replacement for an earlier Celtic monastery which had stood on the site until Viking raiders destroyed it in the 10th century. The north and west walls of the nave are still standing. Next to the abbey lies the ruins is the parish church of St Thomas the Martyr. It contains the Sagranus Stone, which bears an inscription that proved to be the key in deciphering the ancient Ogham script in 1848.

Cilgerran

Famous for its superb Norman castle, which is perched above the wooded gorge of the Teifi, Cilgerran is a few miles east of Cardigan and was once a slate quarrymens village. It is the venue for the annual coracle regatta, which takes place in August.

St. Dogmaels

138

PEMBROKESHIRE
EVENTS 2008

JANUARY 2008

Saundersfoot New Years Day Swim 1st Jan
www.visit-saundersfoot.com

Whitesands New years Day Swim 1st Jan
www.penkifeclub.co.uk

St Davids Concert 1st January (Tickets 01437 720480)

FEBUARY 2008

Festival of Daffodils
End of February / beginning of March

MARCH 2008

Saundersfoot St Davids food & craft festival inc
Cawl Cooking Championship 1st – 2nd
www.visit-saundersfoot.com
Easter week at Folly Farm (01834 812731)
admin@folly-farm.co.uk

MAY 2008

St Davids Cathedral festival / a feast of classical
music 23rd May –1st June
www.stdavidscathederal.org.uk

Newport Bay Spring Festival
www.newport-pembs.co.uk

Herb Fayre Carew Castle
St Dogmaels Art Festival
Eisteddfod Gadeiriol Maenclochog

Taking the high road at the Newport Bay Spring Festival

Enjoying a session during the Fishguard Folk Music Festival

Neyland Mayor's Race and Fun run 10K
Neyland Marina
www.neyland.org.uk

Fishguard Folk Festival
23rd-26th
www.pembrokeshire-folk-music.co/uk

Milford Haven Maritime Heritage Week
www.milfordhaven.info

Pembrokeshire Coast path Trek
www.pcnpa.org.uk

JUNE 2008

Pembrokeshire Classic Cars Scolton Manor Museum
& Country Park, Nr Haverfordwest
1st June

Milford Haven Founders Day
www.milfordhaven.info

Pembroke Medieval Fayre, River Rally

Annual Grand Charity Concert and Roast
Penlan Uchaf Gardens, Nr Fishguard

Wales Biodiversity Week
Events at locations throughout the County
www.biodiversitywales.org.uk

Pembroke Dock Festival
www.pembrkedock.org

Pembrokeshire Fish Week various locations throughout
Pembrokeshire
21st –29th June

141

Saundersfoot in Bloom& Flower Festival
www.visit-saundersfoot.com

Hazel beach regatta/cruiser/dingy race also inshore
activities info@pembokeshirewatersports.co.uk

Seafair Haven a host of maritime sailing ships
18th – 25th June Milford Haven
www.seafairhaven.org.uk

Llangwm festival - including the scarecrows 2
7th – 5th July
www.llangwm-villages.org.uk

JULY 2008

Milford Haven Carnival & Founders day see website for
further info including route & entry forms www.milford-havenroundtable.com

Proms in the park, Scolton Manor County Museum
& Country Park, Spittal near Haverfordwest

Tenby Summer Spectaculars July – Aug (1of2)

Lions Paella Festival
Tenby Harbour

Tenby in Bloom & Flower Festival

Shire Horse and Fun Pony Show
Dyfed Shire and Leisure Farm, Eglwyswrw.
Neyland Carnival & Brunel Week
www.neyland.org.uk

Landshipping Fun Day
Pembrokeshire Yachting Federation County Regatta
Neyland

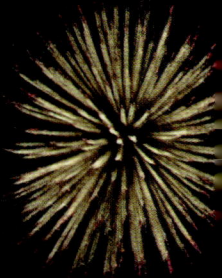

High Tide Festival
Manorbier

Haverfordwest River Festival

Narbeth Civic Week & Carnival
www.narbeth.co.uk

Fishguard International Music Festival
Fishguard, Goodwick, St Davids

AUGUST 2008

County Show 19 - 21st The Pembrokeshire County Show
is the second largest agricultural show in Wales
www.pembrokeshrecountyshow.co.uk

Milford Haven's"Le Grand" Weekend
www.streetfair.org.uk

Tenby Spectacular (2 of 2)

Pembrokeshire jazz n blues festival an international
festival of Jazz & Blues wwwaberjazz.com

Oakwood after dark theme park Nr Narbeth
www.oakwoodthemepark.co.uk

Nevern Show

Pembroke Farmer's Club Town & Country Annual Show
Lamphey

Tenby Firemans Carnival Tenby

The Haven's Carnival
Broad Haven

Fishguard Agricultural and Horticultural Show

Saundersfoot Carnival
www.visit-saundersfoot.com

Lamphey Medieval Fayre

Cilgerran Festival Week

Whitesands Beach Annual Sand Church Competition
Whitesands, near St Davids

Cresswell Quay Boat Rally
Camrose Vintage Working Day

Martletwy & District Agricultural and
Horticultural Show
Cresselly

Open Studios Weekend
Cardigan and North Pembrokeshire
www.westwalesartists.co.uk

Fishguard Carnival
St Davids Carnival
St Dogmaels Medieval Day
Frenni Food Festival at Crymych

SEPTEMBER 2008
Narbeth food festival 10th Anniversary 20th&21st
www.narbethfoodfestival.com

Tenby Arts Festival 20th – 27th
www.tenbyartsfest.co.uk

Pembrokeshire
County Show

Annual Milford Haven to Tenby Classic Car run

Pembroke festival 4th-7th
www.pembroke21c.org

European Heritage Days
Various Locations
www.civictrustwales.org

OCTOBER 2008

Milford Haven 'Ty Hafan' 5k
www.tyhafan.org/milford5krun.htm

"The Big Draw" Events
www.thebigdraw.org.uk

Gwyl ro'r Preseli/ Preseli Festival
Crymych

NOVEMBER 2008

Fireworks display on or around 5th November,
various locations

Tenby Blues festival

DECEMBER 2008

Father Christmas Visits Neyland
Father Christmas Visits Haverfordwest
& Christmas Lights Switch on
Father Christmas Visits MilfordHaven
& Christmas Lights Switch on
Father Christmas visits Pembroke
Charity Torchlight Carol Concert at Carew Castle
Narbeth winter carnival
www.narbeth.co.uk

Opening parade at the Pembroke Festival

Braving the Tenby Boxing Day swim

Tenby winter Carnival Festival
www.tenbyevents.co.uk

St Nicholas Christmas Market
Saundersfoot
www.visit-saundersfoot.com

Carol service at St Davids Bishop's Palace

Pembroke Dock Winter Carnival

Pembroke & District Male Choir
Annual Christmas Concert at Monkton

Candlelit Christmas Concert
St Davids Cathedral

Tenby's Boxing Day Swim
North Beach
www.tenbyboxingdayswim.co.uk

New Year's Eve Celebrations
Saundersfoot, Fishguard & Tenby

Festive fun at Saundersfoot Christmas Market

INLAND PEMBROKESHIRE

In the ancient Welsh tales of The Mabinogion, Pembrokeshire was described as "Gwlad hud a lledrith" - the land of magic and enchantment. Nowhere is this more evident than in the wild, mysterious Preseli Hills. These rolling moorlands, often overlooked by visitors on their way to the coast, are the major upland region of the National Park, presenting a stark contrast to the relatively flat coastal plateau. The hills do not aspire to any great height - the highest summit Foel Cwm Cerwyn, is 1760ft above sea level, but the many remains of hillforts, burial chambers and other monuments are proof that even prehistoric man had a powerful affinity with this bleak and mystical landscape. The evidence left by the earliest settlers suggests man has occupied the hills for at least 5000 years. Neolithic burial chambers, Bronze Age cairns, stone circles, standing stones and Iron Age forts litter this untouched Celtic landscape.

When Neolithic (New Stone Age) farmers arrived in Pembrokeshire, well versed in the art of raising crops and herding animals, they were the first people to work the land here. They fashioned implements such as axes, hammers and hoes from Preseli dolerite (bluestone), and archaeologists believe that two so called axe factories existed on the Preseli Hills, though their sites have never been identified. The dwellings of these distant ancestors were too flimsy to stand up to the ravages of time. But not so their tombs (cromlechau), which are concentrated along the coastal plateau and in the Preseli foothills. Pentre Ifan, on the hills northern slopes, and Carreg Samson, on the coast near Abercastle, are two of the finest prehistoric monuments to be found anywhere in Wales. Later Bronze Age man also left his burial sites on the Preseli Hills, in the form of round cairns. A fine example is to be found on top of Foel Drygarn. There is another on the summit of Foel Cwm Cerwyn, the highest point in all of Pembrokeshire. On exceptionally clear days the views from here are astonishing. You can see west to the Wicklow Mountains of Ireland, north to Snowdonia, east to the Brecon Beacons and south across the Bristol Channel to the counties of the West Country. Another ancient relic adorning the Preseli Hills is the interesting stone circle known as Gors Fawr. This stands on the moorland west of the hamlet of Mynachlogddu. It comprises 16 stones and 2 large outlying pointer stones and its diameter exceeds 70ft. But the biggest mystery of all to emanate from these brooding hills, and one which never seems likely to be answered, concerns the inner circle at Stonehenge, 180 miles from Preseli on Salisbury Plain. Much of this inner circle is made from bluestone, which is dolerite, rhyolite and volcanic ash, found only at Carn Meini on the eastern crests of the Preseli Hills. The mystery is how the 80 stones, weighing up to 4 tonnes each and over 250 tonnes in total, made the incredible journey from Preseli to Salisbury Plain during the third millennium BC. The most likely explanation seems to be that they were taken by boat along rivers up the Bristol Channel, crossing the overland stretches on sledges which had rollers underneath. This would have taken a gargantuan effort by a huge army of labour. Even so, this theory has found much wider acceptance than the two others proposed. One is that the stones were carried to Salisbury Plain by the great Irish Sea Glacier, the biggest

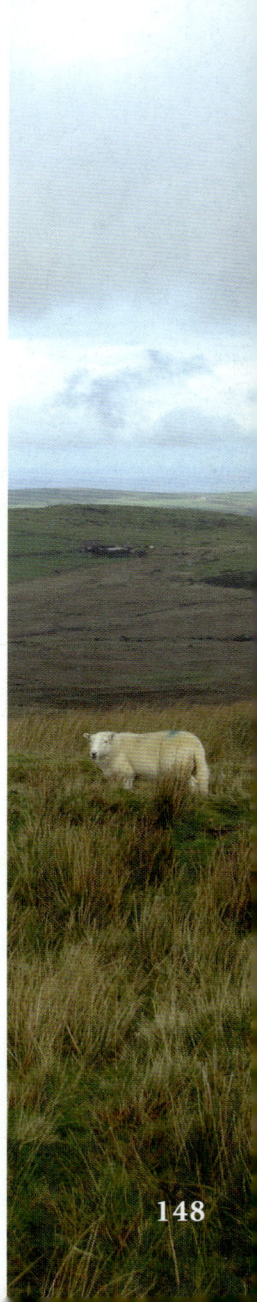

flow of glacial ice ever to cover Britain, long before the builders of Stonehenge set about their task. But even many geologists doubt that this is the case. The other suggestion, and by far the most fanciful, is that levitation is the answer. It is proposed that the builders of Stonehenge had mystical powers and could magically raise stones off the ground merely by thinking about it. Other stories from around the world tell of stones being moved in this way. The Preseli Hills have inspired other myths and legends. Predictably King Arthur has strong associations here. A tale from The Mabinogion tells how he pursued a great black boar across these hills from Ireland and his name is remembered in such places as Carn Arthur. Exploring the Preseli Hills won't bring you into contact with the legendary black boar, but there are certainly other creatures of interest to see. Wild ponies still roam free on the hills, and among the birds which frequent this upland territory are Kestrels, meadow pippits, skylarks and wheat-ears. Close to the resort town

of Newport are such delights as Nevern, with its haunting church and the reconstructed Iron Age hillfort at Castell Henllys. A little further north are the dramatic cliffs of Cemaes Head, where the exposed rocks have been folded by the tremendous forces exerted by movements deep in the earth. The cliffs of the headland are over 500ft high in places, the highest in Pembrokeshire and they look down to the mouth of the Teifi estuary. Like any upland area, the Preseli Hills are best explored on foot, and apart from sheep the most common species you are most likely to encounter in these wilds are hill walkers, Ornithologists, botanists, archaeologists, artists, photographers and others of strange pursuits also seem to find the hills a suitable habitat. However, unless you are familiar with the hills, it is advisable to take a map and compass on your travels. The average rainfall on the hills is nearly twice as much as it is on the coast and the mists have a tendency to come down very suddenly. This is also part of Pembrokeshire where winter

snow falls on anything like a regular basis. An alternative way of exploring the Preseli Hills is to join a guided walk or horse riding lesson which are run by the National Park Authority, as part of its annual activities and events programme. For more information contact any National Park Information Centre.

LLYS-Y-FRAN RESERVOIR & COUNTRY PARK

Close to the picturesque village of Rosebush, beautiful Llys-y-Fran Country Park incorporates the 212 acre reservoir that supplies most of Pembrokeshire's drinking water. Around this man made lake are mature woodlands and open grassland, with superb views of the Preseli Hills and surrounding farmland. In spring the carpets of bluebells in the woods are a sheer delight and throughout the season the country park is vibrant with the colours of countless varieties of wild flowers. In recent years improvements have been made to the park, following a scheme to increase the size of the reservoir. An example of which is the much wider footpath right round the reservoir and the 20,000 broad leafed trees which have been planted. As a result the six and a half mile perimeter walk is now even more enjoyable than ever. Near the main car park is the children's

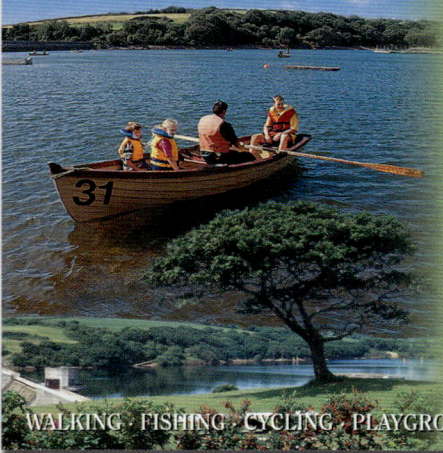

adventure playground to keep youngsters amused. Mountain bikes are another treat that families can enjoy. Bikes can be hired by the hour or by the day and with the reservoir perimeter path serving as a cycle track, this can be a fun activity in which everyone can participate. Fishing is another leisure pursuit which has always been popular here, and Lys-y-Fran attracts anglers from all over Wales and beyond. Little wonder as few fisheries can match the country park's excellent facilities. These include a purpose built boathouse with a fleet of loch-style petrol engine fishing boats ideal for fly fishermen. During the season over 20,000 top quality rainbow trout are released into the freedom of the lake from their rearing cages. A healthy population of brown trout adds variety to the sport. For watersport enthusiasts the reservoir is perfect both for beginners and for more experienced sailors but you must bring your own craft as no hire is available. The park shop does however offer launching permits for dinghies, sailboards and canoes. As you would expect in a country park of Llys-y-Fran's status and reputation, wildlife is of prime concern in the management of the park.

The oak and coniferous woodlands and rough grass provide ideal habitats for a variety of birds. More than 140 species have been recorded here. Llys-y-Fran licensed restaurant enjoys superb views across the reservoir and countryside and is housed in the Visitor Centre alongside the gift and souvenir shop. The restaurant offers excellent service and opens March to the end of October. It is also worth noting that Llys-y-Fran Country Park has strong historical and musical connections. Near the base of the reservoir dam is a tumble down cottage, the birthplace of the famous Welsh composer William "Penfro" Rowlands. It was in gratitude for his son's recovery from a serious illness that he was inspired to write the tune for Blaenwern, one of the best loved of all hymn tunes. A monument to William Rowlands, erected by Welsh Water now stands near the ruins of the old cottage.

for further information
tel: 01437 532273
or 01437 532694

Rosebush

Rosebush enjoys an unusual if modest claim to fame, slates from its quarries were used to roof the Houses of Parliament. But the village could have become a well known tourist attraction in the 19th century had everything gone according to plan. When the Clunderwen - Maenclochog railway opened in 1876 to serve the quarry there were big ambitions to develop Rosebush as an inland spa. A small tourist industry did develop here, but nothing like on the scale imagined. Rosebush is close to Llys-y-Fran Reservoir and Country Park and stands below the summit of Foel Cwm Cerwyn, in a superb setting which is ideal for walking. In 1992 a visitor centre and museum was opened in the village's old post office.

Mynachlogddu

This small pastoral community of the Preseli Hills once belonged to the monastery at St. Dogmaels. It stands east of Rosebush, close to the impressive Gors Fawr Stone Circle, which is over 70ft in diameter. A commemorative stone to the poet Waldo Williams is also nearby.

New Moat

This small village stands in the Preseli foothills, just east of Llys-y-Fran Country Park. A mound marks the site of a Norman motte and bailey castle. The church, distinctive for its tall tower, has an early 17th century altar tomb.

Maenclochog

A small Victorian church on the village green is the central feature of this sprawling community on the southern slopes of the Preseli Hills, a couple of miles north east of Llys-y-Fran Country Park. For many years the village has served the needs of the area and early this century Maenclochog boasted a blacksmith, miller, carpenter, lime burner, wheelwright, draper and no fewer than 10 pubs. A mile from the village is Penrhos, the only thatched cottage in the area and is now a museum.

Crymych

Crymych, situated on the A478 Tenby to Cardigan road, is a 19th century hillside village which grew up around the railway. The Whitland Cardigan line was completed in 1880 and no longer exists, but the village has remained an important agricultural centre and an ideal base from which to

CLARE'S SHOP *Crymych*

UNUSUAL AND UNIQUE

The combination of Welsh craft with quality Fair Trade products from around the world, make the shop a perfect place to browse or seek out an extraordinary and unique gift.

A member of the British Association of Fair Trade Shops, Clare's Shop stocks only products that are Fair Trade or that are made in Wales and the rest of the UK. Homeware and gifts from India and jewellery from Peru sit comfortably with Welsh lovespoons, local turned wood and welsh soap.

Clare's Shop is situated at the north end of Crymch and offers a warm welcome with plenty of parking.

Fair Trade ensures producers are paid a fair price for their products.

FLORIST SERVICE

Clare's Shop offers a full florist service including Weddings , Special Occasions and Tributes. Fresh Cut Flowers are delivered to the shop twice a week.

We deliver for all occasions. Charges vary depending on distance, free of charge for Crymych village up to £8 for longer journeys. Out of the way farms or houses at the end of rough tracks pose no problem, just let us know the postcode and of any big dogs!

For flowers that need to go further afield we use other independent florists or an international relay service, so sending a bouquet to Australia is no problem.

ON THE A478 CARDIGAN TO TENBY ROAD
TEL: 01239 831717   WEBSITE WWW.SIOPCLARE.CO.UK
OPEN ALL YEAR MONDAY TO SATURDAY 9AM -6PM

FAIR TRADE GOODS SOLD HERE

153

explore the Preseli Hills. Within easy reach are Foel Drygarn, where cairns and an early Iron Age fort are to be found and the 1300ft summit of Y Frenni Fawr.

Boncath

Between Crymych and Newcastle Emlyn, Boncath takes its name from the Welsh word for buzzard. A former railway village, it is notable for two houses - Ffynone, designed by John Nash in 1792 and Cilwendeg, a Georgian house built by Morgan Jones.

Eglwyswrw

A compact little village near Castell Henllys Iron Age fort, north of the Preseli Hills, this place with the unpronounceable name, is where St. Wrw is buried. The pre-Christian churchyard is circular and other interesting historical features include the medieval inn, the remains of a motte and bailey castle and a prehistoric ringwork.

CASTELL HENLLYS IRON AGE FORT

This remarkable and archaeological important example of an Iron Age fort is managed by the National Park Authority and has been partially reconstructed with thatched roundhouses, animal pens, a smithy and a grain store, all standing on their original sites. More recently the site was the location of the BBC's "Surviving the Iron Age" series. The Visitor Centre houses an exhibition which serves as an introduction to the life of the early Celts in Wales. Castell Henllys probably flourished between the 4th century BC and the 1st century AD, when the Romans began their conquest of Britain. The Iron Age Celts were a fierce and warlike people and many of their chieftains lived in well defended forts, of which Castell Henllys was typical. Sited on a valley spur, it had natural defences on three sides, and where the spur joined the side of the valley massive earthworks were thrown up, topped with timber palisades. Stone walling protected a narrow gateway which can still be seen. Such elaborate defences would have employed a huge labour force and this suggests that Castell Henllys was occupied by a leader of some importance along with family, retainers and even a band of warriors. The introduction to the site of domestic animals which flourished in the Iron Age has given a further insight into the daily life of these ancient ancestors. A self guided trail takes you through Castell Henllys with information interpretive panels along the way. This is a wonderful place for schools and study groups and an

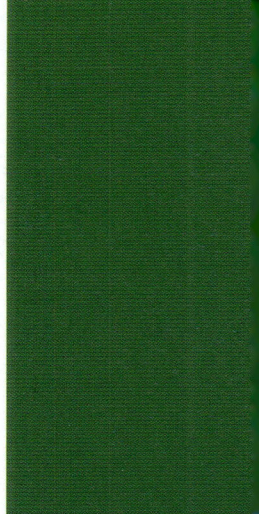

Education Centre has been built in the valley below the fort. To further recapture the atmosphere and spirit of this mystical historic site, which stands in beautiful North Pembrokeshire countryside below the summit Carn Ingli, special events are held throughout the holiday season, including shows given by the Prytani, an Iron Age Celtic reenactment group. Castell Henllys, just off the A486 a few miles east of Newport, is open daily from Easter to October.

tel: 01239 891319
www.castellhenllys.com

The Landsker Borderlands

When the Normans invaded Pembroke in 1093 and took the site on which the magnificent castle now stands, they were quick to consolidate their domination of South Pembrokeshire and the lands they had gained here. To the north of the county the rebellious Welsh proved more troublesome. The Norman response was to build a line of castles to protect their newly won territory, effectively dividing north from south. These formidable fortresses stretched from Llanstephan in the southeast to Roch in the northwest. They marked what has become known as the Landsker Line, a word of Norse origin meaning frontier. Originally a military device, the Landsker evolved into a cultural and linguistic divide and its effects are evident even today. For example, in the north of the county Welsh is still spoken and many of the place nanes are Welsh also. Churches are usually small, with bellcotes and no towers. By comparison in the anglicised south, English is the dominant language as is clear from the names of the towns and villages, and the Norman churches are characterised by tall, square towers which served as lookouts. One of the castles of the Landsker Line was Narberth. Its scant ruins still stand near the centre of this important market town, which is 10 miles north of Tenby. Narberth is at the heart of a beautiful and historic part of Inland Pembrokeshire known as the Landsker Borderlands. The Borderlands spill over into old Carmarthenshire and are bounded by the River Taf to the east, the Daugleddau estuary to the west, hills and valleys to the north and vales and plains to the south. As awareness of the Borderlands increases a growing number of visitors are exploring this largely undiscovered area of great rural delights. The attractive countryside of the Landsker Borderlands, rich in heritage and wildlife, is typified in the north by lush farmland sweeping down from the Preseli Hills. Here you will discover quiet river valleys and tranquil riverside communities, such as those of Lawrenny and Landshipping on the upper reaches of the Daugleddau estuary. South of the Landsker, the rural landscape belies its industrial past. It is hard to believe, for example, that small villages like Reynalton and Jeffreston were once at the heart of the thriving Pembrokeshire coalfield. like all Pembrokeshire, the Landsker Borderlands display evidence of a long history and of occupation by very early settlers. There are prehistoric sites at Holgan Camp Llawhaden, an Iron Age hillfort, and remains of settlements in Canaston Woods, near Canaston Bridge. Medieval ruins are plentiful, including the Sisters House in ancient Minwear Woods, the Hospice Chapel and castle-cum bishop's palace in Llawhaden and the mighty Norman castles of Manorbier and Carew. The Borderlands are also a natural draw for all who appreciate wildlife. During spring and summer the hedgerows and woodlands are ablaze with the colours of snowdrops, primroses, campions, cowslips, foxgloves, bluebells, dog roses, cow parsley, honeysuckle and many varieties of common and rare orchids. In autumn, fungi and ferns brighten the woodland floor and butter

-flies, moths and damselflies bring dashes of colour to the air. Birds and mammals are in abundance too. Buzzards, tawny owls, grey herons, kingfishers, woodpeckers and numerous species of waders and dippers can all be seen in the Borderlands, along with foxes, badgers and even elusive otters. In spring you might also spot the rare Tenby daffodil, which is particular to the area.

Narberth

Distances: Fishguard 24m, Haverfordwest 9m, Milford Haven 14m, Pembroke 15m, St. Davids 25m, Tenby 10m, Carmarthen 21m and London 241m

This delightful little town, with its colour-washed Georgian houses, castle ruins and amazing variety of original shops is an essential visit. In recent years the town has become a centre for artists and craftspeople, many of whose works are sold here. Jewellery, pottery, paintings, fabrics, glassware, clothing and woodworks are all represented. Some of the shops and galleries sell a variety of goods while others specialise in the makers own work. This

Canaston Woods

Narberth Castle

creative movement may be relatively recent but Narberth's history is a long and fascinating one. Standing just south of the Landsker, it falls into the area regarded as "Little England beyond Wales" but its roots lie deep in Welsh history, culture and tradition. The Welsh princes of Dyfed lived here in the dark ages and the town, called by its Welsh name Arberth, features in the ancient stories of the Mabinogion. Narberth castle of which little now remains, was part of the Norman frontier separating north from south. It was captured by the Welsh on numerous occasions and destroyed by Cromwell's forces during the Civil War. Narberth is also remembered for the infamous Rebecca Riots of the 19th century. These began in 1839 with the burning of toll gates in Efailwen, a hamlet in the Preseli foothills a few miles north of the town. This anger was in response to the decision by rich landowners to impose crippling road tolls on the small and impoverished farming communities. The men responsible for torching the toll gates avoided recognition by dressing in women's clothing and blackening their faces, and they addressed their leader as "Rebecca". The dispute quickly became more widespread and other toll gates were destroyed just as quickly as they could be erected. The riots often described as a "true people's revolt" because they had their cause in natural justice, went on for a period of several years. It is one of the ironies of local history that when the authorities called out the troops in a bid to discover the identity of Rebecca and his followers, they were billeted in Narberth's poorhouse. Rebecca's Cell can be seen under the old Town

Narberth

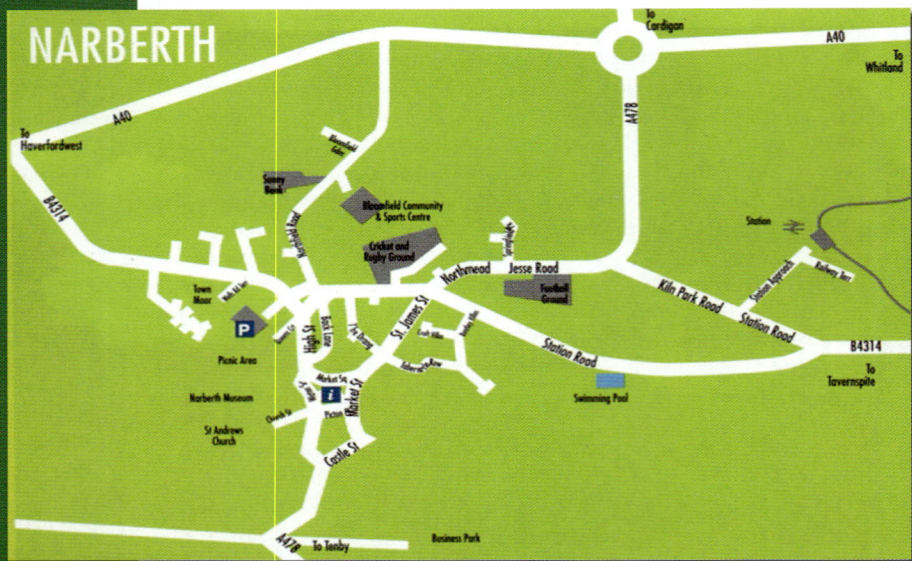

NARBERTH

Finding Your Therapy

Sometimes we seek a little help for a physical, emotional or energetic imbalance or ailment that may be worrying us, or we may simply be seeking enough well-being to be able to 'to wear our scars as reminders of what beautiful people we truly are'. Each Complementary Therapy at Gallery Organics may assist you on your personal journey to a place of inner ease, bodily harmony or physical health. The question is how to decide which therapy is right for you? Complementary Therapies are used to treat the whole of a person, rather than trying to treat the ailment as though separate, as with conventional medicine. The potency of all therapies affects, and is affected by, the entirety of yourself. That is their beauty and their strength. Deciding between therapies will depend on the symptoms that present themselves, the advice of your therapist and your natural preference. We try to make that decision a little easier at Gallery Organics. To help you, we have created an inexpensive booklet that describes therapies carried out upstairs in our therapy treatment and consultations rooms. There is also a handy list of ailments beside each therapy. Further, our team of independent trained and insured therapists have a great deal of integrity and are in easy contact on the premises, or on the phone, to answer your questions. We hope you will help us to help you.

Hall which now houses a craft shop.Narberth Castle of which little now remains, was part of the Norman frontier separating north from south. It was captured by the Welsh on numerous occasions and destroyed in the Civil War by Cromwell's forces. The castle ruins have been consolidated and are now open to the public all year. Narberth's small but attractive town centre is distinctive for its Town Hall and pleasant Georgian houses. With the promotion of the Landsker Borderlands and other rural areas, Narberth has been revitalised. PLANED (Pembrokeshire Local Action Network for Enterprise and Development) has its headquarters here and the town is very close to a number of the county's most popular attractions such as, Heron's Brook Golf Course, Oakwood, CC2000, Blackpool Mill,Picton Castle, Llawhaden Castle, Holgan Camp Iron Age Hillfort and Folly Farm. These

Narberth Town Hall

158

are in addition to those places of interest in Narberth itself, which include a wealth of interesting and unusual shops featuring antiques, art and crafts and galleries as well as many varied and interesting places to eat.

THE QUEENS HALL

A great arts, music and entertainment venue situated in High Street (next to the town's free car park) with a variety of events to suit all tastes. Gallery and cafe.

for more information
tel: 01834 861212

CREATIVE CAFE

If the creativity of Narberth inspires you there is even a cafe, Creative Cafe, where you can decorate a pot or plate yourself while enjoying your coffee and call back to fetch it after firing. A studio/cafe with a difference, where you can be the artist whether you're artistic or not.
Enjoy painting your own designs on ready made pottery egg cups, pet bowls, house signs etc. Leave it with us to glaze and fire, then collect 1-3 days later. A delicious range of teas, special coffees, snacks and home-made cakes are available. Booking is advisable on wet days.

for more
information
tel: 01834 861651

Clunderwen

Situated just inside Carmathenshire and known until the 1870's as Narbeth Road. The village of Clunderwen developed with the coming of the railway in 1852. An interesting histori cal anecdote is that it was here in 1913 that the James Brothers first flew their biplane - one of the earliest flights in Wales.

Efailwen

A small community north of Narberth, in the southern Preseli foothills, Efailwen is recorded in the history books as the place where the erection of a toll gate in 1839 sparked off the Rebecca Riots. Nearby at Glandy Cross is a group of Neolithic and Bronze Age sites, regarded as the most important in South Wales.

Lampeter Velfrey

It is as if the Landsker Line, were it ever drawn, would pass through the parish of Lampeter Velfrey, which is a few miles due east of Narberth. There are several prehistoric sites in the immediate area, including tumuli, a Bronze Age hearth and three Neolithic burial chambers.

Llanboidy

Llanboidy lies across the border in old Carmarthenshire, about 5 miles north of Whitland, in the small Gronw Valley. A well in the village was the focus of many medieval pilgrimages. Close to Llanboidy are two ancient sites, a cromlech at Cefn Brafle and Arthur's Table, a tumulus, which is in a wood at Dolwilym. Today the village enjoys fame as the home of Pemberton's Victorian Chocolates.

for more information
tel: 01994 448800

Gelli

Located just north of Llawhaden, the small community of Gelli developed around a large woollen mill. This worked from the late 19th century until 1937 and was one of several mills which flourished in the Landsker Borderlands at that time. Fishing was another important industry here. In the late 19th century 6 pairs of Cleddau coracles fished here between Gelli and Llawhaden.

Llawhaden

Llawhaden was an important medieval settlement standing on the Landsker Line. The original Norman castle was later developed as a magnificent bishops palace by the Bishop's of St. Davids. The ruins which stand today are evidence of the grandeur of this fortified palatial residence. You can also see the remains of a medieval hospice chapel. The Norman church of St. Aidan stands in the valley below, on the banks of the Eastern Cleddau, in a very picturesque position.

LLAWHADEN CASTLE

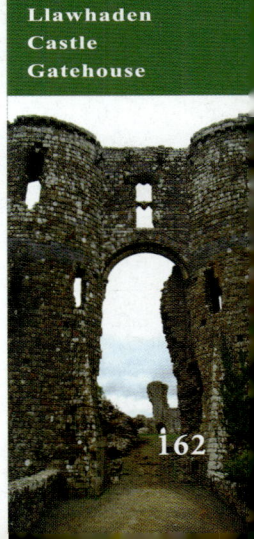

Originally a wooden structure built in Norman times, the castle was rebuilt by the Bishops of St. Davids between the late 13th and 15th centuries and transformed into a great fortified palace. This comprised several buildings set around a five sided courtyard, strengthened with angled corners. The ruins now in the care of CADW (Welsh Historic Monuments), include the front of the gate house which still stands to its full height, the Great Hall, bakehouse, barracks, visitors' lodgings and the Chapel of the Blessed Virgin. After using the castle for more than 250 years, the bishops dis mantled it and stripped the lead from the roof. Close to the castle are two other historic attractions – a restored medieval hospice and Holgan Camp, an Iron Age fort to which visitors now have access thanks to the opening of a new public footpath. The site of the camp was overgrown for centuries until cleared and fenced by PLANED and CADW. Holgan Camp had formidable defences and is a well preserved example of an Iron Age defended enclosure. Many such camps were established in the area.

Llawhaden Castle

Llawhaden Castle Gatehouse

162

Llanddewi Velfrey

Located between Narberth and Whitland on the busy A40, Llanddewi Velfrey originally grew around its ancient church and there is evidence of occupation during the Iron Age. The Quaker burial ground also reflects a strong tradition of non-conformity. The area around the village is ideal for country walks with stunning views of the Marlais Valley to the south and the Preseli Hills to the north.

Llandissilio

This village stands on the A478 north of Narberth, a road which has developed from a prehistoric route that linked the Preseli Hills and the Cleddau estuary. Castle sites and earthworks suggest that the parish has a long history, an idea supported by the inscribed stones in the church which date back from the 5th or 6th century.

Llangolman

From Efailwen, on the A478, the road to Llangolman gives breathtaking views of the approaching Preseli Hills. Until a few years ago, this small village encompassed the last working Pembrokeshire slate quarry Gilfach. The slate, which was formed from volcanic ash,

Ludchurch

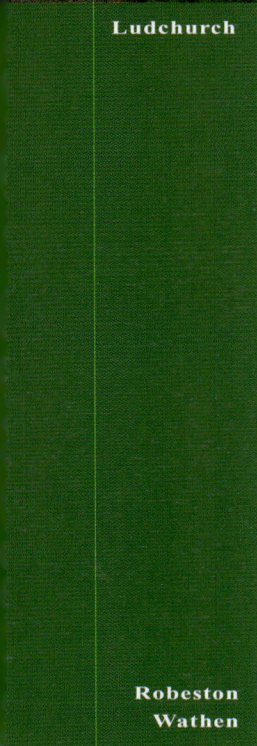

Robeston Wathen

is a lovely soft green colour and was highly prized. The slate was used to roof the National Library of Wales in Aberystwyth and to line the Suez Canal. The Slate Workshop, on the outskirts of the village, still uses some of the green Pembrokeshire slate, although the majority now comes from other Welsh quarries.

Robeston Wathen

The earliest record of Robeston Wathen dates back as far as 1282. The small hilltop community, on the A40, has a Norman Church and distinctive tower. The part of the parish name Robeston is of Norman origin, whose Kings sought to impose their rule on this part of Wales. The Parish was called at this time Villa Robti or "Robert's Ton" although no records indicate who Robert was. However in the 13th century a family by the name Wathen was granted the titular Lordship of the Manor, and so the village has been named Robeston Wathen ever since. This family had interests in the production and weaving of wool, which was to remain the major export of England and Wales for several centuries. Some indication of the importance of this trade can be seen from the fact that Geoffrey Chaucer, the author of Canterbury Tales, earned his living as the Kings Wool Talleyman. Today he would have been called a Chief Inspector of Customs and Excise. The Wathen family moved to the Cotswolds, Gloucester and Bristol in Elizabethan times - then great centres of the wool trade. The Wathen family have served with distinction in Church, State and banking. One John de Wathen became Bishop of Salisbury and his 14th century tomb can be seen in Westminster Abbey.

Reynalton

Reynalton, situated west of Begelly and south of Narberth, is now a small, quiet hamlet in the midst of farmland. Yet earlier in the century coal mining was a thriving local industry, as the village stands in the old South Pembrokeshire coal-field.

Tavernspite

Tavernspite is on the Pembs/Carms border at the junction of the B4328 and B4314. At one time this was also on the route of the mail coaches which travelled from London to Ireland via Milford Haven. The local community here takes great pride in the village; in recent years Tavernspite has won awards in competitions for Wales In Bloom and Best Kept Village. Tavernspite is also notable for its chapel, one of the most remote and picturesque in Pembrokeshire.

Ludchurch

Located less than 3 miles south-east of Narberth, Ludchurch stands on the route of the Knightway footpath. A curious fact is that prior to the 1950's the name Ludchurch referred only to the Norman church and parish and the village itself was known as Egypt. There are definitely no pyramids here, but there are some fine lime kilns to be seen in the old quarry. The name Ludchurch is also becoming increasingly known among people with good taste. The reason is Princes Gate Water - a spring water of exceptioally pure quality which has proved so popular that it is now supplied all over Wales and to markets as far apart as London and North America. The water comes from 3 acres of farmland in the parish which are satu rated with clear natural springs.

Tavernspite

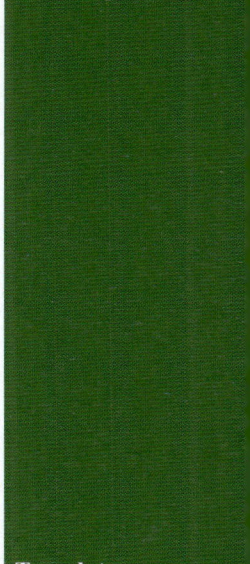

Templeton

164

Canaston Bridge

Just west of Narberth Canaston Bridge marks the junctions of the A40 and A4075. This attractive wooded area is the northern boundary of the Eastern Cleddau and from here you can join the Knightsway - a 9 mile walk linking the Daugleddau Trail with the coast path at Amroth. Nearby, on the south side of the A40 is a picnic area and restored Blackpool Mill. A mile or so from the north side is the impressive ruins of Llawhaden Castle. A few miles south on the A4075 are the neighbouring attractions of Oakwood and CC2000. Also within the area are several interesting woodland walks, including a relatively short path which takes you to Blackpool Mill.

OAKWOOD & CC2000

One of the top ten theme parks in the UK, Oakwood has over 40 rides and attractions for all the family. Next door is CC2000, Oakwood's indoor bowling and family enter tainment centre.

see Pembrokshire's Premier Attractions section on page 57 for details

BLACKPOOL MILL

In a beautiful setting on the banks of the Eastern Cleddau, this is one of the finest examples in Wales of a mill complete with all of its machinery. You can visit their museum, gift shop and tea room.

for more information tel: 01437 541233

TEA ROOM AND SHOP OPEN

OPEN 11 TO 4

Templeton

The layout of Templeton which is a mile south of Narberth, is a fine example of village planning in the Middle Ages. It is believed that the Knights Templars had a hospice here, possibly on the site now occupied by St. John's church, and in the 13th century the village was known as the settlement of the Templars. Hence the name Templeton today. There are several ancient sites here, including Sentence Castle, originally a raised fortification which also probably dates from the time of the Knights Templars. The Knightsway Trail passes through the village.

Wiston

The village of Wiston, five miles northeast of Haverfordwest, was an important settlement in medieval times. Wiston Castle was at a strategic point on the Landsker Line and as such was the scene of much bloodshed in the 12th and 13th centuries. The remains of this impressive motte and bailey castle are a short walk from the car park in the centre of the village and now administered by CADW. Admission is free.

The Daugleddau

The Daugleddau estuary is an area of great natural beauty, comprising the fascinating stretch of waterway which extends inland from the Haven and encompasses four rivers Western Cleddau, Eastern Cleddau, Carew and Cresswell. It is an inner sanctuary, often described as the hidden treasure of the Pembrokeshire Coast National Park. Daugleddau

Beside the Daugleddau

(which means two rivers at the Cleddau) begins east of the Cleddau tool bridge, and has become known as The Secret Waterway. In recognition of the Daugleddau's remarkable diversity of flora and fauna, many parts of the waterway are designated Sites of Special Scientific Interest. These include the Carew and Cresswell rivers, Lawrenny Wood, Minwear Wood, parts of Slebech Park and West Williamston Quarries. In Tudor times Lawrenny was famous for its oysters. By the 19th century sailing vessels of all shapes and sizes, brigantines, ketches, sloops, schooners and coasters, were busily importing and exporting coal, grain, limestone, timber and general goods. Towards the latter part of the century, Willy Boys (flat barge like craft) - carried local produce and ran a shuttle service between seagoing vessels and the Daugleddau's upper reaches. The poor acidic soils of West Wales made lime a valuable and highly saleable commodity. Limestone was quarried at West Williamston, Garron Pill and Llangwm Ferry and burned in hundreds of kilns along the waterway and coastline, from South Pembrokeshire to Cardigan Bay. The remains of several kilns are still visible. The band of carboniferous coal measures which runs across Pembrokeshire from St. Bride's Bay to Saundersfoot cuts through the uppermost reaches of the Daugleddau, and mining around Landshipping was at its height in the first half of the 19th century, particularly after the introduction in 1800 of the first steam engine to be used in a Pembrokeshire coalfield. The high quality anthracite was in great demand. A tragic accident at the Garden Pit near Landshipping in 1844 and a series of insurmountable geological problems which plagued the coalfield throughout its working life led to a rapid decline of the industry by the early 20th century. The last colliery to work, at Hook on the Western Cleddau, was closed by the National Coal Board in 1949. The waterway's rich oak woodlands helped encourage boatbuilding and cutters, smacks and schooners were built at yards and quays along the Daugleddau. At Lawrenny alone, over 40 sailing vessels were built during the first half of

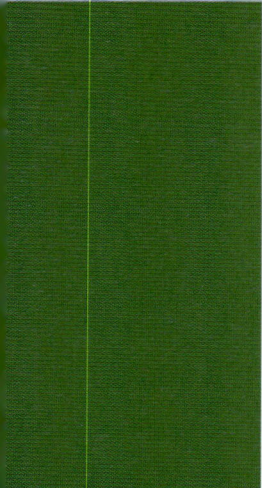

the 19th century. Other industries flourished too, from a chemical works at Whalecomb to a furnace and forge which operated on the site now occupied by Blackpool Mill.

During the 19th century over 100 men earned their living by compass net fishing, a traditional method, suited to rivers with fast flowing tidal currents, which required considerable skill and courage. Much of the working life of the Daugleddau centred around Lawrenny Quay, which in its heyday had more than one quay. Today it is noted for its Yacht Station and excellent facilities for pleasure craft and seeing the waterway from the comfort of a boat will take you to places inaccessible by any other means. Whatever your method of exploration, the Daugleddau will provide endless relaxation and enjoyment. Sights worth seeking out are many and varied, including Lawrenny village and its well restored cottages and huge Norman church. A National Park picnic site gives superb views over the Carew and Cresswell rivers. At Cresswell Quay, a picnic site

and pub are just yards from the water's edge where Kingfishers and herons feed in full view. The long distance Daugleddau Trail and other footpaths reveal a succession of delights, from the evocative ruins of magnificent Carew Castle to the ancient woodland of Minwear. There are many other historic sites to enjoy, such as the exotic gardens of Upton Castle and Picton Castle and the restored mills at Carew and Blackpool. The lime stone quarries have long since fallen silent, but today West Williamston is the centre of other important work for the waterway, the rescue, nursing and rehabilitation of injured and contaminated seabirds, at the Oiled Bird Rescue Centre. Regular visitors to the centre each year are substantial numbers of Manx shearwaters, which once blown inland by autumn gales are unable to take off again and are often stranded in brightly lit harbours and resorts such as Tenby.

Burton

Sitting just across the Cleddau toll bridge from Pembroke Dock, and close to Neyland, Burton is a small hillside village which enjoys superb views over the waterway. It is best known as a boating centre and for its popular waterfront pub, which as well as good food boasts a large beer garden and panoramic views over the estuary to the south, east and west.

Burton

Carew

The most southerly point of the Daugleddau section of the National Park, Carew is famous for its magnificent riverside castle, fine Celtic cross and restored tidal mill. There is also a picnic site and car park here, accessible from the village across the old narrow bridge. The village itself is small, neat and has a distinct charm, with a pub

Carew Castle

and a restaurant offering plenty of local hospitality. Close to Carew, on the south side of the A477, is the slumbering hamlet of Carew Cheriton. The church here dates from the late 14th century and is distinctive for its very tall tower, which has a corner steeple. In the churchyard there is a detached mortuary chapel.

CAREW CASTLE

Here is a castle which has everything: magnificent ruins, an evocative setting, a long and important history, examples of medieval and Elizabethan architecture, a Celtic cross which is one of the finest in Wales and archaeological deposits dating back over the last 2000 years.

Carew is undoubtedly a king among castles. It stands on a low limestone ridge at the head of a tidal inlet of the Carew river - a strategic position, as it guarded a crossing of the river and the main road to Pembroke, 5 miles away. In times of war it could also be supplied by boat, as it has access to the open sea via the Daugleddau and the Haven waterway. Carew Castle was occupied continuously from the 12th century to the end of the 17th century, during which time it was gradually transformed from a medieval fortress to an Elizabethan mansion of considerable splendour. Most photographs today tend to emphasise the latter, as the castle is often shot from across the water of Carew Pill to capture on of the ruin's most striking features - the great Renaissance north wing which Sir John Perrot began building in 1588. Perrot died in 1592 of natural causes while imprisoned in the Tower of London and the wing was never completed. In April 1507 the castle and nearby Carew Meadows were the site of the Great Tournament - a spectacular 5 day event, attended by over 600 noblemen. The occasion was in honour of the Tudor monarchy and also to celebrate the fact that Henry VII had bestowed upon Sir Rhys ap Thomas, who held the castle at the time, the Order of the Knight of the Garter. Sir Rhys had played a major part in Henry's victory at Bosworth and was knighted on the battlefield; it is even said that Richard III died at his hands. Although the king himself was not in attendance, the tournament was a grand affair on a scale not previously seen in Wales. The huge assembly enjoyed jousting, sword displays, hunting and other sports of the day, and the Great Hall was the scene of a sumptuous banquet. This was the last event of its kind ever staged in Britain. During the Civil War years of 1644 and 1645, the castle changed hands between royalist and parliamentarian forces no fewer than four times. Towards the end of the century it was abandoned by the Carew family and fell into decline. The history of any castle which enjoyed such a long period of occupancy is obviously complex, involving many families, characters and events. But the exciting thing about Carew Castle is that much is still being

discovered about its very early history. Since 1986 it has been the subject of a phased but very intensive archaeological survey involving excavation, a stone by stone study of the surviving walls and buildings and examination of documents. To date, two major surprises have been unearthed. One is that the Norman part of the castle is much bigger and older than previously suspected. The other discovery of pre-Norman fortifications, adding weight to speculation that the site had a royal significance long before the Normans arrived and was the seat of Welsh kings throughout the Roman and Dark Age periods. This idea is supported by the famous Carew Cross, which stands within the Castle Field and is a memorial to a Welsh king who died in 1035, more than half a century before the Normans took Pembroke in 1093. In the near future, visitors to the castle will be able to see some of the discoveries made by the archaeological survey, as there are plans to build an Interpretation Centre on site. The castle is still privately owned by descendants of the Carew family, but is leased to the Pembrokeshire Coast National Park Authority under a 99 year agreement so that the castle and its surrounding earthworks can be conserved for everyone's enjoyment. Carew is the only castle managed by the National Park Authority.

for more information tel: 01646 651782

CAREW CROSS

Carew's famous 11th century Celtic Cross stands close to the castle. It is a royal memorial commemorating Maredudd ap Edwin, who in 1033 became joint ruler with his brother of Deheubarth, the kingdom of southwest Wales. Just two years later he was killed in battle. The cross comprises two separate pieces and the inscriptions are predominantly Celtic but also reflect Scandinavian influence.

CAREW TIDAL MILL

This is the only tidal mill to remain intact in Wales, and it stands on the causeway which dams the 23 acre millpond. The present mill is 19th century but the site was previously occupied by a medieval building which operated in Elizabethan times. The mill's machinery was powered by water stored at flood tide and released through sluices to drive two undershot mill wheels. It continued to grind commercially until 1937 and was restored in 1972. Today it is often known as the French mill - a reference to either the architectural style of the building or the mill's grinding stones imported from France. As with Carew Castle the mill is managed by the National Park Authority. It is open to visitors throughout the season and is a popular and fascinating attraction.

for more information
tel: 01646 651657

UPTON CASTLE GROUNDS
Cosheston Nr Pembroke

Upton Castle grounds and gardens occupy a secluded wooded valley which runs down to a tributary of the Carew River. There is free parking on site and the grounds contain over 250 different species of trees and shrubs.

Cresswell Quay

This is a beautiful spot for a picnic, or to enjoy a pint or Sunday lunch at the old riverside pub. The tidal Cresswell River attracts herons and a variety of other waders and brilliantly coloured kingfishers often catch the eye as they dive for prey and seek out the best perches along the banks. Across the water, high above the steep wooded slopes, buzzards soar effortlessly over the trees of Scotland Wood.

Hook

There is much evidence here of the area's long and intensive coalmining activities, including the remains of two quays, tramways and bellshaped mines from the 17th and 18th centuries. Hook pit did not close until 1949 and in its later days was linked to the Milford Haven railway. It is a small settlement on the eastern banks of the Daugleddau, near the confluence of the Western and Eastern

Upton Castle Gardens

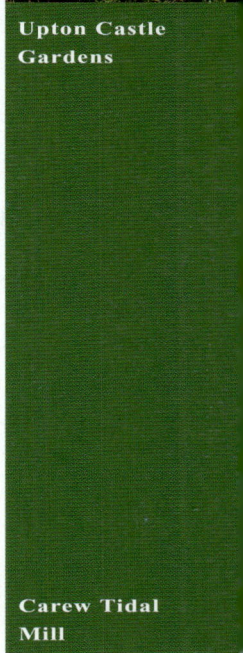

Carew Tidal Mill

Cleddau rivers. Across the river, close to Picton Point is the site from which the Picton Ferry once operated. Coal was a valuable commodity here as the mining industry thrived for a period in the 19th century and Landshipping Quay exported coal from several pits. Close by is the site of the terrible Garden Pit colliery disaster of 1844, when high tide flooded the mine and 40 lives were lost, including those of several young boys.

Lawrenny

Lawrenny has an impressive church with a large Norman tower. Using the Site once occupied by Lawrenny Castle - an 18th century mansion now demolished - the National Park Authority did establish a picnic area. Please note however that this area has been in private ownership since 1995 and is no longer open to the public. Earlier last century, at Lawrenny House Farm, Mr. J.F. Lort-Phillips trained racehorses and put the village on the map when Kirkland won the Grand National in 1905. Another horseracing connection, nearby Coedcanlas was the birthplace of famous jockey turned best selling author Dick Francis.

LAWRENNY QUAY

Close to Lawrenny village, Lawrenny Quay is a popular area for boating which once

Quayside Tearooms overlooking the estuary

boasted a thriving shipbuilding industry. During the Second World War, Lawrenny Quay served as a marine air base for 764 Squadron of the Fleet Air Arm. Up to 15 Walrus seaplanes could be seen moored on the river, and the officers were billeted at Lawrenny Castle.

Llangwm

Llangwm has a long history, and is said to have been a Flemish settlement in the Middle Ages. Traditionally the main occupations of the villagers were oyster and herring fishing, with mining rising in importance in the 19th century. Llangwm is well known for its reputedly tough breed of fisherwomen, who until this century were a familiar sight on Pembrokeshire roads, carrying baskets of fish on their heads to sell in the towns. Near to Llangwm is Black Tar, a popular spot for boating and watersport enthusiasts.

Martletwy

A small agricultural community east of Landshipping, Martletwy is now the unlikely home of a vineyard - Cwm Deri - the only commercial vineyard in Pembrokeshire. Another product associated with Martletwy is coal, though this industry has long since vanished. Among the interesting historic buildings here is the church.

Minwear

A large area of the precious and ancient Minwear Wood is a designated SSSI - Site of Special Scientific Interest and in the heart of the wood is the 12th century church. Close by are the ruins of the medieval Sisters' Houses, which once accommodated pilgrims bound for the monastic community at St. Davids. Minwear Wood is close to Blackpool Mill and Canaston Bridge.

West Williamston

When the limestone quarries were established here, this medieval farming hamlet was transformed into a busy quarrymen's village with smithies, inns and its own church. Today the area has reverted to farming, and is also the home of the important Oiled Bird Rescue Centre.

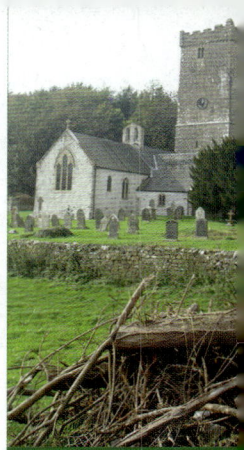

Lawrenny

Llangwm

174

THE HOME OF **WELSH WINE** AND **LIQUEURS**

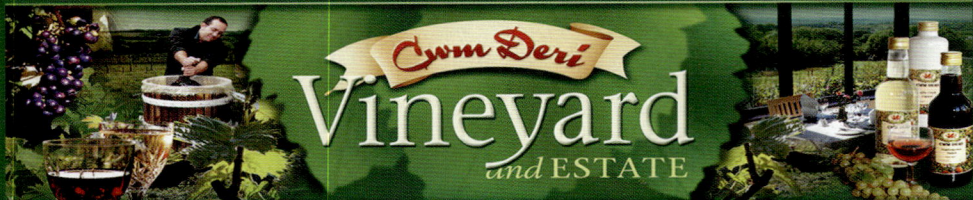

Cwm Deri
Vineyard
and ESTATE

BUY ON LINE www.cwm-deri.co.uk

A chance to stroll through a vineyard in our home climate is rare, and to be able to do it surrounded by the beauty of the Pembrokeshire National Park makes Cwm Deri a unique attraction.

Cwm Deri Estate is a working smallholding, which first opened to the public in 1992 and the vineyard is now one of Wales' foremost attractions.

For the very best of Pembrokeshire produce, whether it's liqueurs, alcohol-free wines, preserves, cheese, cakes or ice-cream, Cwm Deri has something to appeal to all the family, whatever their age.

Enjoy a tasting of our wines and liqueurs, either in our shop or on our patio and terrace, with a commanding view over the vineyard, animals and beyond to the National Park. For freshly prepared and home cooked food then you must try our stunning conservatory restaurant.

Relax with your drink and take a leisurely lunch or afternoon tea, secure in the knowledge that Cwm Deri's younger guests will be happily occupied in Pet's Corner.

BUY ON LINE www.cwm-deri.co.uk

SUMMER OPENING * MARCH 1 - OCTOBER 31
Monday - Saturday 11am - 5pm Sunday 12pm - 5pm

WINTER OPENING * NOVEMBER 1 - FEBRUARY 28
Please phone for our opening times

Cwm Deri Vineyard, Martletwy, Pembrokeshire, SA67 8AP
Tel: 01834 891274 www.cwm-deri.co.uk

175

Pembrokeshire Greenways
Lonydd Glas Sir Benfro

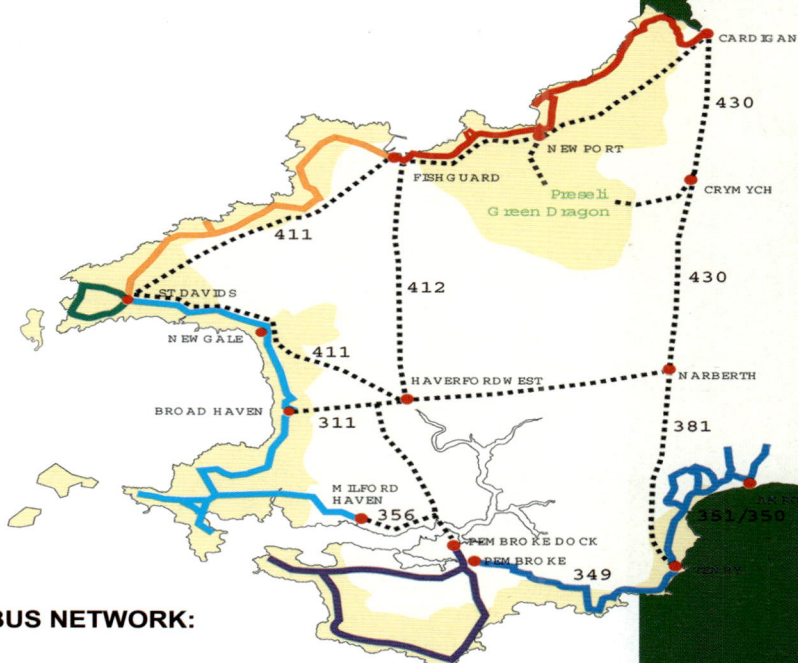

CARDIGAN

430

NEWPORT

FISHGUARD

Preseli
Green Dragon

CRYMYCH

411

430

ST DAVIDS

412

NEWGALE

411

NARBERTH

HAVERFORDWEST

BROAD HAVEN

311

381

MILFORD
HAVEN

356

AMROTH

351/350

PEMBROKE DOCK

PEMBROKE

349

TENBY

COASTAL BUS NETWORK:

Poppit Rocket	**Cardigan - Fishguard**
Strumble Shuttle	**Fishguard - St Davids**
Celtic Coaster	**St Davids Peninsula**
Puffin Shuttle	**St Davids - Milford Haven**
356	**Milford Haven - Pembroke Dock**
Coastal Cruiser	**Pembroke Peninsula**
349	**Haverfordwest - Pembroke - Tenby**
350/351	**Tenby - Saundersfoot - Amroth**

FEEDER ROUTES:

412	**Cardigan - Haverfordwest**
Preseli Green Dragon	**Crymych - Newport**
411	**Fishguard - Haverfordwest**
311	**Haverfordwest - Broad Haven**
315 / 316	**Haverfordwest - Milford Haven - Dale**
381	**Haverfordwest - Narberth - Tenby**
390	**Tenby - Narberth - Cardigan**

176

INLAND PEMBROKESHIRE

PUFFIN SHUTTLE
St. Davids - Milford Haven.
The route passes through the beautiful sights of Newgale, Broad Haven, Little Haven, Marloes and Dale, so all you have to do is sit back and enjoy the ride

CELTIC COASTER
Around the St. Davids Peninsula.
This 14 seater minibus runs from St. Davids to Porthclais, St. Justinians and Whitesands, enabling you to walk the Peninsula, catch the boat trips to Ramsey island or enjoy a day on the beach. The bus can carry 1 x wheelchair.

STRUMBLE SHUTTLE
St Davids - Fishguard
The bus takes you to Abereiddy beach, Porthgain, Trefin, Mathry, Tregwnt Woolen Mill (for Porth Mawr beach) St Nicholas, Trefasser Cross (for Pwll Deri YHA) and as close to Stumble Head as we can get before taking you into Goodwick and Fishguard.

POPPIT ROCKET
Fishguard - Cardigan
Calling at Pwllgwaelod, Newport, Moylegrove, Poppit Sands (for the start of the coast path) and St Dogmaels.

DAY TRIPPER INFO
If you're planning to visit Pembrokeshire's attractions this summer, the Day Tripper bus provides a great link between many of the leading holiday parks and some of the area's top attractions. The bus can also be used to travel to and from the popular resorts of Tenby and Saundersfoot. So give the car a holiday, hop on the Day Tripper and discover the smart way to enjoy Pembrokeshire's attractions. The service is timed to allow a visit to one attraction in the morning, and the opportunity to move on a second venue in the afternoon. Alternatively, passengers can stay at the same venue all-day or return back to their accommodation in the early afternoon. Therefore every Tuesday, Wednesday and Thursday, during July August give the bus a go.

COASTAL CRUISER
This "Surf & Bike" bus runs out of Pembroke to Angle, Bosherston, Stackpole and Freshwater East. The bus carries surfboards, 2 x bikes, 1 x wheelchair and all your beach gear. Look out for the buses that display the Puffin logo and the eye-catching Puffin bus stops - this means that they are part of the coastal bus services. Catching a bus in Pembrokeshire is easy. You don't even have to find the bus stops as all Coastal Buses are on a "Hail & Ride" basis, so all you have to do is signal to the driver to stop. Passengers can be picked up or set down at any point along the bus route, providing it is safe to do so. Once on board your driver will have plenty of local knowledge to help you find your destination or recommend one.

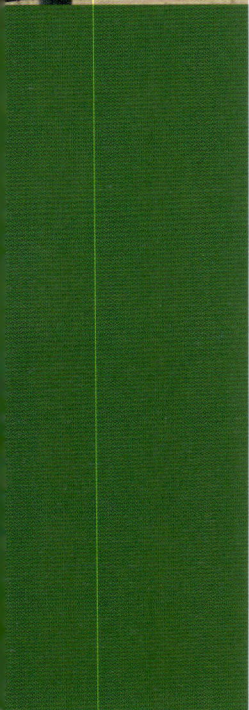

The Coastal Cruiser, Puffin Shuttle, Celtic Coaster, Pocket Rocket and Strumble Shuttle coastal bus services run 7 days a week during the holiday season with a reduced service in the winter. In the south of the county local bus services provide a year round service.

PRESELI HILLS WALKER'S BUS

If you are heading to the Preseli Hills this summer then look out for the Walker's bus service. The Preseli Green Dragon bus is an important link for walkers on the Preseli Hills, providing transport to the start of the walk without having to use a car and enabling you to enjoy walks such as the "Golden Road" ridgeline, without retracing your steps. The bus route hugs the foothills from Crymych to Mynachlog-ddu, Maenclochog, Rosebush, Llys-y-fran, Brynberian, Cilgwyn, Nevern and Newport. In addition to this the bus will also provide a service to Sychpant in the Gwaun Valley. The bus will operate as a Dial-a-Ride service with passengers

required to book a seat in advance. To book your seat telephone 0845 602 7008 at least one hour before the bus is due to run. Details are available from *www.prta.co.uk*

TAKE THE TRAIN FOR A WALK

This summer why not use the train to get yourself around Pembrokeshire. The Greenways "Walk and Ride" leaflets detail walks from Whitland, Narberth, Saundersfoot, Tenby, Manorbier, Lamphey, Haverfordwest and Milford Haven train stations. It also includes walks by bus in the Preseli Hills and St. Dogmaels. You can enjoy discounted travel with the "Greenways Day Ranger" ticket, which enables you to have unlimited day travel along this stretch of line. Pembrokeshire Greenways is a project that encourages people to access the countryside through walking, cycling, bus and train travel.

for details and information pick up a leaflet from any TIC, or tel: 01437 776313 or visit www.pembrokeshiregreenways.co.uk

The Preseli Hills

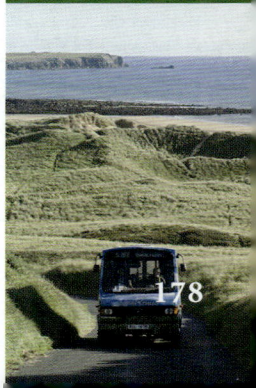

PEMBROKESHIRE'S ISLANDS & WILDLIFE

Pembrokeshire certainly has many virtues, one of its main attractions is the outstanding natural beauty of its coastline and surrounding islands. The wildlife to be found in the area is a major reason for the large number of visitors. The islands such as Ramsey, Grassholm and Skomer are positively teeming with extraordinary wildlife, both on land, in the sea and in the air.

Ramsey Island

260 hectares of fascinating island, now accessible by a regular boat service from the lifeboat slip at St. Justinian's, about three miles west of St. Davids. The island is across the infamous but spectacular Ramsey Sound, with its equally infamous and treacherous reef known as The Bitches. Ramsey was farmed until very recently. To the east, steep sheltered spring fed valleys and cliffs are covered in a wonderful tangle of rich vegetation. To the north east are sheep grazed fields. Ramsey is the only Pembrokeshire island with breeding lapwings. Chough also find Ramsey extremely attractive and both species breed and winter here in good numbers. The western coastline is rugged and spectacular with two small mountains, Carn Llundain and Carn Ysgubor, sheltering the island from the main blast of the prevailing westerly winds. The island is also home to several thousand seabirds in the season, including razorbills, kittiwakes, fulmars and guillemots. On a clear day the mountain top views are superb. To the north and east are St. Davids and the Preseli Hills. To the west, the rocks and islets of the Bishops and Clerks and the main South Bishop rock, where Manx shearwaters and storm petrels breed. To the south, the small offshore islands of Ynys Cantwr and Ynys Beri with Skomer and Midland Isle beyond them across St. Bride's Bay. The caves and beaches around Ramsey are breeding grounds for the largest population of grey seals in southwestern Britain. More than 300 seal pups are born here each season. In 1992 the Royal Society for the Protection of Birds bought Ramsey. There is now a resident warden on the island, who meets every visitor, though there are necessary restrictions on the number of people allowed on the island each day. For those lucky enough to make it, there are refreshments and a shop. Unpaid assistant wardens can arrange to stay and help with work on the reserve.

PEMBROKESHIRE'S ISLANDS & WILDLIFE

VOYAGES OF DISCOVERY

The Ramsey Island Boat Booking Office, opposite Lloyds TSB Bank in the centre of St. Davids
tel: 0800 854367
or
01437 721911

If you mention Dolphins to most people they immediately think of the captive animals that perform tricks in Sea-life Parks. Tell them that you are going Whale and Dolphin watching and they assume you have to jet off to some exotic location in a far-flung corner of the globe.

Well they would be wrong; Pembrokeshire's coastal waters are home to large numbers of these enigmatic creatures and sightings of several hundred animals at a time have been recorded.

The nutrient - rich waters flowing in from the Atlantic produce a prolific ecosystem noted as a Site of Special Scientific Interest. Here on the edge of the Celtic Deep is one of the few places in the UK where cetaceans, seals and birdlife can be found in large numbers. As well as hundreds of Common Dolphin, sightings include Minkie, Sei and Fin Whale. Bottlenose Dolphin, Orca, Rissos Dolphin, and the occasional Basking Shark.

During the winter months some of these animals can be seen off many of our head-lands, where the strong tidal currents pull up nutrients from the sea bed providing food for the shoals of fish on which they feed.

For close encounters a boat trip out to deeper waters can produce some breathtaking scenes. Dolphins are a highly intelligent and very social animal and will very often seek out contact with vessels.

Typically, calves are born in early summer. A single calf is produced every 3 years or so after a gestation period of around a year. The calf suckles for 2 or more years, but starts to eat fish within 3 months and during summer months mothers with young calves have been observed in 'nursery groups' swimming along with vessels for short periods, as if introducing their calves to the correct etiquette for contact with humans. These calves will stay with their mothers for up to 5 years, learning the complex social skills needed to be part of Dolphin society.

To try to describe the emotions experienced when observing these magnificent creatures in their wild and natural state would exhaust a dictionary. The exhilaration as Dolphin bow ride, play and generally show off to their audience, leaping completely out of the water as they race along side you almost close enough to touch will leave you breathless.

Voyages Of Discovery have pioneered Cetacean watching off the Pembrokeshire coast for several years. A family run company with a fleet of specially built RHIB's crewed by expert conservationists, fully guided wildlife tours are run all year round. Offshore Island Voyages to the Grassholm Gannet colony and including Whale and Dolphin watching, run from the end of May to late September.

For more information call their booking office or visit the website:

www.ramseyisland.co.uk

182

Cardigan Island

A small island of less than 16 hectares, situated at the mouth of the River Teifi. The island is leased by The Wildlife Trust of South and West Wales, who annually census its small colonies of seabirds. The lesser black-backed gulls are the dominant species, with only a few hundred herring gulls and very small numbers of other seabirds. In 1934, when the motor vessel Herefordshire was wrecked on the northern rocks, brown rats came ashore and annihilated the islands population of puffins. There have been various attempts to reinstate both puffins and Manx shearwaters. A few have been bred but it is a long and slow process to establish healthy breeding colonies here again.

Grassholm

Currently the island of Grassholm is not open to the public, but a trip around the island remains a truly unforgettable experience. Situated around eleven miles offshore, Grassholm is a reserve of the Royal Society for the Protection of Birds, and is the only Gannet colony in Wales. Viewed from afar the island appears to be snow covered or having a white halo, this in fact is the Gannet colony. Approximately 34,000 pairs of Gannets crowd into the tiny, waterless island to lay their single egg. The noise and sheer spectacle of vast numbers of these magnificent seabirds is something that once experienced can never be forgotten. Gannets are brilliant white in colour and dive for fish in the waters around Grassholm from heights of up to 30 metres. When one realises that a full grown Gannet is about the size of the average Christmas goose the spectacle becomes even more amazing. Writer Dr. Brian John describes the scene thus; "there can be few more beautiful sights than Gannets diving close inshore, wheeling and swooping on the bright clean wind of a Pembrokeshire summer day". The second largest Gannet colony in Britain, Grassholm is a major success story. In 1924 there were 1,000 pairs recorded on the island to an officially recorded 32,000 pairs in 2005. Although Gannets dominate the island to such a degree that even from the mainland it has been described as resembling

an iced bun, other breeding birds include small numbers of Kittiwake, Razorbill and Shag together with Herring and Great Black-backed Gulls. From the boats that take visitors around the island there are often sightings of porpoise, basking shark and even the occasional sunfish. Plus of course a variety of birds such as Puffin or Shearwater, which may be resident on the other neighbouring islands.

Skomer Island

This is the largest of Pembrokeshire's islands, a National Nature Reserve owned by the Countryside Council for Wales but run by The Wildlife Trust of South and West Wales, who employ a permanent warden and staff. The island ferry runs from Martin's Haven on the Marloes Peninsula every day except Monday, though during bank holidays the island is open to visitors all the time, please note that the island will be closed from 20th - 22nd May 2008 for the sea bird census. There is a charge for the boat trip and also for landing, but children under 16 are exempt from the latter. There are guided tours around Skomer, usually operated by the National Park Authority, but in the main visitors are greeted

and given a brief informative talk, which includes information on where to find all of the island's interesting sights and wildlife. From then until the boats leave in the afternoon, you are free to explore via the well defined footpaths. Skomer has some very well preserved archaeological remains dating back to the early Iron Age, in the form of standing stones, hut circles, burial cairns, walls and numerous lynchets. The island was farmed until the mid 1950's, but is now grazed only by rabbits, albeit thousands of them. The flora is not rich, but the carpets of spring and early summer flowering bluebells, red campion, white sea campion and thrift are some of the most colourful in the west. The island's cliff scenery is spectacular, both scenically and for its many thousands of breeding guillemots, Razorbills, Kittiwakes and Fulmars. More than 20,000 pairs of lesser Black-backed Gulls nest in the middle of the island, the largest colony of this species in Europe. Other gulls, such as the Greater Black-backed and Herring are also well represented. Skomer, in fact, boasts the largest colony of breeding seabirds in southern Britain. This is in spite of many years farming

184

activity during which no species of ground predators, even rats or cats, ever managed to establish themselves. Hence ground and burrow nesting sites are numerous. There are over 10,000 puffins and at least 100,000 Manx shearwaters, the world's biggest colony. Of the ground nesting birds, there are good numbers of short-eared owls, curlews and oystercatchers, to name but a few. The island is also home to a unique island race of bank voles, common shrews and wood mice, and on the beaches during the autumn over 150 grey seal pups are born, making this the second most important seal breeding colony in southwestern Britain. Another notable colony is that established by shags on Midland Island, a much smaller island south of Skomer. Skomer, Grassholm and Skokholm are all included in a Special Protection Area designated by a European directive, a further indication of the value of Pembrokeshre's offshore islands to international wildlife.

Skokholm

This small island has been owned by the Dale Castle Estates since the 1970's and is now leased by The Wildlife Trust of South and West Wales, who employ a cook and a warden. There is full board accommodation for up to 16 people a week. Skokholm has all the richness and profusion of wildlife and beauty of Skomer, but in a smaller more gentle way. The only seabird not common to both is the Kittiwake, and in the quarry on the westerly cliffs below the lighthouse there is a colony of several thousand storm petrels, the largest colony in the Irish Sea. In 1936 the island was set up as Britain's first ever bird observatory by a group of people which included Ronald(R.M) Lockley. This of course is Lockley's Dream Island, which was occupied and farmed by him until 1940.

St. Magaret's Island

St. Margaret's Island and its much bigger neighbour Caldey, lay some way to the south of the county. The island has the largest colony of cormorants in Wales, located on top of its steep limestone cliffs, while other seabirds include Greater Black-backed and Herring Gulls, Guillemots, Razorbills, Kittiwakes and Fulmars on the vertical cliffs. There are very few puffins, but burrow nesting birds are restricted by the presence of rats. The island and its wildlife and the coastline of Caldey are best seen from one of the pleasure boat, which run regularly from Tenby harbour between April and early Autumn, but no landings are allowed on St. Magaret's.

Caldey Island

Caldey is owned and run by the small community of Cistercian monks, who farm the island with the help of a few people in the village. A day out here is totally different from anything else you will experience in Pembrokeshire. Several boats a day take many curious visitors to this atmospheric and religious centre, and landings and access are simple compared to other islands. Leaving the boat you will walk towards the village and monastery passing Priory Beach, a beautiful, gently curving stretch of sand backed by dunes, and the island's only safe bathing beach. The easy stroll up through the trees has a distinctly Mediterranean feel to it, which is emphasied when you see the monastery. The imposing but attractive monastic buildings are all whitewashed and have terracotta roofs. The village itself has everything to offer visitors including shops and a cafe with open air seating under swaying whispering trees.

Come with us into a world *of* island wildlife

187

PEMBROKESHIRE ARTS & CRAFTS

Pembrokeshire is well known for its wealth of creative talent with an array of arts and crafts as diverse as the landscape. So whether it's candle making, wood turning, paintings, photography or pottery you're after you will find it all here in fabulous Pembrokeshire. The following is a brief guide to just some of the many attractions to be found across the county

Creative Cafe
Narberth

Tenby & the South Coast

ART MATTERS
South Parade, Tenby
tel: 01834 843375
A wide variety of quality original art in West Wales promoting the work of new and established artists.

AUGUSTUS GALLERIES
St. George's Street, Tenby
tel: 01834 845164 or 842204
A collection which includes some 250 paintings, drawings and prints by distinguished 19th/20th century artists.

EQUINOX
St. Julians Street, Tenby
tel: 01834 843878
A fascinating collection of gifts and crafts

GIFT OF GLASS
Corner Trafalgar & Upper Park Road, Tenby
tel: 01834 845886
Hand crafted glassware and gifts. Free glassblowing demonstrations.

HARBOUR VIEW CERAMIC CAFE
3 Crackwell Street, Tenby
tel: 01834 845968
36 Blue Street, Carmarthen
tel: 01267 229103
Paint your own pottery, explore your creative talent in a relaxed and fun atmosphere

TENBY MUSEUM & ART GALLERY
Castle Hill, Tenby
tel: 01834 842809
Established in 1878, this national award winning museum situated on a spectacular site overlooking Carmarthen Bay has two art galleries with regular changing exhibitions including a permanent collection of work by local artists such as Gwen John, Augustus John, David Jones and John Piper. Open throughout the year, daily during the summer season, and on week days from January to Easter. Full access for disabled visitors. Admission charges and concessions apply.
tel: 01834 842809

Haverfordwest & the West Coast

ANDREW G. BAILEY
23 Riverside Quay, Haverfordwest
tel: 01437 766889
Original watercolours, prints and cards by the artist together with a variety of Pembrokeshire made crafts.

189

CELTIC IMAGES GALLERY

Hilton Court Gardens, Roch Haverfordwest
tel: 01348 837116
A showcase for Pembrokeshire's top photographic and artistic talent.

THE OLD SMITHY

Simpson Cross, Haverfordwest
tel: 01437 710628
Welsh crafts, gifts and new purpose built gallery showing local artists
see advert page 75

THE SHEEP SHOP & WILSONS GALLERY

32 Bridge Street Haverfordwest
tel: 01437 766844
Great range of goods including crafts, lovespoons, prints, etc.
see advert page 71

St. Davids & The North Coast

CARNINGLI CENTRE

East Street, Newport
tel: 01239 820724
Art gallery, antiques showroom, interesting collectables.

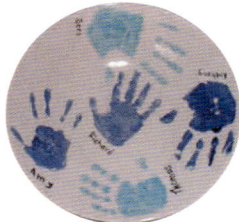

HARBOUR LIGHTS GALLERY

Porthgain, Nr St. Davids
tel: 01348 831549
The best of Pembrokeshire art is featured in the harbourside gallery.

ORIEL-Y-FELIN GALLERY & TEAROOM

Trefin, Nr St. Davids
tel: 01348 837500
A constantly changing selection of paintings, ceramics, cards and prints
see advert page 126

Time plays tricks, something that might seem ordinary in its own time can become valued, even unique by virtue of age and a change of ways. A recent discovery at Oriel-y-Felin is such an example. At the bottom of the garden is an old earth closet, a ty bach - in Welsh, literally a "small house" - and its walls are covered with drawings of late 19th century and early 20th century sailing vessels. It's an incredible record of the ships sailed by a past owner of the house, Captain John George and his son Gwylim. Conservationists from the National Museum of Welsh Life are helping to preserve the drawings and

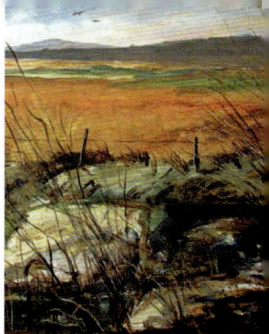

*Original artwork by Pauline Beynon at Oriel-y-Felin Gallery
Top:
"Autumn Moorland"
Above:
"Birds above the bay"*

190

visitors to the gallery can see them by request. Perhaps time moved more slowly back then, and more of it could be spent in the small house!

PEMBROKESHIRE CANDLE CENTRE
Cilgwyn, Newport
tel: 01239 820470
An Aladdin's cave of candles, candlesticks and candle related items.

SOLVA WOOLEN MILL
Middle Mill, Solva
tel: 01437 721112
A working mill weaving carpets and floor rugs.

Inland Pembrokeshire

CREATIVE CAFE
Spring Gardens, Narberth
tel: 01834 861651
Paint your own pottery. Choose from over 200 items, plenty of help and ideas provided, no artistic skill necessary.
see advert page 159

FABRIC HOUSE
6 High Street, Narberth
tel: 01834 861063
Interiors and gifts for home and friends

HAULFRYN
13 High Street, Narberth
tel: 01834 861902
Unusual, hand-made jewellery, antique silver, jewellery repairs

QUEENS HALL GALLERY
High Street, Narberth
tel: 01834 861212
Exhibitions by local and other artists, situated in one of Pembrokeshire's top arts and entertainment venues.

WRIGGLY-TIN.COM
32 High Street, Narberth
Tel:01834 860123
wriggly-tin.com offers a unique collection of images - available on Canvas, Acrylic, Photographic papers and as Garden Art too! We can also work with your own images to create contemporary artwork!
See advert page 160

The Slate Workshop

THE SLATE WORKSHOP

Pont Hywel Mill,
Llangolman,
Clunderwen
tel: 01994 419543

By the side of the Eastern Cleddau River at Llangolman, near Clunderwen. Inspired by the lovely surroundings and by Celtic themes, Richard and Fran Boultbee produce fine lettering and designs in Welsh slate for house nameplates, plaques, memorials, sundials and clocks. Richard sculpts the slate into wonderful tactile pieces and in the showroom their meticulously finished craft items such as vases, bookends, cheeseboards and tealight holders are for sale.
see advert page 161

Ceredigion

MIDDLE EARTH

Priory Street, Cardigan
tel: 01239 614080

Colourful, bohemian gifts and crafts from around the world

TY CUSTOM HOUSE

44 St. Mary Street,
Cardigan
tel: 01239 615541

Shop and Gallery - Art, contemporary design, exclusive home accessories.

Carmarthenshire

ORIEL MYRDDIN GALLERY

Church Lane, Carmarthen
tel: 01267 222775
see advert page 226

WORLD OF WALES

3 Market Street,
Laugharne
tel: 01994 427632

An authentic range of Welsh crafts and gifts set in a relaxed old world atmosphere.

GLYN COCH STUDIOS

Pwll Trap, St. Clears
tel: 01994 231867

Everything from art to wool, including clothes, jewellery, wood, iron and more, all made in Wales, or make and decorate it yourself.
see advert page 233

LAUGHARNE GLASS STUDIO

Market Square, Laugharne
tel: 01994 427476

Originators of silver ornamented glass and glassblowing demonstrations

Laugharne
Glass

192

PEMBROKESHIRE CASTLES & MUSEUMS

Pembrokeshire is not only rich in beautiful scenery; it also has more than its fair share of historic castles and ancient sites together with museums to suit visitors of all ages.

Carew Castle

Carew is one of Pembrokeshire's finest castles with a wealth of detail and atmosphere. Owned and administered by the Pembrokeshire National Park Authority, to get there take the A477 from Pembroke Dock; or the Haverfordwest to St. Clears road, then turn off the A4075.

tel: 01646 651782
see advert page 195

Haverfordwest Castle

Haverfordwest Castle, which overlooks the town, was once used as a prison and more recently as a police station. Owned and administered by Pembrokeshire County Council. It now houses a small museum and the County Records Office.

tel: 01437 763087

Llawhaden Castle

Llawhaden is one of the Landsker castles along the Landsker Line, which is claimed to have divided North and South Pembrokeshire. It fell into disrepair in the mid 16th century after being used as a bishop's residence. Owned and administered by CADW, it can be reached via the A40 from Haverfordwest or St. Clears, then B4313

tel: 02920 500200

Manorbier Castle

Manorbier Castle is where the BBC filmed part of the children's series "The Lion the Witch and the Wardrobe". Set in a stunning area, it can be reached off the A4139 five miles from Tenby.

tel: 01834 871394
see advert page 36

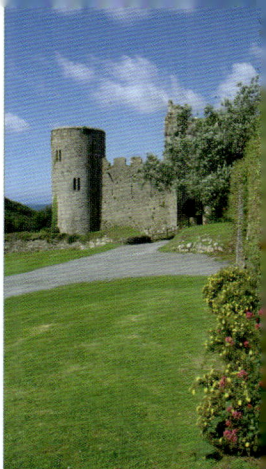

Manorbier Castle

Carew Castle

194

CILGERRAN CASTLE

Cilgerran Castle, three miles southeast of Cardigan, is perched in a dramatic position on a high bluff above the River Teifi. Seen from the deep wooded gorge below - as it was for centuries by the coracle fishermen - it presents a spectacular sight, which inspired great landscape artists such as Turner and Richard Wilson. Equally, the views, which visitors can enjoy from its ruined towers, are magnificent.

The castle, small by comparison withPembroke and the great Norman fortresses of North Wales, is mainly 13th century, but despite its apparently unassailable position, it changed hands many times between the 12th and 14th centuries. Taken from the Normans by Lord Rhys in 1164, it was recaptured in 1204 by William Marshall; used as a base by Llewllyn the Great in 1215, when he summoned a Council of all Wales at Aberystwyth; taken again by the Normans in 1223, following which the present towers were built. After a period of decline and then refortification in the 14th century, the castle was captured again for a brief period by the Welsh in 1405 during the uprising of Owain Glyndwr.

Narberth Castle

Narberth Castle was built in the 13th Century. Its most notable Castellan being Sir Rhys ap Thomas who was given the castle by Henry VIII. By the 17th Century the castle had fallen into ruins, the remnants of which can be seen today and is now open to the public

Nevern Castle

Very little remains of the castle but it provides an interesting view of the siting and layout of early medieval fortifications. To get there follow the Cardigan road out of Fishguard, once past Newport follow the signs to Nevern.

Newport Castle

Newport Castle is another that is in private ownership and not open to the public.

Pembroke Castle

Pembroke Castle is one of the best preserved medieval castles in Wales. Open to visitors all year round, it is an intriguing place to explore. The wide walls are honeycombed with a seemingly endless system of rooms, passageways and spiralling flights of narrow stone steps; interpretative displays and information panels give a fascinating insight into the castle's origins and long history. One of the most impressive features is the distinctive round keep, which was built soon after 1200. It is 75ft high and the views from the top in all directions are nothing less than magnificent.

tel: 01646 681510
or 684585
see advert page 42

Picton Castle

Picton Castle is privately owned and opened to the public six days a week. The beautifully laid out 40 acres of woodland gardens are well worth a visit. The castle lies three miles east of Haverfordwest.

tel: 01437 751326
see advert page 73

Roch Castle

Roch Castle is also a private residence. It is situated on the A487 from Haverfordwest to St. Davids.

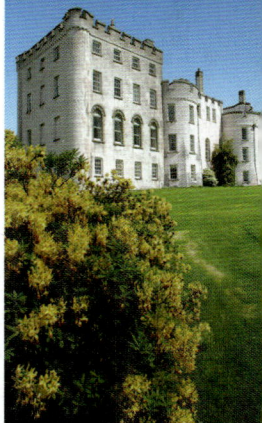

Picton Castle

Pembroke Castle

Wiston Castle

Although very little remains, the castle is worth a visit if only to see the remains of the shell keep built to help protect the motte and bailey castle. Owned by CADW, it be reached from Haverfordwest by taking the A40 towards Carmarthen and turning off at Wiston.

tel: 01443 336000

Carreg Samson

Situated in the coastal village of Abercastle, Carreg Samson is a Neolithic Cromlech overlooking the picturesque fishing village. To get there follow the A487 St. Davids road from Fishguard and then the signs to Abercastle.

Castell Henllys

Castell Henllys is the site of an Iron Age Fort, which has been recreated using authentic materials and techniques. To get there take the A487 from Fishguard to Cardigan, and look for the signs.

Haverfordwest Museum

Haverfordwest Town Museum is situated in the castle an overlooking the town and has been created to illustrate the history of the area. It houses exhibits explaining the castle and prison, which were once housed there, and the transport and industry into the town together with the institutions and personalities that make up Haverfordwest.

tel: 01437 763087

Lamphey Bishop's Palace

Lamphey Bishop's Palace has been acquired by CADW who have carried out careful renovation work to give visitors a rich insight into what the building looked like in a bygone age.

tel: 01437 720517

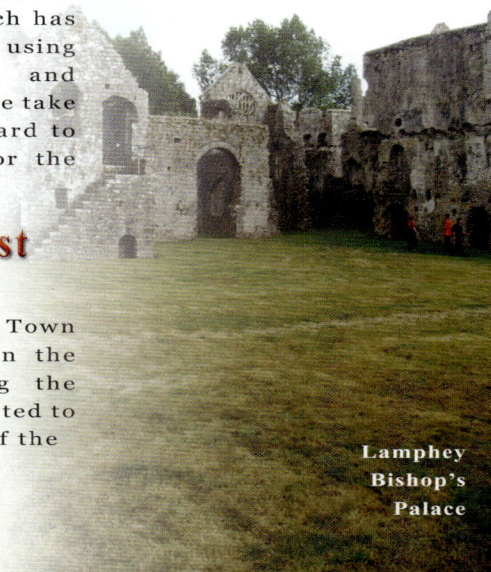

Lamphey Bishop's Palace

197

Milford Haven Museum

The museum brings to life the fascinating story of the historic waterway and the new town's struggle to fulfil its potential. The Milford Haven story is a cycle of hopes dashed and dreams fulfilled and covers its brief period as a whaling port, which ended when gas replaced whale oil for lighting the streets of London. It also covers the town's attempts to become a great Trans-Atlantic port which floundered when the Great Western Railway terminus was built at Neyland and not Milford.

tel: 01646 694496

Penrhos Cottage

This is a typical North Pembrokeshire thatched cottage that has survived almost unchanged since the 19th Century. Built as an overnight cottage in about 1800 and later rebuilt in stone, Penrhos, with its original Welsh oak furniture, provides a unique opportunity to view the cottage's life in the past. The cottage is open by appointment.

For further information contact Scolton Manor Museum tel: 01437 731328

Pentre Ifan

Pentre Ifan is a Neolithic burial chamber dating back from around 3000BC. Administered by CADW, it can be reached via the A487 from Newport, then follow the signs for Pentre Ifan.

tel: 01443 336000

St. Davids Bishop's Palace

Standing in the shadow of St. Davids Cathedral are the remains of the Bishop's Palace that was destroyed during the 16th Century. However much still remains to enable visitors to appreciate the scale of the imposing building.

tel: 01437 720517

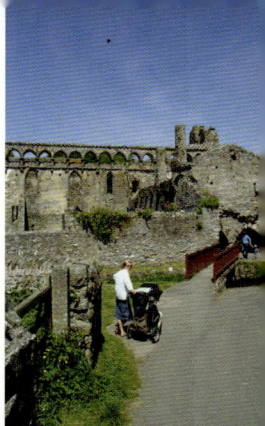
Bishop's Palace St. Davids

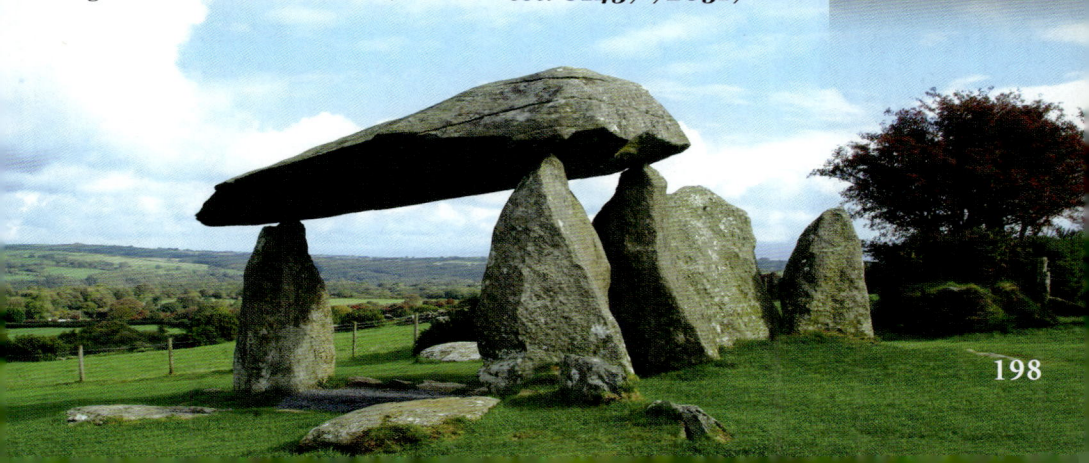
Pentre Ifan

198

Scolton Manor

As the home of Pembrokeshire's County Museum, Scolton has thousands of objects on display illustrating the history of the County in the manor house, stable block and exhibition hall...but Scolton is much more than a visit to a bygone age. It is the place where Pembrokeshire's past meets the future. The museum is completed by the award-winning Eco-Centre where the displays focus on green issues and the wildlife of the park. This 'Greener' lifestyle can also be experienced in the grounds of the Country Park and on the Nature trails through the surrounding woodland. The park also features picnic sites and play areas.

Tenby Museum & Art Gallery

Established in 1878, this national award winning museum is set in the ruins of a medieval castle. Exhibitions of local geology, local archaeology, maritime history, natural history and a social history exhibition called "The Story of Tenby". Events programme include talks, workshops and lectures for children and adults. Museum shop with books, cards, souvenirs and giftware. The Museum and Art Galley is open throughout the year.

for all details
tel: 01834 842809

Tenby Museum

Scolton Manor

County Museum, Manor House, Tea Room, Eco-Centre & Shop

Set in 60 acres of Park and Woodland

ENQUIRIES:
Museum:
01437 731328
Park:
01437 731457

As the home of Pembrokeshire's County Museum, Scolton has thousands of objects on display illustrating the history of the County in the Manor House, Stable Block and Exhibition Hall ...but Scolton is much more than a visit to a bygone age. It is the place where Pembrokeshire's past meets up with the future. The museum is completed by the award-winning Eco-Centre where the displays focus on green issues and the wildlife of the park. This 'Greener' lifestyle can also be experienced in the grounds of the Country Park and on the Nature Trails through the surrounding woodland. The park also features Picnic Sites and Play Areas.

" *The best £2 I have ever spent, wonderful.*
Worth having a rainy day for!
I would recommend it to anybody! "

OPENING TIMES - ECO-CENTRE & COUNTRY PARK: Every day except Christmas Day/Boxing Day. April – October 9.00am – 6.00pm; November – March 9.00am – 4.30pm
MUSEUM: Open every day 10.30am – 5.30pm April - October
ADMISSION: Adults: £2; Children: £1; Concessions £1.50 (additional gate fee charged for entrance to certain events)

HOW TO FIND US: 5 miles north of Haverfordwest on the B4329 Cardigan Road

The Exhibition Hall features displays on the history of Pembrokeshire. Visit the Stable Block and see the stables, carriage house, carpenter's workshop and blacksmith's forge.

GARDENS

GARDENS

BEGELLY COUNTRYSIDE GARDENS
Kilgetty, Nr Narberth
tel: 01834 811320

Set in 12 acres of natural and landscaped features. Tearooms and lakeside picnic area.

BRO MEIGAN GARDENS
Boncath
tel: 01239 841232

Inspirational gardens with a huge range of planting and a tearoom.

COLBY WOODLAND GARDENS
Nr Amroth
tel: 01834 811885

Eight acres of woodland garden set in a tranquil and secluded valley. Gift shop, tearooms, gallery and picnic area. Managed by The National Trust.

MANOROWEN WALLED GARDENS
Fishguard
tel: 01348 872168

Walled garden dating back to 1750. Semi-permanent exhibition of sculpture. Picnic area, teas and plants for sale.

MOORLAND COTTAGE PLANTS
Rhyd u Groes, Brynberian, Crymych
tel: 01239 891363

Small country garden with themed areas. Open for charity and with panoramic views of the Preseil Mountains.

NEWBRIDGE NURSERY
Crundale, Nr Haverfordwest
tel: 01437 731678

A small family run nursery where visitors are welcome to enjoy the adjacent gardens including a wildlife meadow, water and bog garden and a riverside walk.

PENLAN UCHAF GARDENS
Gwaun Valley, Fishguard
tel: 01348 881388

Three acres of landscaped gardens set in the beautiful Gwaun Valley.

PICTON CASTLE
Rhos, Haverfordwest
tel: 01437 751326

40 acres of woodland and walled gardens with a unique collection of

Picton Gardens

Begelly Park Gardens

rhododendrons and azaleas, mature trees, unusual shrubs, wild flowers, fern walk, fernery, maze, restored dewpond and herb collection. Spring and Autumn plant sales.

see advert page 73

PENRALLT GARDEN CENTRE
Moylegrove, Nr Cardigan
tel: 01239 881295

Set in a beautiful location overlooking the sea and coast path above Ceibwr Bay, with a large and comprehensive collection of home grown and unusual plants.

PATIO & GARDEN
Wiston, Haverfordwest
tel: 01437 751343

An extensive range of pots, statues and sundials for patio and garden.

SCOLTON MANOR
Haverfordwest
tel: 01437 731328

Victorian Manor House, Museum and award winning Visitor Centre set in 60 acres of country park and woodlands.

See advert page 199

UPTON CASTLE GARDENS
Cosheston, Pembroke

35 acres of delightful gardens with a variety of attractions and leading to the shores of the Carew river. With a restored 13th Century chapel.

Upton Castle Gardens

Upton Castle Chapel

The National Botanic Garden of Wales was the first botanic garden to open in the 21st century and the first to be created in the UK in nearly 200 years. With a collection of rare and endangered plant species from around the world, it stretches over 500 acres of beautiful, virtually pollution free countryside, across the site of a Regency parkland. Its gardens, lakes, woodlands, undulating hills and organically farmed meadows provide a harmonious blending of the natural and the cultivated. This constantly evolving young garden offers a range of year round attractions to appeal to the broadest interests. The centrepiece is the Great Glasshouse, the largest single span glasshouse in the world. Created by Lord Norman Foster, it houses a stunning display of mediterranean plants from across the globe. In 2007 a stunning Tropical House designed by John Belle was opened in the historic Double Walled Garden. The story of the evolution of flowering plants is told within the enchanting Double Walled Garden; the colourful Broadwalk is one of the longest herbaceous borders in Europe; modern water sculptures complement 200 year old water features and there are also dedicated Japanese, Marsh, Auricula, Bee, Apothecary, Wild, Genetic, Welsh Rare Plant and Slate Gardens. In our unique Edwardian Apothecaries Hall, exhibitions tell the story of the Physicians of Myddfai and Wales's unique knowledge of the links between plants and medicine. We warmly welcome visitors of all ages. Youngsters can scramble around our Adventure Play Zone and enjoy learning about plants in our exciting 360 degrees cinema. Visitors preferring a gentler pace can enjoy a buggy ride and guided tour; browse around our plant sales shop, or daydream beside the beautiful lakes. If you have access to the internet look us up on www.gardenofwales.org.uk to find out about our exciting programme of events and courses.

203

Great attractions
So much to see, and so much to do...

Ar agor drwy gydol y flwyddyn • **Open throughout the year**

Set amongst the gentle hills of the Towy Valley, just 10 minutes from the M4 in Carmarthenshire The National Botanic Garden of Wales is a great day out. See the worlds largest single span glasshouse and the many varied attractions including...

- Tropical Glasshouse
- Lakes, Ponds and Walks
- Millennium Square
- Stables Gallery
- Gift Shop
- Seasons Restaurant
- Mediterranean Cafe
- Double Walled Garden
- Water Discovery Centre
- Bioverse Interactive Exhibition

- Life-long Learning Centre
- Theatre Botanica 360° Cinema
- Japanese Garden
- Childrens Play Area
- Apiary Garden with Bee Hives
- The Living Machine
- Physicians of Myddfai Exhibition

Mae cyfleusterau cynadledda ac arlwyo ar gael ar gyfer hyd at 400 o bobl. Addas iawn ar gyfer ymweliadau ysgol.

Conference and catering facilities for up to 400 people available. School visits highly recommended

Gardd Fotaneg Genedlaethol Cymru
National Botanic Garden of Wales

A Millennium Commission Lottery Project
Project Loteri gan Gomisiwn y Mileniwm

For prices and further information please contact:
Visitor Services, The National Botanic Garden of Wales, Llanarthne, Carmarthenshire SA32 8HG

01558 667148

204

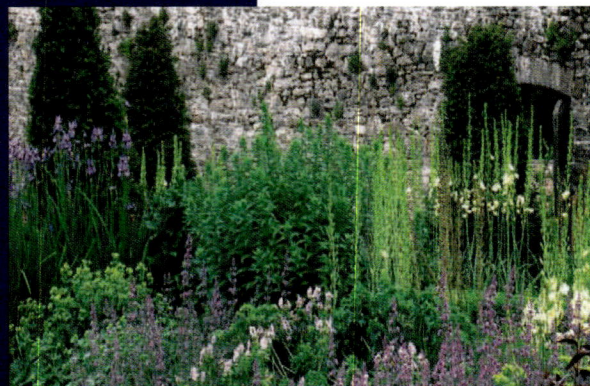

Aberglasney Gardens

Aberglasney is one of the Country's most exciting garden restoration projects which to date has cost over £6 million and has been described as "The Bodnant of South Wales". The restoration of the house and garden started in 1997 and opened to the public in July 1999. Within the ten acres of garden there are three walled gardens and woodland walks, which contain a magnificent collection of plants, many of which are rarely seen in other gardens such as hardy orchids, Magnolias Trilliums and Meconopsis. The garden has been intentionally been planted to be of interest throughout the year.

At its heart is a unique and fully restored Elizabethan /Jacobean cloister and parapet walk, giving wonderful views over the Gardens and is the only example of this style of garden feature left in the U.K. The design of the Cloister Garden took into account the extensive archaeological survey that was carried out on the site during 1999. This survey discovered some of the earliest garden features such as retaining walls and flights of steps, which date back to the late 16th century. Various older artefacts were also discovered including a silver Long Cross Penny dating back to Edward I c1282-1289 and a silver half groat dating back to Henry VII c1485-1509.

In 2005 a unique garden called the Ninfarium was created within the ruinous central rooms and courtyard of the mansion. The remaining walls of the rooms were stabilized and the entire area was covered with a huge glass atrium. This area now contains a fantastic collection of warm temperate and sub-tropical plants including Orchids, Palms, Magnolias and Cycads. In 2006 the Ninfarium won an award for the best garden design/construction project in the UK.

There is a Café in the grounds, which serves delectable light lunches and snacks. In the summer, tea can be taken on the terrace overlooking the Pool Garden. There is also a shop and plant sales area. The Garden and Café at Aberglasney are open every day, (except Christmas Day).

*Llangathen,
Carmarthenshire
Tel: 01558 668998*

see advert page 232

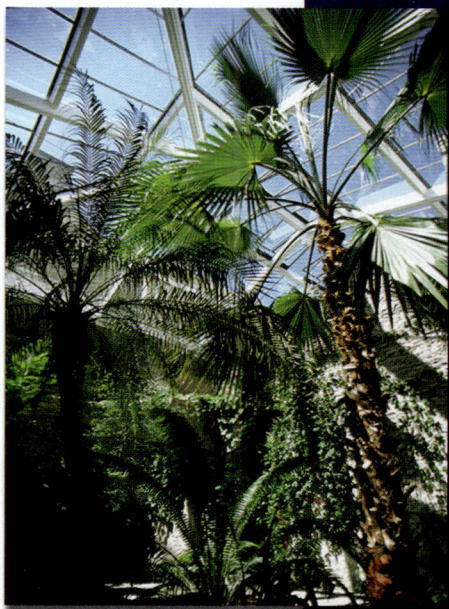

DAY TOURS BY CAR IN PEMBROKESHIRE

For those visitors who like to explore by car, these seven day drives will show you much of Pembrokeshire's varied landscape. The routes suggested, cover the south, west, north and central regions of the county, and each tour brings you back to your original starting point. All are intended as a leisurely drive with plenty of interesting features along the way.

Tour 1

TENBY - CAREW - LLAWHADEN - NARBERTH - AMROTH - SAUNDERSFOOT - TENBY

From Tenby take the B4318 to St. Florence where you can take in the magnificent views across the Ritec Valley. After Manor House Leisure Park, turn left to the pretty village of St. Florence, which features a Flemish style chimney. Leave St. Florence and return to the B4318, turning left for Sageston. At Sageston follow the A477 towards Pembroke for three quarters of a mile then turn right off of the roundabout onto the A4075 for Carew, which has its own castle, Celtic cross and 17th century bridge. Turn left after the bridge for free car parking. After leaving Carew proceed up the hill, turn left on the minor road to Cresswell Quay where the estuary is frequented by herons and king-fishers. Then its on to Lawrenny where at the quay there are yachting facilities, pleasant riverside walks, a picnic site and the fantastic Lawrenny Quay Tearooms. Landshipping Quay, the next village you arrive at, offers a tranquil setting with riverside views. From here follow the signs for Minwear and then on to Blackpool Mill where there is a restored mill, cafe and riverside and woodland walks. Take the A4075 down the hill to the A40 at Canaston Bridge, then turn left towards Haverfordwest and turn right shortly after to Llawhaden where there is a castle and beautiful parish church. Left over the village bridge takes you to Pont-Shan where turning right onto the B4314 takes you to the market town of Narberth. Leave Narberth on the B4314 for Princes Gate, go straight on the crossroads heading for Ludchurch and follow the road for Longstone, go straight over the next cross-roads for Colby Lodge which features National Trust property and gardens. From Colby Lodge proceed up the hill to the T -junction and turn right for Amroth, an unspoilt coastal village with shops, pubs, restaurants,

Saundersfoot

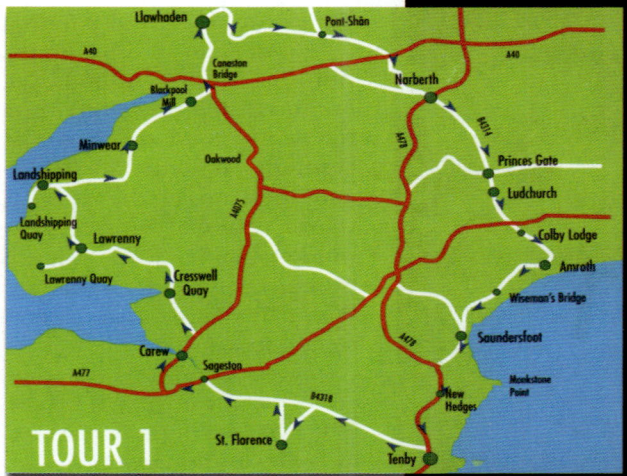

TOUR 1

208

Tenby

DAY TOURS BY CAR IN PEMBROKESHIRE

superb beach at low tide and seafront parking. From Amroth drive up the hill to the Junction at Summerhill, turn left and follow the coast road, passing through Wiseman's Bridge and then on to the popular village resort of Saundersfoot, where you will find superb beaches, tunnel walks to Wiseman's Bridge, shops and restaurants. From Saundersfoot proceed out of the village to New Hedges and return to Tenby on the A478.

Tour 2

TENBY - LYDSTEP - MANORBIER - LAMPHEY - FRESHWATER EAST - STACKPOLE - PEMBROKE - CAREW - TENBY

Leave Tenby on the A4139 signposted Pembroke and

as you approach Lydstep village note the pull in on the left hand side of the road giving superb views of Caldey Island and the cliffs towards Giltar Point. After passing through Lydstep village, turn left at the crossroads to Manorbier, B4585. For a detour to one of the best beaches in Pembrokeshire, follow the signs to Shrinkle Haven where you'll find good parking. Retrace your steps back to the B4585 and turn left to Manorbier village where there is a Norman castle and church, village shops, pub, cafe and beach. Leave Manorbier on the B4585 signposted Pembroke and rejoin the A4139, which takes you through Jameston and Hodgeston and on to Lamphey where there is a ruined medieval Bishop's Palace. From Lamphey rejoin the B4584 to Freshwater East where there is a beach, sand dunes and access to the coastal path. To reach Stackpole Quay cross the narrow bridge by the beach and follow the road through East Trewent for about two miles where

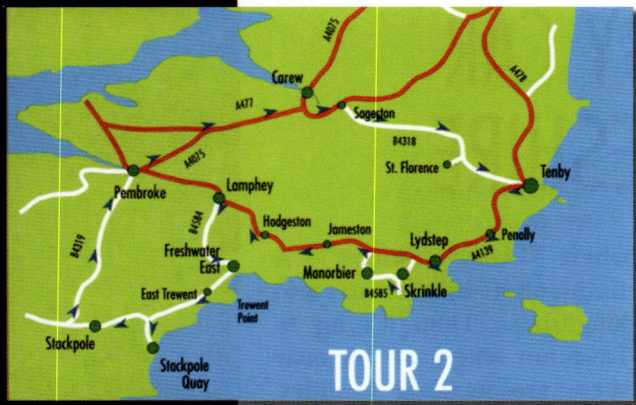

TOUR 2

you will find a small harbour, large car park and coast path to Barafundle beach. Return to the T-junction and turn left to the village of Stackpole, following the road through National Trust woodland to the B4319. Turn right for Pembroke where there is a magnificent medieval castle and tourist information centre. To return to Tenby, leave Pembroke along main street and follow the signpost for St. Clears. At the major junction with the A477, turn right and after about two miles on the A4075 at the roundabout for Carew, where there is another medieval castle and a Celtic cross, tidal mill, walks, pub and riverside picnic area. Return to the A477 and turn left. Turn right off of the roundabout onto the B4318 signposted Tenby and follow all the way into Tenby.

superb walks, wildlife, access to Broad Haven beach, pub and tearooms. Continue through Bosherston, turning left for Broad Haven where there is a large clifftop car park, outstanding views and a superb beach. Re-trace the road back to Bosherston, turning left in the village for St. Govans Head which has a remarkable chapel in the cliffs and spectacular views over dramatic coastal features such as Huntsman's Leap. Back through Bosherston to the B4319 turn left for Castlemartin. After you pass Merrion Camp, where two tanks are on display at the entrance, turn left for Stack Rocks. The road passes medieval Flimston Chapel and leads to a large clifftop car park. Stack Rocks, two vertical columns

Pembroke Castle

Tour 3

PEMBROKE - BOSHERSTON - ST. GOVANS - STACK ROCKS - CASTLEMARTIN - FRESHWATER WEST - ANGLE - PEMBROKE

From Pembroke take the B4319 for Bosherston. After about 3 miles note St. Petrox Church on your right. Continue, turning left at the signpost for Bosherston, where there are lily ponds, a church, fishing,

TOUR 3

DAY TOURS BY CAR IN PEMBROKESHIRE

Haverfordwest

that are home to thousands of breeding seabirds in early summer, stand just offshore a few hundred yards to your left. A short distance to your right is a viewing platform for the Green Bridge of Wales, a spectacular lime-stone arch. Return to the B4319 and turn left for Castlemartin where an 18th century circular stone cattle pound is now a traffic round-about. Fork left for Freshwater West, noted for its long wide beach backed by rolling sand dunes, with a restored beach hut once used for drying seaweed to make laverbread. Continue along the coast road, which gives more superb views as it climbs again towards a T-junction. Turn left here on the B4320 for Angle , passing the huge Texaco refinery and views across the estuary towards Milford Haven and

the busy shipping lanes. In the old fishing village of Angle, which lies between East Angle Bay and West Angle Bay, interesting sights include the church and the remains of the medieval Tower House. West Angle Bay has a beach, cafe, parking, together with views of Thorn Island and the Haven, whilst East Angle Bay is home to a lifeboat station, yacht moorings, outstanding views and walks. Return to Pembroke on the B4320 via Hundleton.

Tour 4

HAVERFORDWEST - MILFORD HAVEN - DALE - MARLOES - LITTLE HAVEN - BROAD HAVEN - NOLTON HAVEN - NEWGALE - HAVERFORDWEST

Leave Haverfordwest on the A4076, passing through Johnston towards Milford Haven, which offers easy parking at both the Rath and the marina. Attractions here include a museum, adventure playground, choice of eateries, boat trips and pleasant walks and views along the Haven waterway. From Milford Haven follow the road sign-posted Herbrandston and

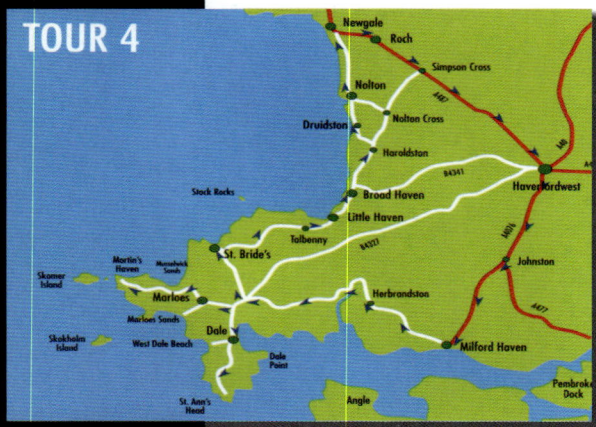

TOUR 4

211

Dale, eventually joining the B4327 from Haverfordwest about two and a half miles from Dale which is a mecca for watersports enthusiasts. Then its on to St. Ann's Head which features a lighthouse, together with outstanding views of the Atlantic and the entrance to the Haven waterway. Retrace your journey to Dale from where you can take a detour to West Dale Beach by turning left by the church and leaving your car at the end of the road. After Dale take the B4327 for about one and a half miles and turn left to Marloes where you will discover one of Pembrokeshire's most beautiful beaches at Marloes Sands. Martins Haven is well worth a visit for here the coast road culminates in a National Trust car park, and a walk from Martin's Haven to the headland will give you outstanding views of Skomer, Skokholm and St. Bride's Bay. Return to Marloes and follow the signs for Dale, turning left at the T-junction. After about a quarter of a mile turn left for St. Bride's. Your next port of call is the small, pretty seaside village of Little Haven, which is accessible via various country lanes that take you through Talbenny. From Little Haven follow the road to Broad Haven, where there is easy parking and a haven for watersport enthusiasts featuring a long beach, outstanding views and walks, interesting rock formations, shops and other facilities.

From Broad Haven take the coast road north for Nolton Haven, which takes you on to Newgale another long beach offering watersports and views towards nearby St. Davids, From Newgale take the A487 to Haverfordwest returning via Roch and Simpson Cross.

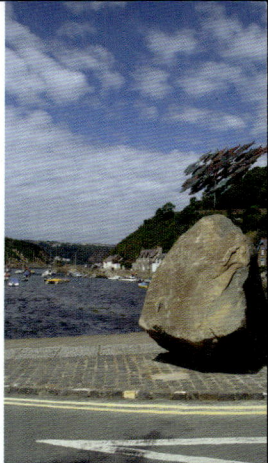

Fishguard

Tour 5

HAVERFORDWEST - CLARBESTON ROAD - LLYS-Y-FRAN - MAENCLOCHOG - ROSEBUSH - GWAUN VALLEY - DINAS CROSS - FISHGUARD - STRUMBLE HEAD - MATHRY - LETTERSTON - TREFFGARNE GORGE - HAVERFORDWEST

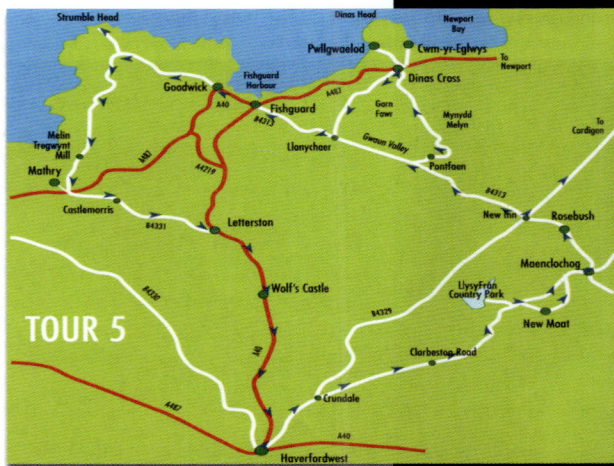

DAY TOURS BY CAR IN PEMBROKESHIRE

Leave Haverfordwest on the Withybush and Crundale road, the B4329, turning right on the minor road signposted Clarbeston Road and Llys-y-Fran. Carefully follow the signs for Llys-y-Fran Country Park, where there is a reservoir used for fishing and a visitor centre and restaurant. From the country park rejoin the road to nearby Gwastad where a short detour to New Moat is well worthwhile. Return to the Gwastad road and go on to the pretty village of Maenclochog. Follow the B4313 to Rosebush, a village whose claim to fame is that slates from its quarries were used to roof the House of Parliament, and continue to the crossroads at New Inn. Here you turn right and climb to one of the highest points of the Preseli Hills, which offer superb views. Return to the crossroads at New Inn, turning right on the B4313 for Fishguard. Continue along the B4313 for about 5 miles and turn left down the hill for Pontfaen. After the village bridge go straight on at the crossroads and up the very steep hill for Dinas Cross. This moorland road gives outstanding views across Newport Bay before descending to Dinas Cross.

At the T-junction turn right onto the A487 and turn immediately left for Pwllgwaelod. Return to the A487, turn left and then go to left again for Cwm-yr-Eglwys, a picturesque beach famed for a ruined church. Retrace your steps back to the main road where you turn right for Fishguard. Follow the road for about 2 miles then turn left to Llanychaer. This road is very narrow and steep in places. After passing over the bridge in the village rejoin the B4313, turning right for Fishguard, home of the Rosslare to Fishguard Ferry Terminal, passing through picturesque Lower Fishguard, a popular film location. At the roundabout by the Stena Line terminal, proceed up the hill and follow the signs for Strumble Head where there is a lighthouse and spectacular views of the coastline. Retracing your steps follow the coast road towards Mathry, which features an unusual parish church, stunning views and an ancient burial site nearby. From there follow the signs for Letterston where you turn right at the crossroads in the village onto the A40 and head back to

Pwllgwaelod

Cwm-yr-Eglwys

Haverfordwest via Treffgarne Gorge which offers striking rock formations and spectacular views.

Tour 6

HAVERFORDWEST NEWGALE - SOLVA MIDDLE MILL - ST. DAVIDS - ABEREIDDY - PORTHGAIN ABERCASTLE - TREFIN HAVERFORDWEST

Take the A487 out of Haverfordwest signposted St. Davids passing through Simpson Cross and Roch, on to Newgale which offers superb views over St. Bride's Bay. Next stop is Solva where there is a beautiful natural harbour, pretty village, shops and excellent walks. Continuing on this road brings you to the tiny city of St. Davids, which boasts a cathedral, Bishop's Palace, shops, restaurants, art galleries and outdoor activities, together with an information centre. From St. Davids you can take the minor road to Porth Clais, another picturesque little harbour, and St. Justinian, where there is a RNLI lifeboat station and views across Ramsey Sound. Returning to St. Davids follow the signs to Fishguard for a short distance before turning left for Whitesands Bay. Here you will find one of the finest beaches in Britain and many other watersport activities. Return towards the A487 follow the signs for Abereiddy where adjacent to the pebble beach is the Blue Lagoon. From Abereiddy,

Abereiddy

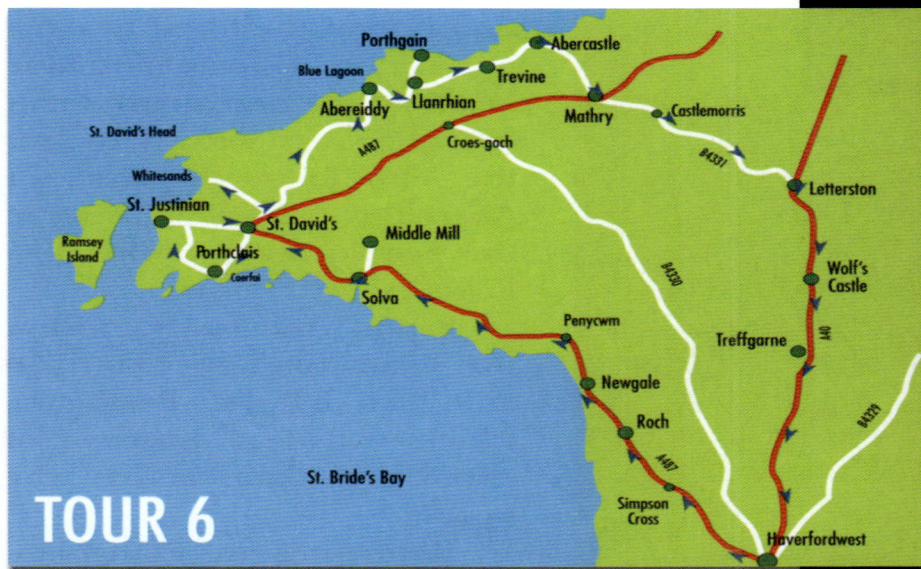

TOUR 6

214

the coast road to Llanrhian and turn left for Porthgain which has a history of exporting slate across the world. Returning to Llanrhian turn left at the crossroads for Trefin where there is a youth hostel, partly restored mill, hand weaving centre, gallery and craft shop. The next harbour along this rugged coastline is Abercastle, home to the Carreg Samson burial chamber. Follow the road out of Abercastle for the village of of Mathry which brings you back to the B4331 to Letterston where you turn right onto the A40 and on to Haverforwest via Treffgarne Gorge and the Nant-y-Coy Mill.

Tour 7

FISHGUARD - DINAS CROSS - NEWPORT - NEVERN - MOYLEGROVE - POPPIT SANDS - ST. DOGMAELS - CARDIGAN -

GWBERT - MWNT - LLECHRYD - CILGERRAN - BLAENFFOS - PRESELI HILLS - ROSEBUSH - GWAUN VALLEY - FISHGUARD

Leave Fishguard on the A487 towards Cardigan. Continue to Newport and Nevern where there is a Celtic Cross and Pilgrims Cross. En route two detours are recommended. The first is to one of Britain's best prehistoric burial chambers, Pentre Ifan, which can be found by turning right off the A487 before the Nevern turnoff and following the narrow country lanes to the top of the hill. The second detour is to Castell Henllys, a reconstructed Iron Age Fort managed by the National Park Authority. After Nevern proceed on the B4582 and take the third left hand turn

Newport Sands

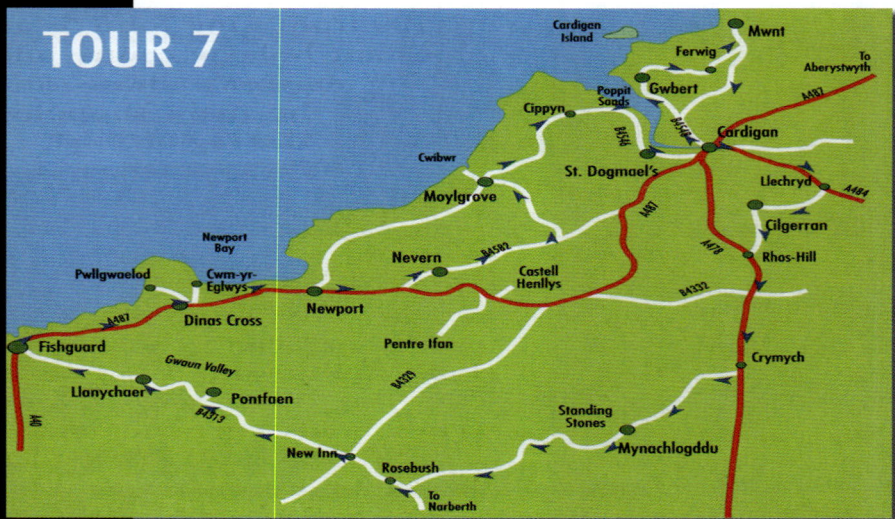

TOUR 7

215

signposted Moylegrove, an attractive coastal village dating back to Norman times. In the village turn left along the narrow road to the pebble beach at Ceibwr Bay. From Moylegrove follow the narrow country lanes to Poppit Sands, a large sandy beach with car park and lifeboat station, together with views of the Teifi estuary. Close to Poppit Sands is St. Dogmael's, an attractive hillside village that features the ruins of a 12th century Benedictine abbey and parish church containing the Sagranus Stone. From St. Dogmael's the road takes you over the bridge to the historic market town of Cardigan and along the northern bank of the River Teifi to Gwbert and then Mwnt. Returning to Cardigan take the A484 to Llechryd and Cilgerran, home to coracles on the Teifi and the Welsh Wildlife Centre. From Cilgerran drive to Rhos-Hill where you join the A478 and the village of Crymych. On leaving the village, go through Mynachlogddu along a country road that takes you through the heart of the Preseli Hills. Return towards the village and follow the signpost for Rosebush. Continue to the crossroads at New Inn and go straight on for Fishguard where the road takes you alongside the beautiful Gwuan Valley, and offers detours to the villages of Pontfaen and Llanychaer.

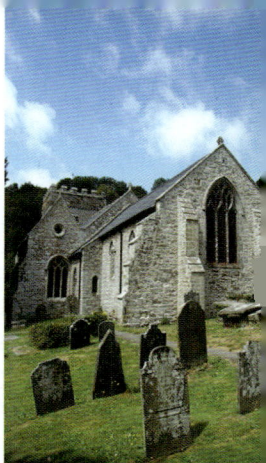
Nevern Church

Pentre Ifan

216

CEREDIGION & CARDIGAN BAY

Just across the Teifi estuary from Poppit Sands and St. Dogmaels is the ancient county of Cardiganshire, or Ceredigion as it is now known in Welsh. Like Pembrokeshire it is a county with a rich and varied landscape together with a long and dramatic history and it is well known to countless holidaymakers as the home of such popular resorts as New Quay, Aberaeron and Aberystwyth. Its spectacular coastline is marked by many fine beaches

EXPLORING CEREDIGION

Historic Cardigan, which received its first Royal Charter in 1199 from King John, is an important holiday centre and thriving market town and is one of the main shopping centres for the region. Beautifully sited near the mouth of the River Teifi with some of Wales' most attractive coast and countryside right on the doorstep, its shops and narrow streets retain the town's character. The Market Hall, built in 1859 and featuring impressive stone arches, holds a general market twice weekly and a livestock market once a week. Visitor attractions include the Theatr Mwldan (housed in the same building as the Tourist Information Centre - both of which are open all year round), an indoor leisure centre, a golf club at nearby Gwbert and a large annual arts festival, Gwyl Fawr Aberteifi. Crossing the Teifi below the castle is the striking multi-arched stone bridge. Sources disagree as to whether this is the original Norman Bridge, strengthened and widened in later years, or whether it was constructed in the 17th or even 18th century. The history of Cardigan Castle raises less argument. The ruins that now remain date from 1240, and it must have been in an earlier castle that the very first National Eisteddfod - advertised, for a whole year beforehand throughout Wales, England and Scotland, was hosted byRhys ap Gruffudd in 1176. The National Eisteddfod

Aberaeron

Aberporth

CEREDIGION

Aberaeron

is now the major cultural event in the Welsh calendar, as well as being Europe's largest peripatetic cultural festival. Cardigan Castle, like so many others, was destroyed by Cromwell, and now all that remains is privately owned. More recently, Cardigan was one of Wales' most prominent ports having as many as 300 ships registered there. Shipbuilding thrived in the 19th century when the busy warehouses along the waterfront handled everything from exports of herring, corn, butter and slate to imports of limestone, salt, coal, timber for shipbuilding, and manufactured goods. Human cargo was carried too: emigrant ships sailed from Cardigan to New York in the USA and New Brunswick in Canada. This prosperous period for Cardigan was relatively short-lived. Inevitably, booming trade meant that ships were getting bigger all the time while the gradual silting of the estuary was making access to Cardigan more and more restricted. The final nail in the town's coffin as a commercial port was the coming of the railway in 1885 - but today, as a popular holiday destination, Cardigan is once again a busy centre of attention, boasting many attractions within easy reach. Several of these stand near the banks of the Teifi such as St. Dogmael's Abbey, Poppit Sands, the Welsh Wildlife Centre, Cilgerran Castle and Cenarth Falls.

New Quay

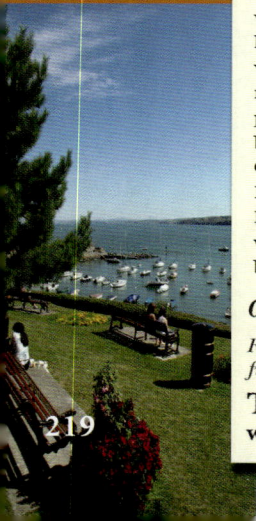

FELINWYNT RAINFOREST CENTRE

Visit this mini-rainforest and experience a different world. Wander amongst exotic plants and tropical butterflies accompanied by the sounds of the Peruvian Amazon. Waterfalls and streams enhance the humidity and someone is on hand to explain the mysteries of butterflies and to answer any questions. Watch the fascinating Leaf Cutter Ants. The visitor centre comprises the nature gift shop and an excellent cafe serving meals and snacks all day (why not try one of Dorothy's homemade cakes). The centre is suitable for the disabled.

Crayons and paper are provided free for children to create pictures for display in the gallery. The centre can be found 6 miles from Cardigan and 4 miles from Aberporth; follow the brown signs from the A487 at Blanannerch.

for more information ring 01239 810250 or 810882

TALYLLYN RAILWAY WHARF STATION TYWYN

The main station of the narrow gauge Talyllyn Railway is at Tywyn on the mid-Wales coast. From there, the line runs inland for over seven miles to Nant Gwernol, most of the route being in Snowdonia National Park. Built in 1865 to bring slate to the coast, the Railway was taken over by the Talyllyn Railway Preservation Society in 1951, becoming the first preserved railway in the world. The railway operates daily from the 17th of March to the 8th of November, and at Christmas. All passenger trains are hauled by coal fired steam locomotives. Tywyn Wharf station has a shop and new enlarged cafe. Also new is The Narrow Gauge Railway Museum with exhibits from over 70 railways. A special section is devoted to

Talyllyn Railway

Talyllyn Railway

Rev. W Audrey and his "Railway Series" of children's books, many of which were inspired by the Talyllyn where Rev. Audrey worked as a volunteer guard. Abergynolwyn has a cafe and shop and the popular Railway Adventure children's playground. At Dolgoch there are spectacular waterfalls with a tea room at the nearby Dolgoch Falls Hotel. A booklet detailing walks from every station on the line is available, and as every round trip ticket is a Day Rover, there are lots of opportunities to explore this beautiful part of Wales.

For details of timetable and special events ring 01654 710472 or visit www.talyllyn.co.uk

CANOLFANNAU CROESO CEREDIGION TOURIST INFORMATION CENTRES

ABERYSTWYTH TIC
Terrace Road
Aberystwyth
SY23 2AG
01970 612125
aberystwythtic@ceredigion.gov.uk

ABERAERON TIC
The Quay
Aberaeron
SA46 0BT
01545 570602
aberaerontic@ceredigion.gov.uk

CARDIGAN TIC
Theatr Mwldan
Cardigan
SA43 2JY
01239 613230
cardigantic@ceredigion.gov.uk

EASTER – SEPTEMBER

BORTH TIC
High Street
Borth
SY24 5HY
01970 871174
borthtic@ceredigion.gov.uk

NEW QUAY TIC
Church Street
New Quay
SA45 9NZ
01545 560865
borthtic@ceredigion.gov.uk

VALE OF RHEIDOL RAILWAY
Aberystwyth

An unforgettable journey through the spectacular Rheidol Valley by narrow gauge steam train on one of the "Great Little Trains of Wales". The journey between Aberystwyth and Devil's Bridge takes about an hour in each direction and the train overcomes a height difference of 600ft giving superb views of the Rheidol Valley. The Railway which opened in 1902 to serve the lead mining industry, was the last steam train railway owned by British Rail. It has undergone major renovation with improvement work continuing. Trains depart from the centre of Aberystwyth adjacent to the British Rail station. Ample parking is available in their car parks off Park Avenue and at Devil's Bridge.

Trains run most days Easter - Oct.

CARMARTHENSHIRE

Carmarthenshire is a very attractive holiday destination for visitors who appreciate history, culture and a green and beautiful environment. Covering an area of 1,000 square miles, the county is a veritable feast of delights and discovery. The 50 miles of stunning coastline embrace vast stretches of safe golden sands such as the beaches of Cefn Sidan and Pendine, punctuated by the Taf and Towy estuaries, which so inspired the legendary writer Dylan Thomas. The county is also rich in bustling market towns, such as Newcastle Emlyn, Llandysul, Whitland, Llandeilo, Llandovery and Llanybydder and of course Carmarthen. The other attractions and activities to be enjoyed are many and varied, from castles, museums and art galleries, steam railways, country parks, fishing and golf, to the beautiful gardens at Aberglasney and The National Botanic Garden of Wales, Llanarthne.

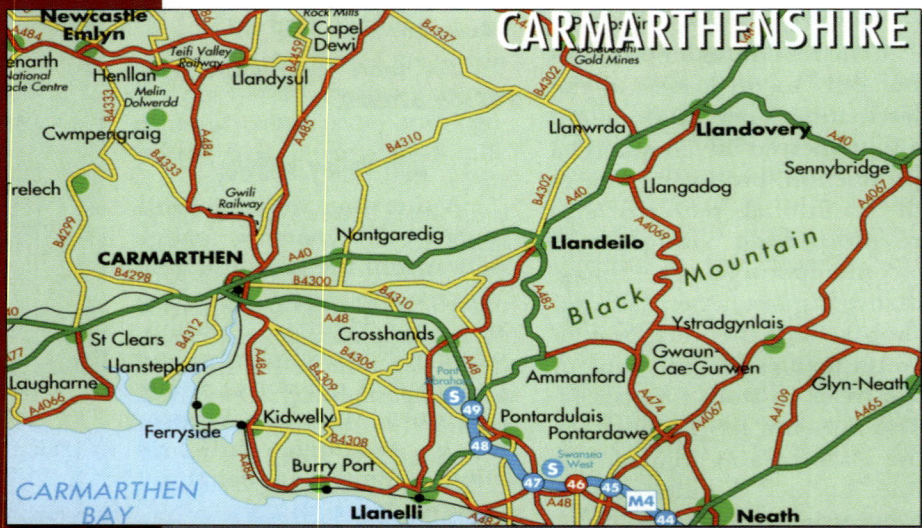

Carmarthen

At the heart of the county is the ancient township of Carmarthen, the reputed birthplace of Merlin - wizard and counsellor to King Arthur. The town stands eight miles inland on the River Towy - a position that inspired the Romans to make it their strategic capital. They also built an amphitheatre here, rediscovered in 1936 but not excavated until 1968. Today Carmarthen's quaint old narrow streets are full of Welsh character and tradition. There's also a first-class modern shopping centre with its many familiar high street names, which expanded with the opening of the Greyfriars shopping complex. Carmarthen's famous market, which is open six days a week, complements the town centre and attracts people from all over Wales. In Carmarthen you're also likely to catch more than a smattering of Welsh, as it is still widely spoken here. It is believed that the oldest manuscript in the Welsh language - The Black Book of Carmarthen - now in the National Library of Wales in Aberystwyth - was written in the town. For sport, there's the town's modern leisure centre, with its outstanding all weather facilities. A few miles west is Derllys Court Golf Club, near Bancyfelin, which has an interesting 18 hole, pay as you play, set in a beautiful location amongst rolling countryside. There is a

Pendine

225

licensed bar together with catering facilities and a warm welcome is extended to visitors.

for more information ring 01267 211575

Another attraction virtually on Carmarthen's doorstep is the Gwili Railway at Bronwydd Arms (just off the A484) - one of Wales' last remaining standard gauge steam railways where a train takes you to a wooded riverside area deep in the valley where there is also a picnic site. The railway opened in 1860 and eventually became the property of British Railways, but after the remaining milk traffic was transferred to road, the line closed in 1973. The Gwili Railway Company was set up in 1975 and in 1978, and thanks to volunteers a section of the line just over a mile long was reopened between the Bronwydd Arms and the riverside station at Llwyfan Cerrig. An extension towards Cynwyl Elfed is progressing well.

Cenarth

Dylan Thomas Boathouse at Laugharne

Laugharne

An ancient and interesting township standing on the west bank of the Taf estuary. Originally a fortified Roman station, the township is thought to have been founded by the Princes of Dynevor prior to the Norman conquest. It has enjoyed several names over the centuries, Abercorran (at the mouth of the Corran) Tallachar, Thalacharne and modern day Laugharne. The town is dominated by the castle which was built in Norman times as part of a line of fortified garrisons along the Carmarthenshire and Pembrokeshire coast designed to keep the local inhabitants under control. It has had a varied history and played a prominent role in the Civil War when it withstood a Cromwellian siege for seven days. More recently, CADW spent twenty years carrying out sympathetic restoration work and it is now open to the public. Laugharne and Malmesbury in Wiltshire are the only towns in the UK to retain their ancient Charter, granted not by Parliament, but by Royal decree and which allows them to be governed by a Corporation in addition to the normal local government bodies.

The Corporation is headed by the Portreeve with a Foreman, a Recorder, two Common Attorneys, four Constables, a Baliff and a Jury consisting of twenty Burgesses. This august body of men meets on a monthly basis and many matters of local interest are discussed and decided upon. These sittings are held in the Town Hall where the original Charter is displayed together with many other articles of historic interest. Once every three years, the local population of Laugharne take part in the Common Walk when the boundaries of the Township are walked and identified. This is a walk of some twenty six miles through very rough and difficult countryside and for those brave enough to take part, refreshments are served during the route. In more recent times Laugharne became the home of the famous Welsh poet Dylan Thomas and his well known work - Under Milk Wood - was undoubtedly inspired by the Township and its inhabitants. His home, The Boathouse, is now a museum to his life and works and is open to the public.

EXPLORING CARMARTHENSHIRE

From Laugharne, the road west cuts a picturesque route to Pendine Sands, where Sir Malcom Campbell and others made several attempts on the world landspeed record, the most recent being in 1998. The fatal crash of Parry Thomas-Jones in 1927 ended Pendine's racing career, but the exciting new Museum of Speed recalls this village resort's days of fame and glory. On the eastern side of Carmarthen Bay are the estuaries of the Gwendraeth and Loughor, and the superb seven mile beach of Cefn Sidan Sands - one of the best beaches in Britain.

Whitland

Whitland, which stands on the River Taf inside the Carmarthenshire border, west of St. Clears, rose in prominence as a market town in the 19th century. The coming of the railway established it as an important junction. The town's most significant place in history goes back to the 10th century, when the great Welsh king Hywel Dda (Hywel the Good) called an assembly of wise men here to draw up a unified legal code for Wales, based on the ancient tribal laws and customs already in existence. The assembly took place at Ty Gwyn ar Daf (The White House on the Taf) - Hywel Dda's hunting lodge. It is thought that the house could have been the site chosen two centuries later for Whitland Abbey. The Hywel Dda Interpretive Gardens and Centre, in the centre of the town, now commemorate this great assembly. Whitland Abbey was the first Cistercian monastery in Wales and gave rise to seven others, including Strata Florida which was founded in 1140, but unfortunately virtually nothing remains of the abbey today, its ruins standing to the north of Whitland.

Pendine

Llanelli

Once the tinplate capital of the world and arguably the home of Welsh rugby, Llanelli is a thriving town with an impressive pedestrianised shopping centre and bustling indoor and outdoor markets. Standing on the beautiful Loughor estuary, Llanelli has a pleasant beach and is close to many major attractions. These include the recently developed Millennium Coastal Park, Pembrey Country Park, magnificent Cefn Sidan Sands, the Pembrey Motorsports Centre and Kidwelly Castle. Places to visit include Parc Howard and Sandy Water Park.

Cenarth

Cenarth is one of the most popular beauty spots in the whole of West Wales. Standing on the River Teifi, it is a very pretty village, famous for its salmon leap falls. It is also recognised as the traditional home of the Teifi coracle, and here you will find the National Coracle Centre, which despite its name is a private enterprise, though no less important or interesting for that. Unspoilt Cenarth is a designated conservation area, with many of its buildings listed. The fine old bridge is believed to be 18th century, and the flourmill, which houses the Coracle Centre dates from the 1600's. Also of historical interest are St. Llawddog's church and its mysterious Sarsen Stone.

CORACLE CENTRE
&
MILL, CENARTH

The strange, round fishing boat, known as the coracle, has been a familiar sight on the River Teifi for centuries. It is light, manoeuvrable and ideal in shallow water, though mastering the art of coracle fishing can take years of practice. Today

230

McDonald's

CARMARTHEN
MYRTLE HILL, PENSARN

TELEPHONE: **01267 220861**

OPEN 6.30am - 11pm SEVEN DAYS A WEEK

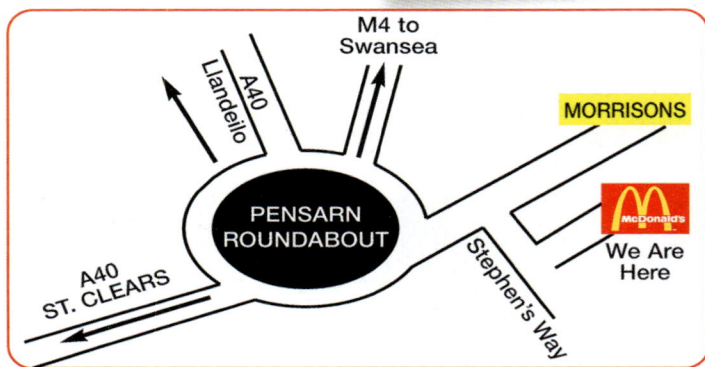

there are still 12 pairs licensed to fish on the Teifi, but the best place to see coracles is the National Coracle Centre which houses over 20 different types of coracle, in varying shapes and sizes, from all over the world - India, Vietnam, Tibet, Iraq and North America - as well as 9 varieties of Welsh coracle and examples from England and Scotland. An added bonus for visitors is that in the workshop you can see how coracles are made. The Coracle Centre stands on the ground floor of a 17th century flourmill, which is also open to visitors, and there are arts, crafts, souvenirs and gifts for sale.

for more information ring 01239 710980 or 710507

MUSEUM OF THE WELSH WOOLLEN INDUSTRY
Drefach Velindre

The new museum promises not only to do justice to the fascinating story of wool but also continue in commercial production, producing fabrics in traditional patterns and re-interpreting designs for a contemporary market. Imaginative displays, a new cafe and shop selling the very best of Welsh textiles are just some of the treats in store for visitors. The museum has facilities for the disabled and admission is free. Located 4 miles east of Newcastle Emlyn, 16 miles west of Carmarthen. Follow the brown tourist signs.

For more information ring 01559 370929

232

GLYN-COCH
CRAFT CENTRE
Pwll-Trap, St Clears

The Jones family invite you to our craft centre, set in tranquil countryside, and signposted from the A40, 1mile west of St Clears. Our Craft Shop sells over 1000 stock lines made by about 30 local suppliers. Some only sell through us. Glyn-Coch Design China was decorated here from 1980 until they moved to Tenby in 1995. We maintain the tradition by Hand Painting China and Glass, and producing our own earthenware.

"You can have a go or attend a variety of informal courses"

We also sell wool, woollen garments and craft kits using wool from our Rare Norfolk Horn Sheep, which can be seen from our prize winning circular Woodland Walk and Nature Trail. Afterwards you can relax in our friendly Tearoom, or visit our small displays of Radios, Computers or Vintage Farm Machinery. Open 6 days a week all year.

Closed on Tuesdays.
tel: 01994 231867

THE BUNCH OF GRAPES
Newcastle Emlyn

The Bunch of Grapes is an attractive Public House built with stone from the castle and oak stolen from Kent! It retains a traditional feel in both its ambience and tasteful decor with a wealth of oak beams. The colourful garden at the rear is very sheltered and an excellent suntrap. The pub always has "Directors" and two guest ales on tap, has "Cask Marque" accreditation, and was CAMRA Pub of the Year 2004. The food is rather special as well with constantly changing menu of homemade dishes, made with fresh local produce, to tempt every palate. Booking is advised, especially for evening meals in the non-smoking restaurant and also for the traditional Sunday carvery. The Bunch of Grapes also provides live music every Thursday and Saturday evening.

tel: 01239 711185

WHERE TO EAT GUIDE

CARMARTHENSHIRE

Carmarthen

McDONALDs

Good fast food for the family in a hurry

see page 231

Laugharne

THE STABLE DOOR RESTAURANT

Imaginative home cooked meals with a varied wine list in a conservatory dining area overlooking the castle and estuary

Newcastle Emlyn

THE BUNCH OF GRAPES

Genuine homemade dishes and vegetarian specialities served in the bar or restaurant

see page 233

Pwll-Trap

GLYN COCH STUDIOS

Small tea room offering a variety of light snacks and cream teas which are also served in a sheltered garden.

see page 233

Llanddarog

THE WHITE HART THATCHED INN & BREWERY

Dating from medieval times, the White Hart is believed to be among the oldest inns in South Wales. Restaurant and bar meals are available using fresh local produce.

THE BUTCHERS ARMS

Over the years The Butchers has been awarded many awards, including several from Egon Ronay and 'A taste of Wales', to name but a few and been included in many good Pub Food Guides.

DAY TRIPS TO IRELAND

Stena Line

With a choice of fast and superferry crossings, unrivalled service and value fares, Stena Line's Fishguard - Rosslare route is the best choice for travel to the south-east and south-west of Ireland.

The luxury superferry Stena Europe is ideal for motorists wanting a rest and relaxing break, especially those with children. Alternatively between the months of May and September, holidaymakers in Pembrokeshire can spend a day in the sunny South East of Ireland by taking advantage of the hi-speed Stena Express catamaran service which travels across the Irish Sea to Rosslare in a time of just 2 hours.

For longer stays, Stena Line Holidays offers a great choice of short breaks in hotels and self catering holidays for all the family, throughout Ireland. Just click www.stenaline.com or call 08705 707070.

There are a number of facilities on board both vessels, including bars, restaurants, cabins, Stena Shopping and our exclusive Stena Plus Lounge where you can travel in style and relax in comfort.

SOUTH EAST IRELAND

Explore 10,000 years of Irish history in a day! Begin with the Irish National Heritage Park in Wexford and discover how the Irish lived from the Stone Age to the 12th century. Travel to Waterford and its fabulous Museum of Treasures, tracing the history of Ireland's most ancient city, before lunch in a centuries old pub. See how the world famous Waterford Crystal is made, then journey to the marvellous castles of Lismore and Cahir and then the magical Rock of Cashel before ending your day at Kilkenny Castle, dining at one of medieval Kilkenny's superb restaurants. A medieval fortress that has stood witness to many key moments in Irish history, a beautifully restored castle that has stood guard over a city for over 900 years... History you can touch and feel is all around in the south east region, an area linked by a network of five ancient river valleys and containing Ireland's oldest city, Waterford. Follow the trail of previous visitors, Celts, Vikings and Normans through magnificent castles and monuments, heritage museums and great country houses. Discover the creative heart of Ireland's traditional crafts and some of Europe's most beautiful gardens, cruise on Ireland's second largest river or enjoy game, sea and coarse angling in the cleaning of rivers and lakes or off miles of stunning coastline. Here's just a taste of what is in store: Follow the epic story of five generations of Kennedy's at the Ancestral Home of JF. Kennedy in Wexford. You can still see the original farmyard of the President's Great Grandfather. The John F Kennedy Arboterum in Wexford, dedicated to the memory of the late President, has over 4,000 individual species of trees from around the world. Follow the footsteps of the famine period emigrants on the Dunbrody Famine Ship in Wexford, a full scale reconstruction of a 19th famine ship. Learn the heroic tale of the 1798 rebel lion in Ireland at the interactive displays at the award-winning National 1798 Visitor Centre in Wexford. Lismore Heritage Centre in Co Waterford, tells the fascinating story of the town's history from its Celtic origins onwards. Part of that story is the 17th century Lismore

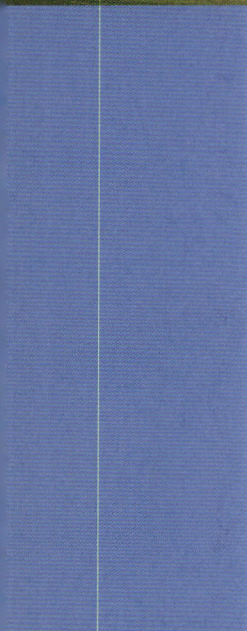

Castle, with its fabulous gardens, including the Yew Walk where Edmund Spenser is said to have written the 'Faerie Queen.'

13th century Hook Lighthouse in Wexford is the oldest working lighthouse in Northern Europe and now has a craft shop and restaurant.

Now fully restored to its former glory, as are its beautiful public gardens, Kilkenny Castle has stood guard over the lovely city of Kilkenny for over 900 years. Kilkenny is also known for atmospheric traditional pubs and fabulous restaurants, as well as for some of Ireland's finest craft producers. Most of these can be found at the world famous Kilkenny Design Centre, housed in the old castle stables.

County Kilkenny is also home to one of Ireland's finest monastic settlements, Jerpoint Abbey and the magical Dunmore Cave, whose underground chambers were formed over millions of years. You can also explore massive caverns at one of Europe's most famous showcaves, Mitchelstown Cave in Tipperary. There's a mystical aura around the Rock Of Cashel in Tipperary, a spectacular settlement of medieval buildings, including a 12th century round tower, 13th century Gothic cathedral and 15th century castle. The Brú Ború Cultural Centre, adjoining it, offers a folk theatre, genealogy suite and underground theatre and an exhibition telling the story of Irish song and dance. Nearby, the Cashel Folk Village, a collection of thatched buildings recreates traditional Irish village life.

Castle Cahir, imposingly situated on a rocky island on the river Suir in Tipperary, is one of Ireland's largest and best preserved castles, with an impressive keep, tower and much of its defensive structure still intact. In Carlow, fascinating Huntingdon Castle and Gardens, rebuilt in 1625, boasts an ancient vine in its conservatory and a famous avenue of yew trees in its beautiful gardens. In Tipperary, famous Dungarvan Castle, an Anglo-Norman fortification, was built by King John in the 12th century.

Irish Ferries

Irish Ferries operate to Rosslare on the south east coast of Ireland with the luxury 34,000 ton cruise ferry, the m.v Isle of Inishmore. You have the choice of afternoon or early morning sailings and the crossing takes you down the Milford Haven Waterway and out past the 2 bird sanctuary islands of Skokholm and Skomer before heading across St Georges Channel to the Tusker Rock Lighthouse which is seen approximately half an hour before arriving in Rosslare Harbour. The vessel has 2 restaurants, bars and lounges, plus a children's free cinema and a "Cyber Zone" with electronic games and entertainment.

During the summer period there is a live entertainment programme onboard, also a Tourist Information Centre giving information on South Wales and South East Ireland. Throughout the year we offer low cost Day Trips for visitors to the area, and early spring or autumn moneysaving offers for passengers with cars. Irish Ferries Holidays also have a great choice of inclusive short and long break holidays in hotels, self catering and motoring holidays for all the family throughout Ireland.

INDEX

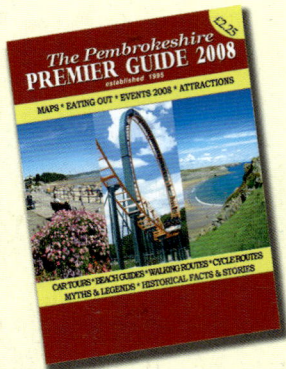

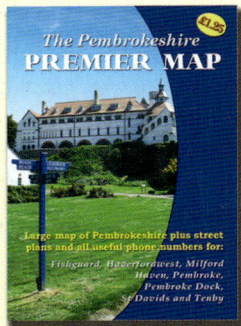

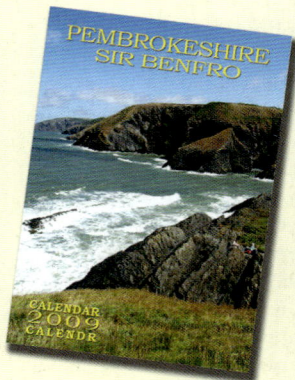